TI

BEST BOOK

Version no. 1

1600-2017

John Joe

CW00402526

John Joe

The Best Book: Version no. 1

First edition: 2020

Translated by **Jane Joe**
Proofread and corrected by **Georgia Skalidi** and **Manos Kounougakis**
Cover designed by **Maria Siorba** (based on the cover of the Greek version designed by **A4ARTDESIGN**)
Photos edited by **Christina Katsara**, **Dimitris Kakarelis** and **Dimitris Milidonis**

© 2020, Saint Paul Educational Establishment

All rights reserved. The republication, subsequent translation and any other use of this piece of work without the permission in writing of the publisher, in accordance with Law 2121/93, international conventions on intellectual property and any other law, are not permitted.

Although every precaution has been taken in the preparation of this book, the publisher and author assume no responsibility for errors or omissions. Neither is any liability assumed for damages resulting from the use of this information contained herein.

ISBN: 9798574481271

CONTENTS

PREAMBLE

"The most important thing about any biography is the biographer". This paradoxical reply was given by the famous English biographer Peter Ackroyd when asked to offer the definition of biography.

This biography of Markos Vamvakaris by Dimitris Varthalitis is the most emphatic confirmation of his statement, as it reveals not only the face of the biographer, but also the era and the face of the biographer himself, his perspective and ideological surroundings.

Markos Vamvakaris, one of the cornerstones of Greek rebetiko[1] music, is now considered to be the leading figure of modern Greek music tradition. Composer, songwriter, virtuoso of the bouzouki and singer of his own compositions, he included lived experiences and sounds in his work that were

---

[1] A form of urban folk music from Greece that appeared in the 1920s following migratory waves from predominantly Greek populations expelled from Asia Minor. Rebetiko was developed in the first half of the 20th century, as the (essentially rural) population of Greece became more and more concentrated in the cities, in particular in the large ports of continental Greece (Piraeus, Thessaloniki), as well as in the United States where, in fact, some of the first rebetiko recordings were made. The development of rebetiko at the port of Piraeus was the consequence of the meeting of refugees from Asia Minor and the Greek emigrants from the islands and the mainland coming to seek a better life in Athens. In 2017, rebetiko was inscribed to UNESCO's list of the intangible cultural heritage of humanity.

influenced by his musical expertise both from his native island, Syros, as well as from Piraeus and the various tekedes[2].

Dimitris Varthalitis, by composing Markos's biography, operates as a cultural historian who researches, interprets, re-evaluates persons and events, and illuminates an entire epoch through Markos, as well as by his own lights. Armed with the deepest knowledge and love for the artist's work, the biographer-writer embarks on the adventure of interpreting the life and works of Markos Vamvakaris without feeling the need to construct his own version. His own storytelling consists of factual data, archival research, empirical documentation and historical recording. The pursuit and expectation of the truth and of "objectivity" is the author's priority.

The book contains unique testimonies of various events, locations and situations with reference to Markos Vamvakaris, his work, the places he lived, and the people he met and consorted with. Magical moments of the past starring this enfant terrible of rebetiko music come alive through the pages of the book. The image of Markos as an unruly son in the neighborhoods of Syros, as a young man in love in the streets of Piraeus, as a family man and loving father who cares for his boys' education and prepares their future is also highlighted in the best possible way. The exemplary character of the narration follows the way Markos directed himself and his life and opens us to a bulimic tendency for more biographical details as well as other specific incidents.

By quoting third-party testimonies as such, the author

---

[2] Tekes (pl. tekedes) = originally a Turkish word meaning a place to housing religious specialists and scholars, a kind of equivalent to Christian convents. Later, in Greece, the word meant a place to smoke hashish, generally a slum where hashish smokers used to go to smoke the hookah.

flirts with impartiality and bias, but avoids the risk of a hagiography or of the identification with a subjective and relative truth.

In the process of interpreting life and artistic creation events, it is precisely this self-evident narrative truth that is called into question, somehow ascertaining Pascal's quote that "the opposite of truth is not a lie but another truth".

Biographies are, perhaps, the literary genre that express the spirit of each era better than other texts as they metonymically make up the narrative of a country's public and hidden life. They consent and at the same time contrast public with private, secret with known, real with fictional, past with present.

This biography meets the multifaceted needs of the action of the "ego" (biographer and readership). Beyond the aesthetic enjoyment of reading it and beyond its importance as a record of historiographical-testimonial value, it significantly contributes to the study and understanding of the morals, the psychology and the sociocultural priorities of Greek society and of the cultural underground of the first half of the 20th century.

At the same time, the book urges us to meet with Markos in the context of his artistic work, precisely because it acts as a mediator in this respect and supports causal links between personal life, external events and the work itself.

With his passion and love, Dimitris Varthalitis reshapes the man and artist Markos Vamvakaris, combining empirical documentation with historical recording and history with myth.

Sissy Papathanasiou

"KNOW THYSELF"

Socrates, underlining the importance of "knowing thyself", urged us to discover ourselves properly by confessing the truth primarily to ourselves, therefore to our consciousness. But confession still seems to be important as a self-determination process. A characteristic example following the archaic period is the work of Roman Emperor Marcus Aurelius entitled "To Himself", in which he was a confessor of himself.

Christianity is inextricably tied to confession as an act of repentance. James, in his Catholic Letter, chapter E, verse 16, urges believers to confess their sins to one another. Thus, the first Christians confessed publicly. In support of the above, I shall add that Saint Augustine, a theologian, states in his work "Confessions", book X: "This wish I to do in confession in my heart before You, and in my writing before many witnesses."

When studying Markos Vamvakaris's autobiography, I was moved and I admired how he chose to pour out the story of his life. When reading the beginning of the book, where he describes his biography as a confession ("I want this world to be my confessor", p. 34), I was overwhelmed by this thought: Having studied Jean-Jacques Rousseau's (1712-1778) book entitled "The Confessions" ("Les Confessions de Jean-Jacques Rousseau"), I noticed that in his introduction he admits to writing his biography in order to bring the verdict "an innumerable throng of my fellow-mortals, let them listen to my confessions" (p. 9) to the discretion of the public.

The above associations led me to strive for a parallel between the introductions of the two biographies in order to highlight Markos Vamvakaris's wisdom and greatness of soul. It is known that the great rebetis[3] went to school only until the fourth grade. He therefore did not receive any basic education and his connection to the French philosopher, author and composer seems utopian. For this reason, however, the spiritual "encounter" of the two in the preamble of their works generates interest and curiosity, since they have the same motivation: confession.

Markos Vamvakaris, in telling the story of his life, tries to expose his personal truths to a world that loves and follows him bravely: "I should be ashamed to confess many things. But I'll find the courage [...] to expose my sins to the world" (p. 33). Rousseau, in turn: "Whenever the last trumpet shall sound, I will present myself before the sovereign judge with this book in my hand, and loudly proclaim, thus have I acted; these were my thoughts; such was I. With equal freedom and veracity have I related what was laudable or wicked, I have concealed no crimes, added no virtues; and if I have sometimes introduced superfluous ornament, it was merely to occupy a void occasioned by defect of memory: I may have supposed that certain, which I only knew to be probable, but have never asserted as truth, a conscious falsehood. Such as I was, I have declared myself; sometimes vile and despicable, at others, virtuous, generous and sublime; even as thou hast read my inmost soul: Power eternal! assemble round thy throne an innumerable throng of my fellow-mortals, let them listen to my confessions, let them blush at my depravity, let them tremble at my sufferings" (p. 9) Thus, they both recognize the boldness of their venture. They also identify when, in the context of their self-criticism, they attribute the public confession of their actions to their diversity. Markos

---

[3] Rebetis (pl. rebetes) = the player, singer and/or composer of rebetiko. A free-spirited individual who embodies the bohemian life of the subculture that produced the rebetiko.

Vamvakaris states: "But I was different" (p. 148). And Rousseau: "I am not made like any one I have been acquainted with, perhaps like no one in existence; if not better, I at least claim originality" (p. 9).

The fact that we are in the process of contrasting Markos Vamvakaris with Jean-Jacques Rousseau, as we realize his spiritual stature 45 years after his death, could only be considered as honorary. With that in mind, it is a natural consequence for the great rebetis to receive an invitation from the State University of New York at Buffalo to teach music. The French philosopher and his work "The Confessions" is taught in a similar way at the National and Kapodistrian University of Athens. At this point it is worth noting that Markos Vamvakaris disproved Rousseau's expectation, who believed that no one other than him would dare a public confession. "I have entered upon a performance which is without example, whose accomplishment will have no imitator. I mean to present my fellow-mortals with a man in all the integrity of nature; and this man shall be myself" (p. 9), claims Rousseau, for Markos Vamvakaris to answer: "I have the desire to tell the story of my life [...] A man, if he's to be called a real man, has to be able to step into the shoes of his fellow man [...] I'll tell you about my faults and my sufferings" (p. 33).

Through his autobiography, Markos Vamvakaris opened his heart to us by making his own public confession, in imitation of the first Christians: "The kind lady who's acting as my scribe says the first Christians used to confess their sins aloud, in front of everybody, and then everybody forgave them and they got it off their chests" (p. 33). Thus, he reveals unknown aspects of his life.

Speaking about his life, the enfant terrible of rebetiko music gives his consent to the writing and publishing of this book. Thus, in this book, one can read stories about the family of Markos Vamvakaris, his wife Evangelia, his children

Vassilis, Domenikos and Stelios, his relatives and neighbors in Aspra Chomata[4], his "students" who spent every waking hour in his basement and organized great events for him, the singers who visited him in his studio in order to consult him, the common people, especially Syrans[5], who encountered him either in Syros or in Athens and who were entertained by his music and songs, 12-year-old children who were rushing over to meet him and the top scholars of his day who worshiped him and were visiting in order to listen to him.

The book also includes: researches on the work of the great rebetis, an important and unique study of the family tree of Markos Vamvakaris from 1600 until today, a journey through the space and time of Syros via a journey to Markos's past and present. The book's thematic variety is complemented by photographic material and a few corrections concerning inaccurate information about his life and works.

The interviews of the ordinary people in this book impel us to see Markos behind the name Vamvakaris and are somewhat like the Christmas tree lights: if one is missing all go off and all of them illuminate aspects of Markos Vamvakaris's soul. Each interview is unique and offers a unique perspective on his personality.

The book was published by the Saint Paul Educational Establishment, which created the non-profit association C.I.R.E.L. - Aesop-La Fontaine International Research Center (Centre International de Recherche Ésope-La Fontaine), founded by Dimitrios Vikentiou[6] Varthalitis. Aesop's fables,

---

[4] A neighborhood of Piraeus.

[5] Those who come from Syros.

[6] The word "Vikentiou" is the genitive case form of Vikentios and an actual patronymic. Actual patronymics are used in official documents

where the protagonists are animals, are known for their educational character. Likewise, one could think that music plays its own role in shaping people's psyche through its healing properties. Thus, rebetiko music, whose main representative is Markos Vamvakaris, uses the bouzouki and manages to entertain and redeem us from the sorrows of the soul.

With Markos in mind and heart, we embark on a journey into the memories of his life story, 45 years after his death, and a guided tour of the researches attempting to explain the uniqueness of the great rebetis.

A special word of thank you goes to the adorable sons of Markos Vamvakaris, Vassilis, Stelios and Domenikos, his nieces, Elpida, Athanasia, Margitsa, his nephew Dominikos F. Vamvakaris, his brother-in-law in Kyparissia and Georgia Palaiologou. Many thanks are due to the former bishop of Syros father Frangiskos Papamanolis, the former Catholic archbishop of Athens father Nikolaos Foskolos, the Catholic bishop of Syros father Petros Stefanou, the vicar of Syros father Antonios Voutsinos, father Ioannis Patsis and father Nikolaos Roussos. Thank you to those who gave me studies and interviews, paintings or sketches. We are all fans of Markos Vamvakaris. I would like to thank the staff of the Archives of the Catholic Diocese of Syros, the Archives of the Catholic Archdiocese of Athens, the Archives of the Catholic Church of Saint Sebastian in Apano Chora[7], the Archives of the Catholic Church of Saint Paul in Piraeus, the Historical Archive

---

as "middle names" preceding the surname. For example, the children of a certain Ioannis Papadopoulos are, say, Katerina Ioannou Papadopoulou and Petros Ioannou Papadopoulos.

[7] The capital of any Greek island is generally called Chora. Historically, the Chora was a high up ("ano" or "apano") place which was far from the sea due to the danger of pirates or other invaders. However,

of the Cyclades, the Registry Office of Ano Syros, the Land Registry of Ermoupoli[8], the Chamber of Commerce and Industry of the Cyclades, the Museum of Markos Vamvakaris in Apano Syros, the Registry Office of the Municipality of Nikaia and the Registry Office of Piraeus. I would like to warmly thank the historian-theatrologist and Head of the Ministry of Culture Sissy Papathanasiou, the painter Sotiris Sorogas for his work on the cover of the Greek version of the book and Maria Siorba for redesigning the cover of the English version, the tireless expert in Syros's history and a personal friend of mine Michalis M. Roussos, the gallerist Giorgos Kartalos, the journalist Giorgos A. Kiousis and especially Michalis Fragias, Markos K. Freris, Irini Sakka, Katerina Flouraki, Angeliki Psilopoulou, Ioanna Chasapidou, Sophia Zaloni, AHEPA's[9] past President Anastasios Vasilas, the photographer Christina Katsara who originally edited the photos, Konstantinos M. Freris who edited the Greek version of the entire book, mainly the archive and the album, Nikolaos Poulakis for the painstaking pagination of the Greek version of the book and finally Christos Poulakis for the translation and the set-up of the English version of the book.

Dimitris. V. Varthalitis

in the case of Syros, Ermoupoli was a big port in the 19th century, even larger than the one of Piraeus. It became the capital of the Cyclades and replaced the old Chora, now known as the Apano or Ano Chora (or Syros). The two are very close to each other.

[8] The capital of Syros.

[9] The American Hellenic Educational Progressive Association (AHEPA) is a fraternal organization founded on July 26, 1922, in Atlanta, Georgia, USA. AHEPA was founded to assist Greek immigrants' assimilation into American society.

Educator, researcher, author, publisher and director of the Lycée Franco-Hellénique Eugène Delacroix for twelve years. Since 1997, Dimitris V. Varthalitis is the owner and director of the Saint Paul Greek-French School in Athens, which in 2020 was granted the official international accreditation "Label FrancEducation", a seal of quality for schools offering a French bilingual program (awarded by the French Ministry of Foreign Affairs through its Agency for French Education Abroad). He is also the publisher of the magazine "Syriana Grammata"[10] (during its first period, 1988-1998, as well as during its revival since 2017) and the founder of the C.I.R.E.L. - Aesop-La Fontaine International Research Center (Centre International de Recherche Ésope-La Fontaine) in 2009. Multifaceted and skillful, Dimitris V. Varthalitis is passionate about education, his island Syros and Markos Vamvakaris.

He has devoted years to researching the history of his home territory and has conducted, on his own and in collaboration with other researchers, in a large number of studies on the history, the traditions, the toponyms and the linguistic idioms of the island.

He has participated in presentations and lectures at events in Greece and abroad, supporting his research results and highlighting issues that concern him, often in a highly imaginative and creative way. In 2013, he directed a "meeting" between Aesop and Vamvakaris at an international conference in Sorbonne, accompanied by a speech about Aesop to the strains of Markos's music.

In 2007 he was awarded with the Academic Palms of the French Republic for his contribution to Education and for the dissemination and support of French Culture in Greece.

---

[10] "Syran Letters".

xxi

This publication is the result of his long and thorough involvement in the work and life of the great rebetis and as the author himself states: "The book constitutes a stopover on the way to establishing the Markos Vamvakaris Foundation in Syros."

TRANSLATOR'S NOTE

I share two passions with Dimitris Varthalitis: the French language (he is the owner and director of the Saint Paul Greek-French School in Athens, and I, for my part, studied in various French schools around the world before starting my studies) and, mainly, our common love for Markos Vamvakaris. We owe our acquaintanceship to Stelios Vamvakaris, one of Markos's three sons: shortly before his sudden death in June 2019, and during a visit to his house, Stelios felt the need to offer me Dimitris Varthalitis's book as a gift. I told him, however, that I already had it, and though it was a present from him, I politely refused to accept it. "Maybe someone else who hasn't read it should have it, it would be a waste if I took it", I told him. He looked at me and replied: "Manga[11], okay, no worries. But I'll give you another gift: here's Dimitris Varthalitis's phone number. Call him whenever you like, I believe he'll be glad to meet you and, who knows, maybe you could even collaborate sometime." It so happened that we actually met in person for the first time shortly after, during Stelios's funeral...

I had read the Greek edition of Dimitris Varthalitis's book throughout the summer of 2017. I was impressed by the size of the two-volume book, by the multitude of documents, by the unpublished (up to that time) photos, but mainly by the interviews of many people who had not come to the fore for so many years, who had not been given a chance to speak about Markos and their testimonies were nowhere to be

---

[11] Manga(s) (pl. manghes) = someone who is a master of himself and who has little respect for any authority beyond his own inclinations and personal principles. He enjoys the finer things in life, does not speak a lot and does not cause problems unless he is provoked.

found in the literature. I thought that such a book, with this kind of documentation, was really important for all those who are delving into Markos Vamvakaris in particular and into rebetiko in general.

After some time, my interaction with Dimitris Varthalitis became more frequent, as did my visits to his school, which by chance happens to be within walking distance of my office. After the necessary discussions and consultations, the plan was drawn up and the "order" was finally given: "I want you to translate, if you of course would also like to, my book into English!" Would I!

But where to start from? The Greek version of the book contained numerous pages, the text was dense and I thought that all this information would be overwhelming to the Anglo-Saxon readers. Fortunately, Dimitris Varthalitis immediately provided me with the freedom to reorganize the structure of the book as I thought fit, always in concert with him. Thus, I removed the largest part of the 1364 pages of the Greek edition, essentially generating a book of ▌ pages. For someone who is not really proficient in Markos Vamvakaris's turbulent life, reading an English version of more than 1000 pages would be tedious, taking in consideration, for example, the countless documents (catalogs, official documents, photos, glossaries, etc.) which were collected over decades by Dimitris Varthalitis (and which concern not only Markos but also Syros, Piraeus, the Catholic Church, etc.) and included in the Greek version. Basic texts containing the testimonies of people who met Markos Vamvakaris, several of the photographs, the family trees of the Vamvakaris and Provelengios families (pages ▌-▌), as well as a cumulative and updated timeline have of course been retained. Some other minor changes involved removing repetitions, moving sentences within a paragraph and moving or even linking up one paragraph with another. In addition, some excerpts from the original text were converted into footnotes in order to better fit, emphasize and not interrupt the reading flow in an abrupt manner.

Yet, what should be noted is that new interviews taken by Dimitris Varthalitis, as well as new texts which are not included in the Greek version of the book and which come from the magazine "Syriana Grammata" (Issue 7, July 2020), as well as some unpublished ones, have been added to this edition. Thus, as the research still carries on, the readers have the opportunity to learn new facts and information about Markos Vamvakaris's life and works.

In the process of translating I did my best to stay as faithful as possible to the original. More particularly, as regards the part of the interviews, I made every effort to maintain the style of expression of each interviewee. It is not always easy to find the right words to illustrate aspects of the character of a person who narrates his/her own experience with or view of Markos. I should also note that I chose to leave some words belonging to the rebetiko slang untranslated and simply transliterate them into English; their explanations are given in footnotes at the bottom of the pages concerned.

I have to thank Grigoris Kourkoulas for his general support, as well as Georgia Skalidi and Manos Kounougakis for the corrections and the proofreading of the final text. I am also grateful to Dimitris Kakarelis and Dimitris Milidonis for their help in the editing and formatting of some of the photos and the family trees, as well as to Efi Katsikari for her kind cooperation in organizing and resolving various issues raised during the translation process of the book. Finally, I would like to particularly thank the restless Dimitris Varthalitis who entrusted me with this important endeavor; I hope I lived up to his expectations, as well as to those of the readers.

Christos Poulakis

Christos Poulakis was born in Greece in 1987. He grew up in Venezuela, Morocco and Belgium, where he graduated from the European School of Brussels III (2005). He then moved to Athens to study Communication, Media and Culture at the Panteion University of Social and Political Sciences (2011) and completed his postgraduate studies in Translation at the University of Strasbourg (2012). He has been working since as a translator, proofreader and publisher. In 2109, he translated in French and published Markos Vamvakaris's autobiography under the title "Markos Vamvakaris : le patriarche du rébétiko – Autobiographie". He was interested in music since his teens and learned to play the bouzouki, the tzoura and the baglama. He has played rebetiko in various bands and now also offers bouzouki lessons.

To Vikentios

To Petros

1

FROM MYTH TO HISTORY

I

It's the second Wednesday of August 1909. I'm around four years of age. Our faithful dog Arapis is sitting on my lap. An improvised bouzouki is hanging from my left shoulder and I'm holding Rokos's halter in my right hand; that's the name of the donkey barba[12] Pieros Vamvakaris has lent us. My mother Elpida is sitting on the saddle holding Leonardos, still a baby, in her arms. I'll sit on the donkey's hindquarters once we get started.

My father Domenikos is standing very skeptical behind the donkey; I can hear him say: "Last Tuesday afternoon, when I was cutting osiers in the stream below Saint Kirykos, I felt tired and went into the cave where I was born and sat next to the sheep. I fell asleep and had a dream about leaving this place. Speranza[13], I have a swelling in my heart leaving Danakos[14], Saint Kirykos, the cave I was born in, as well as Tsygros, with barba Pieros's house, where we had our two children..."

On hearing these words, I'm sitting down, bending my cap and plucking loudly the stretched strings of my improvised bouzouki with my calloused little fingers, shouting out

---

[12] Barba(s) = term used to designate older men, similar to "uncle".

[13] The name Speranza is an Italian name meaning "hope", i.e. "elpida" in Greek.

[14] Danakos is a small village located on the west side of the island of Syros. Markos Vamvakaris spent the early years of his life in that village.

29

the pain of my infant soul: "Daddy, it would kill me if I didn't strike them so loud. Barba Pieros got us out of his house. Megas took our field with the bucketed water well, Leonardos, our baby, is hungry and there's no milk coming out of the breasts of my twenty-year-old mom. What else can we do but leave?" I look at my mother and I see the hope in her eyes flickering. My father picks me up and sits me cross-legged on Rokos's hips while hugging my mother. He wipes one of his tears and shouts loudly: "Let's go, Rokos!" and off we go like refugees in our homeland.

We reach Vigla, from where Kini can be seen, we cross Chalara and we quench our thirst at the source of Trypiti. We bless ourselves in front of the monastery of Saint Varvara and the chapel of Vouliani, we cross Sifneika, we reach Alithini and we hear the bells ringing. "It's noon and Don Almansis is ringing the Saint Sebastian's bells. It's time for people to eat", my mother says. And while my father cuts slices of barley bread with his hands so we can eat, my mother, waving her right arm around, says in her sweet voice: "Here's Alithini, there's Nichori and next to it is Pateli." We were on her turf. She was feeling nostalgic after five years.

"Mother, what's that downhill under Saint Giorgis?"

"It's Mentonis's Persinos, my child. Portara is right below. If you slip on the rocks a little bit they'll slide down and do great damage. Swear to me you'll never go there."

"I swear, mommy."

As we ate the barley homemade bread with some fresh maronia and gaitania figs, a bunch of Serfiotiko and Roditis[15],

---

[15] The maronia are white figs, the gaitania are black figs, the Serfiotiko is a white-skinned Greek grape variety and the Roditis is a pink-

the boat that was entering into the port honked its horn. My father said: "Today, your uncle Morfinis[16] will travel to America with this boat to go find work and maybe one day you will too, Markos. Our relative Irini Altouva[17] will do the same, as she's also going to Piraeus. Who knows when we'll see them again?"

Don Almansis, Pateli, Nichori, Alithini and Saint Sebastian, the rocks of Persinos, the boat, Piraeus, uncle Morfinis, America, aunt Irini hammered my soul just like the nails were hammered on my wooden bouzouki.

I'm sitting cross-legged on a rock straightening my cap and plucking the string of my bouzouki in a different now; I'm starting to play at my own rebetiko rhythm. My dad's soul is slowly bursting. He raises his hands, starts dancing a zeibekiko[18] and singing with his heavy voice:

---

skinned Greek grape variety traditionally grown in the Peloponnese region.

[16] "My uncle Morfinis, who died in America, also played the bouzouki a little" (Markos Vamvakaris, "Autobiography", compiled by Angeliki Vellou-Keil, second edition, Papazisis publications, Athens, 1978, p. 35). Hereinafter indicated as "op. cit.".

[17] "When I left Syros and came to Piraeus, I stayed with an aunt of mine called Irini Altouva in Fotiou Korytsas Street, down the far end of Tabouria" (op. cit., p. 81).

[18] The dance of the Zeybeks warriors (irregular militiamen and guerrillas living in the Aegean region of the Ottoman Empire from the end of the 17th to the beginning of the 20th century also acting, traditionally, as protectors of the villagers against bandits and tax collectors) in 9/8 or 9/4 time signature. This dance is very popular in Greece and its main characteristic is that it accepts only one dancer. It is danced freely, with the arms outstretched like a hawk. The term also designates a family of rhythms.

The pretty ones are in Finikas[19],
in Della Grazia[20] are the pale ones;
and in lovely Galissas[21]
carnations and potted plants.

The goodies are in Chrousa[22],
the tomatoes are in Galissa;
but the pea plants, in Danakos,
they are full of smoke.

I'll never go to Piskopio[23] again
nor sit on the stone bench,
cos they told lies about me
that I love a serving wench.

Στον Φοίνικα είναι οι όμορφες,
στην Ντελλαγκράτσα οι
άσπρες,
και στον ωραίο Γαληοσά
γαρυφαλλιές και γλάστρες.

Στα Χρούσα είναι τα καλά,
στον Γαληοσά οι ντομάτες,
στον Δανακό οι μπιζελιές
είναι καπνό γεμάτες.

Δεν πάω πια στο Πισκοπειό
να κάτσω στην πεζούλα,
γιατί μου βγάλαν αβανιά
πως αγαπώ μια δούλα.

He stops dancing and singing and signals me to loudly hit the strings. In a delirium, stretching out his arms and pointing to the farthest reaches of earth, he slowly starts singing

---

[19] Finikas is a settlement on the southwestern part of Syros located 12 km from Ermoupoli. In ancient times, it was a port of the Phoenicians, from which it took its name.

[20] Poseidonia (named after the god Poseidon) is a village in Syros located 10 km from Ermoupoli. It was also known as Della Grazia (name taken from the small church of Maria della Grazia) in the past.

[21] Galissa(s) is a seaside village in Syros. It is located on the west side of the island, 7 km from Ermoupoli.

[22] Chrousa is a settlement located on the south side of the island of Syros, 8.5 km from Ermoupoli.

[23] (E)piskopio is a settlement in Syros. It is built on the slopes of a pine-covered hill and is one of the richest sources of greenery on the island. It is located 4.5 km from Emoupoli.

an amanes[24]:

Foreign lands will cherish you,[25]	*Η ξενιτειά θα σε χαρεί*
not I, my bouzouki player.	*κι όχι εγώ, μπουζουξή μου.*
From the bottom of my heart	*Από τα βάθη της καρδιάς*
I'll keep you in my prayer.	*σου δίνω την ευχή μου.*

Markos D. Vamvakaris

II

On December 18, 1966, we had planned to give the grades to the parents of the students of the Saint-Paul French School of Piraeus, where I was teaching French. Domenikos, the son of Markos Vamvakaris, who was a graduate student of the school during the school year 1966-1967, had informed me that his father, who was a bit weary, would come to the School.

Indeed, at one point I saw Markos Vamvakaris getting down from a tricycle and standing behind the School's main gate. I approached him, and after heartily embracing him, we went down to the semi-basement of the school, in the frères'[26] dining room. There, besides Domenikos's future, we discussed about (what else?) Syros and his life. He was 61

---

[24] Special kind of monophonic song, the main characteristic of which is the repetition of the Turkish affirmation "aman" which means "mercy" or "compassion".

[25] "To the people whose joys and sorrows, wealth and poverty, orphanhood and exile I was the first to sing" (op. cit., p. 33).

[26] The Brothers of the Christian Schools (also known as the Frères des Écoles Chrétiennes) is a Catholic religious teaching congregation, founded in France by a priest named Jean-Baptiste de La Salle (1651–1719). Frères means "brothers".

years old and I was 23, when I was starting out. Here's what I remember after 51 years:

"I was born in the house of barba Pieros, at Pouletos, in Tsygros, Danakos, where I spent my childhood. In Danakos there's the church of Saint Kirykos. I wasn't baptized there, but in Saint Sebastian, in Apano Chora, because it was where the parish to which Danakos belonged and the place where my mother was from. Below Saint Kirykos is a ravine crossed by a stream with osiers, and fifty meters above there's a cave where my father Domenikos was born.

When I was young, my family and I used to go to the festivals in the surrounding villages. We also used to go to the festival of Amaliani on the 15th of August, with almost the whole village of Danakos being present. All of them were also attending the festival of Saint Kirykos on the 8th of September. They were very poor, but with some olives and a herring they were drinking a carboy of wine. And what a wine! They were making it on their own. After the service at the festival of Panagia[27] Amaliani, the feast began underneath the centuries-old olive trees. I remember a guy called Bastianos playing the lute. I was sitting spellbound next to him and listening.

When it was time to go to school, in 1909, we left from Danakos and went to Skali[28] in Apano Chora. I had stopped school when the French frères came in 1914 and opened a French school across Saint Sebastian, very close to our house, which was operated by the Josephine nuns as a kindergarten; I went there for one year. The frères were weirdly dressed, they were wearing cassocks, though they were not priests, had a white collar and were wearing a tricorne as a hat. In addition to Catholic students, wealthy Orthodox students

---

[27] Panagia means the "Virgin Mary".
[28] Skali means "step" in Greek.

from Ermoupoli also went on to do their French lessons. I envied them. Some were boarders from the surrounding islands. I reacquainted myself with those frères when the time came to send my three children to school. I came and enrolled them here, in Saint Paul, where frères from Syros are now teaching, such as frère Stefanos Sargolos, frère Petros Roussos, the kindhearted frère Léonard and others. I'm grateful to them.

When I was older, I went back to Syros and sang at Piskopio, at Psariaras's tavern, at the request of shipowner Minas Rethymnis. There was a big difference between the villagers of Danakos and Malia and the wealthy people and shipowners of Piskopio[29]. These people were however also born poor and now they're living large in Piskopio. Night and day... And they were so close! But this injustice still exists everywhere, even now. These frères over here are the exception. They feed the poor students in the same dining room where they eat, with the same dishes and with the same food that they eat, and they provide them with the best education, the Greek-French. When I come to this school, I feel perfection. Oh, if only the whole of society was like that!"

As he was talking, he got up, extended his hands to the ground and assumed the posture so as if he was about to dance a zeibekiko. "When I was dancing zeibekiko it was just me and God." At that moment, I was immersed within his dark-brown eyes to the depth of his soul. He also looked at me and said: "Dimitris, I really liked the bouzouki. With the bouzouki I tried to give joy to my tormented soul and to the people who have suffered. You should freely do something

---

[29] "I remember some rich old guys in Syra, shipowners with loads of money" (op. cit., p. 122).

you like in your life. Build your own school so as to love children."

We got up and we had difficulty climbing the stairs. He grasped the banister with his right hand and he put his left hand around my neck to feel safe. I felt very happy. I was receiving vitality from a giant. And while saying goodbye, he told me: "May you live long, my master."

This happy encounter with Markos awakened in me some other memories related with my family and especially with my father. These memories even explain, to a certain extent, my particular love for Markos Vamvakaris. My father Vikentios, after coming home from work in the afternoon, always wanted to sit in the backyard of our home in Lazareta to play music, whistling in a very special way of his own. He used to stretch his lips as if he was smiling and use his tongue to control the air coming through his teeth and create the sound. So, his mouth was turning into a musical instrument and with that he was playing amazing melodies[30]. I really liked this music and I used to sit on a stool next to him and listen. He usually played Markos Vamvakaris's tunes.

My father, Vikentios Dimitriou Varthalitis, was born in Apano Syros in 1914 and was baptized in the Cathedral of Saint Georgios. When he was 10 years old, an instrumentalist refugee from Asia Minor gave him some bouzouki lessons and his sister Nikoleta bought him a bouzouki. Eventually he became a builder and then a contractor. While serving his military duty, he went with some other fellow soldiers from Syros to Markos's kafeneio[31] in Aspra Chomata and got to

---

[30] "I always did everything I could to be alone wherever I was because I had to either write verses or hum music" (op. cit., p. 257).

[31] Kafeneio(n) (pl. kafeneia) = the kafeneio designates the traditional Greek coffee house. The kafeneion is generally the central social spot of a village or of a neighborhood in a city.

know Markos, the bouzouki player, very well.

In the summer of 1955, I was 12 years old and I was studying to take introductory exams in order to enroll as a boarder at the middle school of the French College De La Salle in Thessaloniki. Markos Vamvakaris was in Syros and was playing and my father wanted to bring him at our house in Lazareta to accommodate him for a few days. My mother Annetta, who rarely refused his wishes, said to him:

"Vinkentios, right now Dimitris is studying for the intro exams, let's not disturb him. Maybe another time." I left for Thessaloniki in August and I didn't see or hear anything about Markos during my childhood. I knew him, however, from the songs my father used to sing and from the conversations that took place at home.

I remember when I heard my mother say that during the Occupation, when my father was a soldier, he had opened a kafeneion in Lazareta, in the cellar of our house, and the wealthy and affluent were coming from Ermoupoli to drink wine. In fact, I remember her saying that Markos Vamvakaris also once went there with his friends in 1941. In the summer, while studying the archives of the Chamber of the Cyclades, I was impressed when I found the license 2305/18-10-1940 that my father had been granted and had opened the kafeneion.

Every time Markos showed up in Syria, my father would go and have a good time with him. He also stayed at our home in Malia. There, he confided his sorrow in my father: half Syrans were enjoying themselves with him at night and the other half were turning away when he walked by.

"But the time will come when they too will listen to my songs. But I'll be dead by then", he said, and a round tear rolled down from his eye. They ate a homemade sausage with thyme from Syros, pikti[32], cracked green olives with fennel, grilled herring also with thyme, kopanisti cheese[33], pasta and drank aromatic red wine. Finally, they drank heavy coffee. "Here's how I prepared it", my father told me. "As always, I had cooked in a clay pot with kudzu vines and the ember was still hot in the stone fireplace. With a special stick, like the ones doctors use for the tongue, I put seven level tablespoons of coffee and very little sugar in the coffee pot, and while the coffee was rising in the coffee pot, I stirred the coffee with a special spoon in order for the blend to mix with the entire amount of the coffee. I took the pot off the ember three times and I also put it back on three times. Then, from above, I poured the coffee into a thick cup in order to create a lot of bubbles and I served it to Markos, who slurped it; his slurp was like the chirping of goldfinches. After drinking it, Markos said to me: "Vikentios, you really know how to make a good coffee." When I met Markos in 1966 at Saint Paul, he remembered it. He also remembered the pastelaries[34] he offered him.

My father told me that one time, when Markos was singing at Kopanakis, told the milkmen: "Go home and feed your children. Don't spend all your money here." And he sang them his song "O grousouzis"[35] (1937), which he had written on Syros.

---

[32] Traditional head cheese.

[33] Kopanisti is a spicy cheese with a pungent, intense peppery taste, reminiscent of Roquefort cheese but also distinct, since it has no particular shape and is spreadable, with a characteristic tan and, sometimes, a pale pink color that darkens as it matures.

[34] Pastelaria (pl. pastelaries) = a kind of sweet consisting of dried figs sprinkled with sesame and cinnamon.

[35] "The loser".

All night long, you loser, you sit and booze it up, leaving your kids at home all famished and locked up.	Βρε γρουσούζη, όλη νύχτα κάθεσαι και μπεκροπίνεις, και στο σπίτι τα παιδιά σου θεονήστικα τ' αφήνεις.
All day long you're drunk, where do you go to hit it up? You cause your family agitation since you lead them to starvation.	Μεθυσμένος όλη μέρα, πού γυρνάς και μπεκρουλιάζεις, και την οικογένειά σου απ' την πείνα την ταράζεις;
Have a care and change your tune, try to collect your thought; and if you've got a dime left, to your kids it should be brought.	Κοίταξε ν' αλλάξεις γνώμη, να μαζέψεις τα μυαλά σου, κι αν σου μείνει μια δεκάρα να τη φέρνεις στα παιδιά σου.
Go find some other girl if you don't like me anymore; I can't stand you any longer, you alcoholic, grumbling bore!	Όταν εγώ δεν σου αρέσω, κοίταξε άλλη να πάρεις· δεν μπορώ πια να σ' αντέξω, να 'σαι μπέκρας και γκρινιάρης!

In 1985, Tsitsanis and Bellou[36] were singing in Charama[37] and I was sitting at the first table after having been invited by the owner of the place. During the break, Tsitsanis came and sat at my table. In the course of conversation, he told me that when Markos used to play in Piraeus he could be heard up to Trikala. I asked him if he went to his funeral. If I remember correctly, he told me that he had sent a wreath, but he could not attend. When he got back on stage, he asked me to dance the song "O Markos mathitis"[38] (1935). The business owner sent three waiters with a stack of dishes each and smashed them at my feet.

As I was going to sit down, Bellou nodded at me; she was sitting with two girlfriends of hers somewhere a little bit

---

[36] Sotiria Bellou (1921-1997) was a famous rebetiko singer.

[37] "Dawn".

[38] "Markos the student".

more private and I went and sat next to her and poured me a glass of red wine. Over our discussion I realized that Bellou loved Markos. She told me at one point: "Markos, whom you had the chance to meet, is expecting something from you. Promise me you won't forget it." She got up and sang "Frangosyriani"[39] in my honor.

During that period, I also went to listen to Stelios at "Perivoli t'ouranou"[40] and he also sang "Frangosyriani" to thank me. I was also lucky enough to speak with Grigoris Bithikotsis[41] at Domenikos Vamvakaris's concert in Michail Voda Street in 1985. This is what he told me: "When I was 15 years old, in addition to Markos's other songs, I also heard 'Frangosyriani' on a neighbor's record player and everything changed in me.

If I hadn't listened to Markos's songs, I'd have never been involved with singing. When I went and found him in Aspra Chomata he was lying in bed with a hose in his mouth. When I left, he threw it away because of his joy. But I too was even more happy that day. A shy little boy was present: it was Domenikos, who we honor today, and who can confirm it."

When, on a Sunday in 1968, I met Markos Vamvakaris at the Piraeus Catholic church, I asked him the following:

---

[39] "Frankosyran girl".

[40] "Orchard of the sky". A very famous tavern in Athens.

[41] Grigoris Bithikotsis (December 11, 1922 – April 7, 2005) was a popular Greek folk singer/songwriter/bouzouki player. He is considered one of the greatest singers of Greek music. He secretly started playing bouzouki at an early age because his father did not like rebetiko. In 1959, he met Mikis Theodorakis and the two collaborated to produce songs that are still very popular. Bithikotsis participated in the creation of the musical genre that followed rebetiko, laiko.

— *Markos, what was the most important thing that happened in Syros before leaving for Piraeus?*

It was in early 1913. I was eight years old. A Turkish warship, "Hamidiye", was informed that the Greek ship "Macedonia" was in the port of Syros to be repaired and came to bomb it[42]. There was also an English ship inside the harbor that had come to load emery. "Hamidiye" ordered the English ship to leave the port. The latter stalled in order for the "Macedonia" to scuttle. It was helping it. When it sank, it left the port. As soon as it came out, the cannons started firing from Fanari[43]. Dimitris, if only you were at Ai Giannis in Apano Syros, in the Capuchins monastery. Up to 2,000 people from Ermoupoli surrounded it and the Capuchins raised the French flag so they wouldn't bombard them. The same thing happened at the French nuns' hospital. When people realized that the "Hamidiye" had left for good, they went back down. The following day I went down to the port and saw the "Macedonia" sunken and I learned that a maid who was cleaning a house nearby had been killed by a projectile. My mother was pregnant and she almost lost the baby[44]. She was also thinking of my father who was a soldier.

— *Markos, which bouzouki player had you singled out in Syros?*

---

[42] See newspapers "Ermoupolitis", issue 528-529-530/1913 and "To Vima", issue 5-12-19/1913.

[43] Fanari (or Didymi or Gaidouri or Gaidouronisi) is a small uninhabited skerry located opposite the port of Ermoupoli, in the eastern part of Syros.

[44] She was thinking about Markos's brother, Antonis, who was born on March 7, 1913 and died on April 7, 1913.

Dimitris, there was a guy named Vafeas, a barber. He had his barber shop inside the market. When he was playing in his barber shop, when I was just a kid, or at Gavrilis's tavern, when I used to come to Syra[45] when I grew up, I couldn't get enough of him. He fascinated me. He had come from Constantinople. I saw Vafeas for the last time during the Occupation, in 1941, when I came to Syra to mourn some of my friends who had died. I had met him every time I came to Syra before the Occupation and we used to have a good time together. He loved me very much.

— *What do you remember from your school in Syros?*

The building was old. We were told that it was one of the first schools built in Greece. I had even heard that a German had designed it. I had two teachers: Nikolas Printezis from Apano Syros and Giorgos Tsagkouros. I loved learning. But I only went to school for four years.

— *Where did you stay when you came to Piraeus?*

At first, I was staying with a friend of mine, Iosif, in a boat. I'd gotten used to the port of Syros and I wasn't so impressed by the hubbub of Piraeus. Iosif's brothers, who had a boat and transported agricultural products from the ships, gave me something to eat... In the meantime, I found an aunt of mine, Irini Altouva, and asked her for a place to sleep. She asked for a small rent in order to get me to start working. So, I went and worked as a coal man to make money. It was a really tough job and I thanked God I'd found it.

Dimitris. V. Varthalitis

---

[45] The island of Syros is also sometimes called Syra.

2

MARKOS LIVED
THROUGH HIS SORROWS

Markos's house was across from ours in Aspra Chomata. I knew his father Domenikos as well as his mother Elpida. She was a very good woman. She used to say to him: "You should marry Vangelio"[46]. My mother Marianthi and my mother-in-law Elpida weren't alive. So, he came and he asked for my hand. He said to my father Lefteris Vergiou: "Mr. Lefteris, I want to marry your daughter Elpida"[47]. He replied: "You're too old for Vangelio." I was born on April 10, 1918. He was born on May 10, 1905. He was 13 years older than me.

My father was sick. He had enterocolitis. Once he got well, Markos came back. He received the same answer. Then my father died and Markos came back again after some time. We were six siblings, three boys and three girls. I was the eldest. We had a meeting. After discussing it, I agreed too and I said yes and we got married within a month[48].

---

[46] "My sister, the older one [Grazia], started on at me saying that Vangelio is a good girl and our mother also wanted it to be her when she was alive [...] you'll be happy" (op. cit., p. 195).

[47] "Vangelio was good. I mean, I wish I'd had her for my first wife because then people would have pointed at me and said 'There goes a lucky man'. Such a good homemaker, this woman I've got now [...] I was much older than her and we lived in harmony" (op. cit., p. 197).

[48] "I got married one Sunday in 1942 [11 July 1943] and I invited my fellow musicians to my in-laws' house – that is, the band I played with. Peristeris, Papaioannou, Keromytis, Kostas Karipis and other

Nearby, 44 Nikis Street and 70A Krinis Street, Nikos Persiadis, of Russian origin, had a grocery store. He removed all of his stuff from inside the store as a favor to Markos and the marriage was held with three priests; the wedding feast followed. There were also bouzoukia.

Markos was brave and kind and a very good husband. He loved God and his children[49]. He loved me very much[50]. He loved animals, flowers, having fun. He loved Syros a tad more. He was a Frankosyran[51]. We always had loukoumia from Syros in our house and we served them to our friends and visitors.

Markos was glutton and a big eater. When he wanted to eat, he made a fuss about being served and eating fast. The children, however, were small and I had to look after them first and then after him. He liked all kinds of food. He especially liked eating pikti, Syran loukoumia[52], dried figs and

---

colleagues too that didn't play with me. That was my wedding with Vangelio, my present wife" (op. cit., p. 196).

[49] "I live quietly, a family man with a good and dear wife and my three boys. Lord love them" (op. cit., p. 34).

[50] "I loved my wife [Vangelio] because she loved me very much and she was a great wife. I wouldn't trade her in for any woman. She was a real gem" (op. cit., p. 202).

[51] The island was conquered by the Venetians after the siege of Constantinople by the Venetians and the Franks in the Fourth Crusade in 1204. It remained part of the Duchy of Naxos until 1522, which explains why most of Syros's residents were Catholics or "Frankosyrans".

[52] Loukoumi is a family of confections based on a gel of starch and sugar. Varieties are often flavored with rosewater, mastic, Bergamot orange, lemon, pistachios, hazelnuts or walnuts bound by the gel. The

drinking sage tea. We also had a lantern in which were several things, and definitely herrings[53]. Markos liked variety.

All three of our children, Vassilis, Stelios and Domenikos, were sent to Saint Paul's French School in Piraeus. I have a weakness for all my children. I spent all my life near Domenikos.

We went through very difficult times together with Markos. He died young. He shouldn't have died so early... He lived through his sorrows.

Evangelia Vamvakari

In memoriam

Evangelia Vamvakaris could be considered as Markos Vamvakaris's second chance in life, because it was thanks to her that he set aside the painful memories of his first marriage. "I believed all women were the same. But later on [...] my sister told me: 'Vangelio is a good girl [...], you'll be happy" (p. 195) and he devoted himself fully to Evangelia, who was different. He brought to life his descendants with her. "And I began to bring children into the world with this woman, something I'd given up hoping for." (p. 197)

He considered and respected her opinion. "Whatever the wife tells me." (p. 252) He had complete confidence in her, as he was confiding in her about his pains, his yearnings and his secrets. "When it's a good dream I talk about it with my wife Vangelio; we discuss what we'll do, what will happen, what we'll make of it." (p. 120) "I told my wife when I got

---

confection is packaged and eaten in small cubes dusted with icing sugar.

[53] "When I was feeling well I used to eat herrings, sardines, olives and garlic" (op. cit., p. 253).

back home and we didn't sleep that night." (p. 204) Evangelia was Markos's pillar of support, his rock, his harbor, his love in which he found refuge.

On February 12, 2012, forty-six years after meeting Markos in Saint Paul's School of Piraeus, I phoned Evangelia Vamvakari. "I'm waiting for you, my child. I'm going to prepare you a cup of coffee in the same cup from which Markos used to drink his coffee." It was noon when I arrived and Evangelia, 94 years old, was lying down. Her soul was vibrant. She got up and hugged me. I had hugged Markos, now I had also hugged Evangelia. How happy I was!

Dimitris. V. Varthalitis

3

MARKOS, THE "PATRIARCH" OF REBETIKO

Markos loved all three of us. He had a special relationship with each one of us[54].

— *Domenikos, tell me one of your childhood memories.*

Markos worked different jobs to raise us. Among these, he had opened a grocery shop in the basement of our house in Aspra Chomata, where his office was. He also had a donkey and his trailer. My older brother Vassilis and I were five or six years old, we used to yoke it, go to the farmer's market and sell potatoes, onions, tangerines, oranges. One time, it started thundering and raining and it startled the donkey, so it started running and stopped just outside the door of our house in Aspra Chomata. As if Markos knew it. He was waiting for us outside and reassured us.

— *At what age did you go to the conservatory?*[55]

I was 18 years old. Vassilis took me and I enrolled. I was shy. I obtained all the diplomas. I studied for 12 years, then

---

[54] "I feel calm now that my kids have grown up and turned out well" (op. cit., p. 240)

[55] "My son Domenikos, who goes to the Conservatory, knows this stuff" (op. cit., p. 271).

I was appointed professor at private educational establishments, and after that, I transitioned to public educational establishments where I successfully worked for 19 years in a row.[56]

— *When did you buy your first piano?*

When I started learning piano at the conservatory, I bought a piano with my own money that I was collecting; I put it in the basement. I got it in 1968 from Giorgos Rovertakis[57], the musician who played with Markos, for 4,000 drachmas. It was a used German-made piano. You cannot imagine how happy Markos was. He was writing songs and playing them on the bouzouki and I was playing accompaniments on the piano.

— *Domenikos, which musical instrument do you love?*

I play the bouzouki and the piano. Out of the two, I guess I have to pick out the bouzouki. And I owe this to Markos.

— *When did you first go to Syros with Markos?*

---

[56] "I'm quite sure the youngest one [Domenikos] will become a great musician. Give it a couple of years and he won't be touching any laika at all. He'll play European songs, the great music. He writes it, he reads it, he goes to the Conservatory. He's on the way to becoming a maestro this one" (op. cit., p. 240).

[57] Giorgos Rovertakis was born in Smyrna in 1911 and died in Athens in 1978. He played the piano, accordion and harmonium.

In 1955, when I was six years old, I accompanied my father on a trip of his to Syros. Stelios also came with us. They had played in Mykonos before. It was the summer season and school was out... I remember the stage they had made out of beer crates at Lilis's tavern in Apano Syros. They went on and played. I was sitting all night watching them, next to my father. I remember Lilis's famous meatballs... I went again back to Syra with Markos for two or three summers. I played in Dili, in a tavern near Anastasi, with a baglama[58]. Recently, I played with Giorgos Dalaras in a three-day event in honor of Markos. It was the first time Giorgos Dalaras sang Markos's songs. I had also sung during the "Apanosyria" festival, when Markos Daskos was mayor.

— *Who was Markos's close friend in Syros?*

In Syra, a close friend of Markos was Artemis, the waterseller. He was born in 1917. He had all of Markos's records and a record player and he would play them over and over again. He also used to drink and have a blast at Tembelis's tavern in Vrontado. I got to know this man very well. My father had slept in his house. He would always welcome him when he was getting off the boat and bid him farewell when he was leaving.

— *Did Markos have flowers and animals in Aspra Chomata?*

He had many flowers, especially rose bushes. I also remember a vine and some olive trees. He had a small one in

---

[58] Baglama(s) (pl. baglamades) = a three-stringed musical instrument. It is a kind of miniature bouzouki.

the yard at home, but also on the sidewalk. The house was ours[59]. He also had a plot a little bit further. This is where he put all the animals. A goat, some rabbits - which I used to clean up and they were stinking - and a donkey. We also drank donkey milk. He was paying someone to clean and feed them. He was keeping the animals out of love. He had acquired this habit and love from Syra. He used to hang bird-cages with goldfinches, chaffinches and canaries outside the house. We're talking about many birds... I used to clean them. I had kind of drawn the short straw.

— *When did you leave from Aspra Chomata?*

I was 19 years old when we left from Aspra Chomata. As soon as I went to the air force[60], we moved to Perivolaki, on Dedalou Street, near the hospital. Markos lived in that house for the rest of his life.

— *How did you learn to play the bouzouki?*

The trigger was listening to Markos's bouzouki. Since we were young, we used to play the baglama and, in the end, we switched over to the bouzouki. This is how we learned to play the bouzouki. We inherited a lot from Markos. Markos had learned to play the baglama and the three-stringed bou-zouki.

— *How did the music tradition of Syros affect Markos*

---

[59] "I liked letters, as I said, music and flowers. Ah yes, flowers... Even now, down at my niece's house, I have pots of jasmine, roses, carnations. [...] And up there on the plot of land I got, I have three olive trees" (op. cit., p. 255).

[60] "The kid calls me, Domenikos, who's still a soldier" (op. cit., p. 252).

Vamvakaris as a composer and performer?

It's from there that he transferred his memories and wrote his songs.

— *Who do you think Markos's music was addressed to?*

To the entire world.

— *How many jobs did Markos change during his life?*

Many jobs. That's why the song "Markos, Jack of all Trades" (1937) exists: he wrote in detail everything he had to do in order to survive. He worked in a grocery store, in a butcher shop, in a convenience store as an apprentice, in a port, where he carried coal, he was a shoe-shiner... He also opened a grocery store in Aspra Chomata and was a green-grocer for some time.

— *At that time, was it enough to only be a musician in order to make a living just from that?*
No.

— *What was Vamvakaris's relation with religion?*

He was religious. He always believed in God. He crossed himself before eating and before sleeping.

— *What kind of audience did Markos like to play music and sing to?*

To the common people.

— *Was Markos asking the opinion of others about the songs he was writing? Whose opinion mattered most?*

There were many times when he would ask for us and play his new songs in the basement, which was his office, where he was composing them. We were telling him our opinion and we mainly were encouraging him.

— *Was Markos interested in the general social, economic and political situation of his day?*

Yes, of course. He had immediacy; his songs prove this. He also wrote political songs, songs about money, about ministers, etc.

— *Did he consider himself a professional, a semi-professional or an amateur musician?*

Professional.

— *Is there a difference between an instrumentalist and a musician?*

An instrumentalist is a musician. There is no difference.

— *What particular techniques did he use when playing? Were these used in some parts of his work or in his entire repertoire?*

He had a special technique, the karadouzenia[61]. He divided the bouzouki into several pitches in order to perform each song. He was the only one to know the karadouzenia, such as arabienne karadouzeni, sirf karadouzeni and many

---

[61] Special bouzouki tunings (also called "douzenia").

others. No one else knew them, no one was playing them. Only Markos did. He had learned them from the old players in Syros and they were in his DNA. He knew them, was playing them, and thus he correctly performed each song to the pitch it had to be played. There was also the Italian tuning where he played normally, just as the others did. But what made Markos special was the karadouzenia. That is the tunings, the special tunings.

— *How was his collaboration with other musicians, singers and instrumentalists in the orchestras in which he participated?*

Flawless, very good.

— *Did he prefer fixed collaborations?*

As far as possible.

— *How much attention did he pay to the virtuosity of an instrumentalist?*

He admired it.

— *What was his opinion on the subsequent addition of new, modern instruments to the laiko[62] orchestras?*

He sometimes disagreed.

---

[62] Urban folk music style, in contrast to the traditional rural music (dimotiko), which followed rebetiko. The word "laiko" means "popular" in Greek. Many use this term to also designate rebetiko.

— *Which singer did he like the most?*

Grigoris Bithikotsis.

— *Did he ever work with Zabetas[63]?*

Yes, on stage. But not on record labels.

— *What musical knowledge did Markos have?*

Everything he retained in his mind from the music he was listening was he was a kid. Markos had an exceptional memory.

— *What was his opinion about the Syran society?*

He went often to Syra. During the summers, when he would leave with a band of four or five people, first they would make a stop to Syros in order to confirm his presence and then they would go to the other islands. He loved Syra and he wrote songs for the island, such as "Markos, o Syrianos" (1933), "Frangosyriani" (1935), "Syros" (1936) and "Koula Frangosyriani" (1940).[64]

---

[63] Giorgos Zabetas (1925-1992) was a music composer, singer and one of the greatest bouzouki artists. He was one of the most recognized musicians of all times, as he appeared in many Greek film productions and also worked with famous Greek composers.

[64] "Markos, the Syran", "Frankosyran girl", "Syros", Koula, the Frankosyran girl".

— The painter Stavros Pasparakis told me: "El Greco[65], Elytis[66], Seferis[67], Markos Vamvakaris, they are one and the same!" What's your opinion on that?

Markos is the "Patriarch" of rebetiko. He's considered as one of the great personalities of the Greek pantheon.

— Was Markos influenced by Byzantine music?

Of course. His songs were influenced by Byzantium. But he was also influenced by western music.

— What does the bouzouki mean to Markos?

For Markos, the bouzouki was the be-all and end-all of his soul.

— Where did Markos use to write his lyrics?

---

[65] Domenikos Theotokopoulos (1541-1614), most widely known as El Greco (meaning "The Greek"), was a Greek painter, sculptor and architect of the Spanish Renaissance. "El Greco" was a nickname referring to his Greek origin.

[66] Odysseas Elytis (born Odysseas Alepoudellis, 1911-1996) was a translator, poet, art critic and writer. He was regarded as a major exponent of romantic modernism in Greece and the world. In 1979, he was awarded the Nobel Prize in Literature.

[67] Giorgos Seferis (born Giorgos Seferiadis, 1900-1971) was a poet and diplomat. He was one of the most important Greek poets of the 20th century and a Nobel laureate. He was a career diplomat in the Greek Foreign Service, culminating in his appointment as Ambassador to the UK, a post which he held from 1957 to 1962. In 1963, he was awarded the Nobel Prize in Literature.

He had a talent for writing music and lyrics[68]. He used to write the lyrics right away and he was playing music by whistling. He used to sit in the kafeneion across from the house and drink his coffee. From that spot, he was observing and writing about all kinds of people on cardboard boxes, cigarettes, papers and notebooks, whatever was in front of him at that moment. A few days later, he would call a musician to write down the music on a sheet music for him. Giorgos Theofilopoulos, Mimis Prokos from Syros, Spyros Peristeris[69]... These guys had studied music. Markos had written the lyrics. They were sitting on the small balcony of our house; Markos was playing his musical inspiration on his bouzouki and they were writing it on the sheet music. Markos had the wind; he wasn't just anyone. He was a natural. He used to go to the record label and show them his lyrics

---

[68] "My first songs. I'd write the lyrics and set them to music and it was all done. I was memorizing and playing them on my bouzouki. [...] I had learned them all by heart with the bouzouki" (op. cit., p. 158).

[69] Spyros Peristeris (1900-1966) was born in Smyrna. He learned to play the mandolin from a young age. Around 1914, his family moved to Constantinople where Peristeris completed his music studies and was already an acclaimed musician at the age of 18. Following the Asia Minor Disaster in 1922, Peristeris moved to Athens, where he soon learned to play the bouzouki and became known as a composer and lyricist. Peristeris could play all fingerboard string instruments as well as the piano, accordion, cello and double bass. From the early 1930s, he worked as local repertory manager and orchestra leader for several recording companies (namely Gramophone, Columbia, His Master's Voice, Odeon, Parlophone) in Greece. From these posts, he strongly influenced rebetiko. He was pivotal in persuading Markos Vamvakaris to record his songs. In parallel with his managerial activities, Peristeris continued to compose and record songs of his own.

and music to get the go-ahead; after that, they told him he could record.

Grigoris Bithikotsis, Poly Panou[70], Katy Grey[71], Stamatis Kokotas[72] used to sing. The label was choosing them. Markos also chose some of them to sing his songs. They would come home, go down to the basement and rehearse. Then they would record the songs at the label.

Markos was a troubadour in the truest sense of the word. He was writing both the lyrics and the music; he was also singing and dancing. He was one hell of a dancer. When he was dancing zeibekiko or chasapiko[73] it was all nobility.

— *How was Markos getting inspired in order to write songs?*

---

[70] Polly Panou (1940-2013) was a famous singer. She was born in Athens but grew up in Patras. Her real name was Polytimi Bitha (or Polytimi Koliopanou, according to others). She started recording in 1952 and founded the record label "Vendetta" in 1966. It is worth noting that Polly Panou was the first to sing the song "Ta paidia tou Pirea" (which translates in English as "Children of Piraeus") by composer Manos Chatzidakis, which later became an international success sung by Melina Mercouri in the movie "Never on Sunday".

[71] Katy Grey (real name: Athanasia Gizili) was born on May 14, 1924. She first became an actress and then recorded her first song in 1952. In the 1960s she was the highest paid singer of the time. She has recorded more than 1500 songs. In 1996, she retired from singing. See also page ▌ for more information.

[72] Stamatis Kokotas (born in 1937) is a Greek singer. His songs were very successful in the 1960s and 1970s.

[73] Chasapiko (pl. chasapika) = the "butcher's dance", originally from Constantinople, in 4/4 or 2/4 time signature. It is danced by at least two people by placing their arms on each other's shoulders.

He was a poet, that was that.

—   *What do you know about the kafeneio where Markos used to hang out?*

There were three brothers, Savvas, Stratos and Avraam. They were the owners of the kafeneio. The place was half a café and half a tavern. The best hearts used to gather at this tavern; they were drinking wine and were inviting Markos in order to play bouzouki for them. They were paying him.

I remember the hunters, who were coming back many afternoons from their hunt in the mountains outside Athens. The tavern-keeper was cooking the birds they'd caught and they were eating them. And Markos was playing the bouzouki and entertaining them. It was always the same folks from the neighborhood. They were drinkers these guys, they were hitting the bottle. They were also starting the phonograph with the old 78-rpm records of Markos and others. Markos wasn't drinking. He was just playing. He liked watching people having fun and that was making him happy. I was just a little kid; I was sitting outside playing and listening to him.

—   *Did Markos use to read newspapers?*

He was reading the newspapers at the kafeneion he was sitting across from our house. He would go and hang out in the corner of the kafeneion and pick up and read three or four newspapers: "Ta Nea", "Acropolis", "Ethnos", "Vradyni", "Apogevmatini".[74] He was blissful when he was reading. He was drawing information, data and coming up with ideas

---

[74] "The News", "Acropolis", "Nation", "Afternoon", "Evening".

from the newspapers and from the books he was reading. He especially loved the collected works of Giorgos Souris[75], who was also from Syros, as well as the collected works of Giorgos Vizyinos[76].

— *Had Markos set up a stage next to your house in Aspra Chomata?*

Yes, he had transformed the area within Mrs. Theodosia's sheepfold into a stage and many people were coming and having a good time. But he was forced to stop because the police didn't give him a permit. Immediately afterwards he began touring across Greece.

— *Were you present during Markos's decisive meeting with Bithikotsis?*

Back then I was an 11-year-old child. We were not used to such visits. I was sitting on the stairs and I heard them talking about collaborating. It was the greatest moment of joy of my childhood. Markos was smiling from ear to ear. Bithikotsis gave me a hug as he was leaving. Takis Labropoulos[77], the successor of Themistoklis Labropoulos in Colombia, came then to our house and I remember him saying that he

---

[75] Giorgos Souris (1853-1919) was one of the most important satirical poets of modern Greece, having been described as the "modern Aristophanes".

[76] Giorgos Vizyinos (born Giorgos Michail Syrmas or Michailidis, 1849-1896), was a Greek novelist, poet and scholar. He is considered one of the most important representatives of Greek literature.

[77] Takis Labropoulos (born in 1930) was the director of the record company Columbia, the administrative responsibility of which he assumed at the age of 28 in 1958.

had come at the instigation of Bithikotsis.

— *What was Bithikotsis opinion about your father?*

He considered him as if he was a tree and all his other colleagues, who did the same job, were the branches. Tsitsanis, for example, was a large bough. But he considered Markos as the pioneer of the genre. Markos first and the rest followed.

— *What are the first Markos's songs that Bithikotsis sang?*

I remember Markos's agony. The first record written and composed by Markos and performed by Grigoris Bithikotsis was released on May 19, 1960 with two songs: "Apelpistika"[78] (1960) and "Kavouras"[79] (1960), both zeibekika. The lyrics of "Apelpistika" allow us to understand the pain of Markos's soul when he was abandoned by everyone.

> Dark as the night is,
> my heart's in its embrace,
> and like the silent rain
> tears run down my face.

> Όσο είναι η νύχτα σκοτεινή,
> έτσι είναι κι η καρδιά μου,
> και σαν τη σιγανή βροχή
> τρέχουν τα δάκρυά μου.

Bithikotsis was often coming at our house. He made his debut with Markos. Then Theodorakis[80] collaborated with

---

[78] "Despair".

[79] Kavouras is a last name. The word literally means "crab".

[80] Mikis Theodorakis (born July 29, 1925) is a famous composer and lyricist who has contributed to contemporary Greek music with over 1000 works. He scored for the films Zorba the Greek (1964), Z (1969), and Serpico (1973). He is viewed as Greece's best-known composer.

him and he became successful. He first sang about 30 Markos's songs and then Theodorakis heard him singing and took him; that's how he became "Bithikotsis". But the first lessons, the first steps of his career, were with Markos. "Frangosyriani" (1935), "Antilaloun oi fylakes" (1935), "Mavra matia, mavra frydia" (1936), "Ta ziliarika sou matia" (1938), "Ta matoklada sou laboun" (1960), significant songs.[81]

— *Who has visited the semi-basement of your home?*

Grigoris Bithikotsis, Katy Grey, Poly Panou. Many had gone down to the basement to rehearse the new songs he was giving them. It was his office. A table, a chair, some bouzoukia and canaries. I used to go and take a peek out of curiosity. I was a kid. Nikos Karanikolas[82], Voula Gika[83], Mario Konstantinidou[84] and Michalis Menidiatis[85] had come. Many

---

[81] "The prisons clang", "Black eyes, black brows", "Your jealous eyes", "Your eyelids shine".

[82] Nikos Karanikolas (1929-2003) was a bouzouki player, singer and composer. He began appearing on stage in the early 1950s and started recording in 1961. He wrote about 60 songs during his 60-year career. He was Voula Gika's husband.

[83] Voula Gika (January 8, 1933) is a singer. Shortly before the Second World War, her family moved to Piraeus from Argos. She began her artistic career at the age of 18 despite the mores of the time. She maintained herself at the forefront of the music scene for more than three decades. She was the wife of Nikos Karanikolas.

[84] Mario Konstantinidou (30 March 1945), most commonly known as "Mario", is a rebetiko singer. She has been given the nickname "the last rebetissa".

[85] Michalis Menidiatis (his real name was Michalis Kalogranis, 1932-2012) was a singer and entrepreneur. He started playing bouzouki

were coming to visit him there[86]. Eftichia Papagianopoulou[87] was passing by to give him lyrics, but Markos wasn't accepting them because he was writing his own.

— *Why do they call him the "Patriarch" of rebetiko?*

Markos is the pioneer of rebetiko. He's the "Patriarch", the bard of music, and then the rest fell into line. They were Markos's disciples, they first learned how to write based on Markos's songs. Tsitsanis, Papaioannou[88], Mitsakis[89]... They

---

from a young age. He first appeared on stage in 1953 and began recording in 1957. In 1964, with his brother Kosmas Kalogranis, he decided to open the nightclub "Fantasia", which became both a symbol of Athens nightlife and a center for the promotion of young artists.

[86] "I am Markos. This house of mine right here is the source of all truth about the bouzouki" (op. cit., p. 243).

[87] Eftichia Papagianopoulou (1893-1972), was a lyricist. She was born in Aydin, near Smyrna. She left Smyrna in 1919 prior to the Greco-Turkish War and emigrated to Athens, where she settled permanently. She wrote the lyrics to many popular Greek songs, collaborating with composers. However, her great contribution to Greek music through her exceptional ability in writing lyrics wasn't broadly known and recognized, even though many of the successful songs of the 1950s and 1960s were composed by her.

[88] Giannis Papaioannou was a rebetiko musician, composer and singer born January 18, 1913 in Kios (Gemlik in present-day Turkey) and died August 3, 1972 in Greece in a car accident. Particularly productive during the 1940s, he wrote many songs, some of which are considered today as "classics" of rebetiko.

[89] Giorgos Mitsakis (1921-1993) was a Greek composer and lyricist of numerous rebetika and folk songs, as well as a skillful bouzouki player.

played Markos's songs for about ten years, they sang them, and after ten years they popped out, they followed Markos's footsteps.

— *What about Tsitsanis?*

Tsitsanis used to go down to the basement of his house in Glyfada. He would lock himself in the basement where his office was, he would listen to Markos's records and then write his own songs. Markos was like a template for him. Markos's songs had been released ten years before Tsitsanis's songs. Tsitsanis used to sing ten songs of his own and ten of Markos's. He wouldn't sing the songs of any other composer.

— *Which Markos's song do you think is his best?*

His big hit is "Frangosyriani". It's a milestone. It's one of the best chasapika ever written in the history of rebetiko. There's no other. It's his best and the one with the most covers worldwide. It has 500 different covers, just the music score or the entire song in Greece as well as abroad, in France, England, Japan, America, Australia.

— *"Frangosyriani" or "Synnefiasmeni Kyriaki"[90]?*

I believe "Frangosyriani" has the lead. It's considered to be the best chasapiko ever written. The original version is from Markos, singing and playing in 1935. The second cover is by Grigoris Bithikotsis in 1960. The song "Ta matoklada sou laboun" (1960) also stands out over others. And he wrote "Syros" (1936) as a tribute to the island of Syra.

---

[90] "Cloudy Sunday". Vassilis Tsitsanis's most famous song.

— *Did Markos ever tell you how he was inspired to write "Frangosyriani"?*

He was inspired and wrote it. He was going back and forth from Syros and knew its toponyms, so he got inspired and wrote it. He almost certainly saw some Frankosyran girl too[91]...

— *Domenikos, have you ever done any research on Markos's work?*

I've written three volumes for the piano with 60 songs, the most popular having been released by Papagrigoriou-Nakas publications and entitled "Markos Vamvakaris: Ta tragoudia mou – Metagrafi gia piano: Domenikos Vamvakaris"[92].

— *Do you have Markos's first bouzouki?*

I have his baglama and his three-stringed bouzouki. These are heirlooms. But I wonder whatever happened to his first bouzouki...

— *Where did you play bouzouki for the first time?*

The first time I appeared on stage was at "Madhubala"; I didn't play with Markos. I sometimes accompanied him to

---

[91] "I wrote 'Frangosyriani' for a girl in Syra in 1935" (op. cit., p. 284).

[92] "Markos Vamvakaris: My songs – Transcription for the piano: Domenikos Vamvakaris". "Now [Domenikos] plays from these books that they give him [at the conservatory], but he also plays my songs. All these new songs I make up, he writes them down for piano" (op. cit., p. 240).

support him, but I didn't play with him.

— *How did the students find him?*

The students discovered that Markos was the forefather of laiko music during their research around 1958-1960. Several of them were gradually coming from the college dorm to visit him. They loved Markos and they were all right. He loved them too. Panagiotis Kounadis also used to come by and he knows Markos's life well.

— *Could you tell me where the manuscripts of his autobiography are?*

We have them here, Angeliki[93] sent them to us from America. The book is printed based upon these exact manuscripts. There's nothing more or less, I've searched. There's nothing more that didn't make it into the book.

— *What was something very characteristic of Markos?*

Markos had an excellent memory, hence the existence of his autobiography.

— *Why did the Catholic Church excommunicate him?*

Markos was excommunicated by the church because he got divorced and remarried in an Orthodox ceremony[94], while his first wife was still alive. A few years before he died, by action of Don Antonis Vamvakaris, who was a pastor at

---

[93] Angeliki Vellou-Keil compiled Markos Vamvakaris's autobiography in 1972. The book came out in 1978.

[94] "And, as is known, our religion doesn't give divorces" (op. cit., p. 196).

the church of Saint Paul in Piraeus and spent many afternoons in the company of Markos, the church took care of the
issue.

— *A few words about Markos's funeral?*

A great lot of people. There was a huge line. Argyris[95], his
brother who was living in America, was also present. Before
he was buried, Stelios and I played "Frangosyriani". A lot of
artists came.

— *When I met Markos in Saint Paul's School, he said
the following to me: "As a kid, I liked to climb up Tsygros
hill, behind the house of barba Pieros, and listen to the rebetiko sounds of the waves of the stormy sea." What does
this remind you of?*

Markos's song "Ta karavotsakismata"[96] (1936).

Bitterness, torture, misery,	Βάσανα, πίκρες, φαρμάκια,
ah, wreckage all around me!	καραβοτσακίσματα, ωχ!
Like a rock lashed	Σαν τον βράχο, που τον δέρνουν
by the waves of the wild sea.	της θάλασσας τα κύματα.
I'm not to blame,	Τι φταίω και με παιδεύεις;
why you make me sore?	Αχ! Τι γυρεύεις,
Ah, what are you looking for?	κι άλλον λατρεύεις;
There's someone else that you adore!	Δεν μ' αγαπάς! Αχ!
You don't love me, say it,	Πες μου το, γιατ' είμαι μόρτης,
I'm just a scum and nothing more.	φουκαράς.

---

[95] Argyris Vamvakaris (1930-1983) was a bouzouki virtuoso and the
brother of Markos Vamvakaris. In the early 1960s, he left for the
United States, where he continued to play for the Greek diaspora. He
returned to Greece in 1981 and died of heart failure in 1983.
[96] "Wreckage".

I'll fade away, I'll live no more, I won't adore, I will forget. At my wreckage, don't laugh yet!	*Θα σβήσω,* *πια δεν θα ζήσω,* *δεν θ' αγαπήσω,* *θα λησμονήσω.* *Στα καραβοτσακίσματα μου* *μην γελάς!*
At home, everyone scolds me and that's on you; they say harsh words, a bitter brew.	*Μες στο σπίτι μου για σένα* *όλοι με μαλώνουνε, ωχ!* *Λένε ζόρικες κουβέντες* *που με φαρμακώνουνε.*

Domenikos M. Vamvakaris

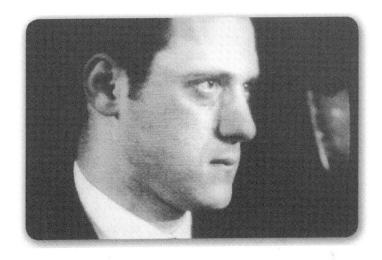

Domenikos M. Vamvakaris, composer, music teacher, instrumentalist and poet.
(Domenikos Vamvakaris's archive)

67

4

SYRANS SHOULD LOVE AND HONOR MARKOS

— *My dear Stelios, how old were you when you saw Syros for the first time?*

I took my first trip to Syra in 1955. I was an eight-year-old kid then. Markos had to make some money in order for him to go to the island of Ikaria to take thermal baths, because his hands and fingers were deformed due to arthritis. They had been all swelled up in the slaughterhouse from all the work he had done in the port, from the coal he had been carrying, from the all-nighters he was pulling and from all the jobs he had done as a child. It was difficult for him to play and support his family.

We didn't take the regular transport ship to go to Syra, but rather a smaller fishing boat because we had no money. We arrived after seventeen hours from Piraeus... The fishing boat was transporting oil, beans, donkeys, dogs, chickens and diesel. When it entered the port of Syra, Markos was moved and began crying. As soon as we got off, I, as a kid, was impressed when I saw a man selling pastelia[97]. We went to a kafeneion and sat down. I remember eating vanilla in a teaspoon submerged in a glass of water. During the night, we slept in the attic of Dalezios's kafeneio. We joined two tables and slept there. We couldn't go to a hotel. It was a question of money; we were very poor...

---

[97] Pasteli (pl. pastelia) = a sesame seed candy which is generally a flat, oblong bar made with honey and often including nuts.

Meanwhile, word hit the street that Markos had come and the next day the bouzouki players from Syros came to see him. Antonis Bertos, Vaggelis Prekas, Kostas Valsamakis, Loukas Nomikos, Kyriakos Mavris, who was playing the guitar, Apostolis Katevatis... I can't forget them. They started forming a rebetiko band. Syrans musicians were renowned. They were poor and they wanted to make some money, so Markos was their window of opportunity. I was holding my father's bouzouki and a baglama, since I was just a kid.

—   *Did Markos ever tell you about Danakos?*

About Danakos... Where he was born and spent his childhood. In the streams, where the shrubs were smelling. My father used to talk to us about the dry riverbed where he was weaving the baskets...

He took me there, where he was born, and started talking to me about his childhood. His father Domenikos wove baskets and, when he didn't have any work, he cut branches and uprooted thyme from the mountains, made bundles and sold them to the bakeries. Markos of course followed and helped him. At Christmas and on New Year's Eve, he would go with his friends and sing carols. During the Carnival celebrations, his father played the gaida and Markos played the drum.

He showed me the deserted and lonely house where he was born in Tsygros. He showed me the threshing floor, the dovecote and the oven they used to lit every Sunday. They used to throw sage into the fire and the aroma wafted through the air. He took me to the cave where his father was born and where he also spent a few summers with his family before leaving Syra.

Finally, he took me to the church of Saint Kirykos where he used to go as a child every Sunday with his father Domenikos, his mother Elpida and his brother Linardos.

We also met Artemis Katevatis, the waterseller, who became Markos's close friend. He had a barrel on his cart and he was selling water. He also had a gramophone and he used to play Markos's records and people could hear them as he was passing. He adored Markos, he was listening to his songs and was fascinated by him. After my father's death, he gave me 78-rpm records of his. I used to call him every month for a long time...

Anyway, it was really busy during the days we worked. Many people came to see Markos sing and play; they danced with his songs. When we received the first day's pay, my father bought me pastitsio[98]. It was the first time I ate this food. I cannot describe its taste. I was like, whoa!

In general, while we were there, he took me to his relatives' houses. He especially loved Santina, the daughter of Antonis Vamvakaris, his father's brother. She welcomed us to her house many times and treated us to lunch. She often came to Kokkinia and always visited us carrying bags full of food.

On July 27, 1955, on the feast day of Saint Panteleimonas, we went to the festival of the church of the village of Finikas. There was a big feast after the service.

— *When did you visit Syros again?*

The second time, in the summer of 1961, we went again to Syra with the boat "Despina" and returned with the "Myrtidiotissa"[99]. We were hosted by his aunt Anneta at her house in Della Grazia. She adored him. Her son was the bouzouki player Argyris Dalezios. We played for a long time at Pateris's tavern in Finikas. Argyris Dalezios and Apostolis

---

[98] A Greek baked pasta dish with ground meat and béchamel sauce.
[99] Myrtidiotissa means "Of the Myrtle Tree".

Katevatis were playing the bouzouki. We went all over the place to play after Finikas: at the festival of Saint Paraskevi, in Piratikos kafeneion, in Gavrilis's and Kopanakis's taverns, in Tempelis's tavern in Vrontados and in Lilis's cellar in Apano Syra. He took me to Skali and showed me the houses they had stayed in before leaving for Piraeus, the Jesuit and the Capuchins monastery, as well as the elementary school he had attended for four years. When he took me to that school, he told me the following incident: In order not to wear his sandals, he used to wear the right one for one week and the left one for the next week. When his beloved teacher Nikolaos Printezis gave a reprimand to him, he tied one foot with a cloth so as to make it look sore. He also took me to the church of Saint Sebastian, where his parents got married and where he was baptized.

We also gave a concert at Panagiotis Daskaleas's open-air movie theater. This happened as we were preparing to leave the island, but Daskaleas, who loved Markos so much, allowed us to give a concert. I played too. The movie theater was full of Syrans. My father was very happy with this concert and we made some money.

— *When did you go for the third time?*

We visited Syra for the third time on August 5, 1962. Marilyn Monroe died that day. We went with the boat "Kolokotronis" and we came back with the "Karaiskakis".[100]

In 1965, we went to Syra for the fourth time and we were hosted by Artemis Katevatis, the waterseller. In the evenings, he would spread a rag outside his house and sit. Then, he would play Markos's records and those who were heading

---

[100] Kolokotronis and Karaiskakis were prominent figures of the Greek Revolution (1821-1832).

to Tempelis's tavern would stop and listen to the music.

— *Do you remember something that impressed you?*

We went to eat lunch at Efstathios Gouraros's house, who used to live behind Vardakas's factory. Efstathios married a child friend of my father, Irini Palamari. Irini was a reveller, she especially liked to dance chasapiko and zeibekiko, just like her sister Elpida, who was very beautiful and Markos loved her very much. It was his idol, his Mona Lisa. My father himself told me what I'm about to tell you: he wrote "Frangosyriani" for her. I wish we could find a photo of hers...

— *How did Markos call those who used to come down to his basement?*

Markos used to say that they were his minions, his apprentices. Everyone visited Markos.

From the bouzouki to the tekes,	*Από το μπουζούκι ως τον τεκέ,*
the minions are all mine,	*δικά μου είναι τα τσιράκια,*
all those who now play	*αυτοί που παίζουν σήμερα*
that fine bouzouki way.	*τα φίνα μπουζουκάκια.*

Markos's second career, as well as the singing career of everyone else, began from the basement of 35 Ofryniou Street in Palia Kokkinia[101], in Aspra Chomata[102]. It gave them

---

[101] A neighborhood of Piraeus.

[102] "However many others sing and strut their stuff, they're not going to know what I know about the bouzouki because I have suffered for this instrument and that's something all these big shots know too. [...]"

strength and vitality; that's how they started singing. That's where the entire history of laiko music was written.

— *Who gave him this strength, this inspiration?*

His soul. His soul never died. Although tired and broken, he was always carrying a bouzouki in his hands and writing songs. Both Domenikos and I were listening to him and we were ecstatic. That's how we became musicians. We loved him very much. He was the sort of man who knew what to do in this field. He was the only one who knew what to do and he was writing the lyrics and the songs he had in mind whenever he wanted. It wasn't just a computer or a tape recorder... He remembered them, all of the songs he had written. Each one of them.

— *How would you characterize Markos?*

He never did anyone any harm. What does that tell you? His parents brought him up well. I never met my grandfather nor my grandmother. Near the end, he used to go a lot to church. He confessed and received communion in the grace of God and the blessing of the Virgin Mary. He was a calm man and he passed away calmly[103].

But I have a big complaint. [...] All these great and well-known bouzouki players are ungrateful. [...] Because I can assure you that, if it weren't for me, where would these millionaires be? [...] But I was the first who set the table and said 'Come on, sit down, let's eat'. And these guys filled their bellies and I stayed hungry" (op. cit., p. 243).

[103] "Anyhow, I believe my soul is pure. I didn't hurt anyone. Whatever was bad I struggled to act on it and make it good" (op. cit., p. 256).

— *Let me get back to Syros. What does this place mean to you?*

Aspra Chomata is the "holy neighborhood", but Syros is Delos, Bethlehem, Mecca. This is where the history of rebetiko began. Syra is the cradle of rebetiko.

I liked that I went in the summer of 2017 and gave a nice concert in Della Grazia, at the Tsiropina Villa[104]. I wanted to honor Markos, but also the Syrans who love him so much. I will never forget this night. While I was playing and singing, the wind stopped blowing and a full moon came out.

I was happy to be in Syra, my father's homeland, and very happy to be able to say a few things both about Markos and the three-stringed bouzouki at the Apollon Theater[105]. Some call him the "Parthenon" and others the "Patriarch" of rebetiko. I am the happiest person in the world because I carry his spirit inside me and I can talk about him, about what he showed me and about what he taught me.

— *Stelios, do you love Syros?*

How could I not love it? All the members of our family love it. My love for our homeland is huge. I love this island, I like it and I support it. Above all, every time I go and the

---

[104] The imposing villa of Antonis Tsiropinas was built in 1915. The family had a tannery and later made a great fortune in shipping. Nowadays, the City Hall and Cultural Center of Poseidonia are housed there.

[105] The Apollon Theater, also known as the Municipal Theater Apollon, is a theater located in Ermoupoli. A cultural icon of the city, it was built in 1862-1864 to the designs of the Italian architect Pietro Sampo and opened on April 20, 1864.

boat enters the port, every time I see Apano Syra and Ermoupoli, I shiver, I feel emotional, just like my father... The Cycladic culture was born in Syros. We both love that place, Dimitris. We utter its name and we shed tears...

— *Describe me a craving of yours.*

My only complaint is that I don't get to see the island of Syros, the one that my father loved, even though I want to. Syrans should love and honor Markos and I say this to you with all my heart: I'd like to see Markos's family tree written out in your book.

Stelios M. Vamvakaris

Stelios M. Vamvakaris, musician, composer and bouzouki virtuoso.

5

MARKOS'S FAMILY TREE

The origin of the name Vamvakaris is unknown to us, as its roots are lost in the depths of centuries. It probably goes back to the Byzantine times and means "cotton seller or processor".

In Syros, the story of the Vamvakaris family begins in the early years of the 17th century, with the marriage of Markos Vamvakaris to the daughter of father Giannoulis Salachas, a priest at the church of Saint Nikolaos, the medieval Castle of Syros (today known as Ano Syros or Apano Chora). After his marriage, Vamvakaris was ordained a priest and began to preach in that same church.

Over time and with the intermarriages of their descendants, members of the Vamvakaris family became numerous.

Today, apart from Ano Syros, the Vamvakaris surname can be found in the settlements Plati Vouni and Chartiana Ano Merias, in Ermoupoli and in the community of Petra, as well as in the villages: Agros, Galissas, Danakos and Kini. People bearing the name Vamvakaris and originating from Syros can be found in Athens, Piraeus, Lavrio, Volos, Thessaloniki and Drama. They also used to live in Smyrna, Constantinople, Nafplio, Beirut in Lebanon and in the commune of Torre del Greco, near Naples, Italy.

Markos's ancestors

Markos Vamvakaris was born on May 10, 1905 in Pouletos, located between the villages of Galissas and Danakos in Syros. 10 days later, his birth was declared by his father at the Registry Office of the Municipality of [Ano] Syros. On May 28, 1905, he was baptized in the Catholic parish church of Saint Sebastian in Ano Syros[106]. The marriage of his parents Domenikos Markou Vamvakaris and Elpida Leonardou Provelengiou took place in this church on July 25, 1904.

Domenikos and Elpida lived in Pouletos after their marriage. But some years later they left this house and settled in Ano Syros, near Elpida's mother and brothers and sisters. Not having a house of their own, they were forced to rent, often changing houses.

Markos's father Domenikos was born on May 20, 1882 in Danakos. In the birth registries of his children, it is mentioned that he was illiterate and that he was working as a farmer (1905), a laborer (1908), a greengrocer (1910) and again a laborer (1914-1918). Domenikos Vamvakaris died in Piraeus on April 19, 1931 at the age of 49.

Markos's mother Elpida was born on December 4, 1889. The records show that at the beginning of the 20th century the family of Markos Vamvakaris's mother did not have a house of her own in Ano Syros. Elpida Vamvakari died in Piraeus in 1942 at the age of 53.

Markos's siblings

After Markos, Domenikos and Elpida Vamvakari had

---

[106] April 27th is listed as the date of birth of Markos Vamvakaris and May 7th as the date of its declaration, according to the Old Style or Julian calendar, which was then kept by the Greek state at the Registry Office of Ano Syros. At the registry book of births of the parish of Saint Sebastian, May 10th is listed as the date of his birth, according to the New Style or Gregorian calendar kept by the Catholic Church. This same date is also given by Markos himself in his autobiography (op. cit., p. 34).

eight more children: Leonardos (January 10, 1908), Frangiskos (July 12, 1910), Antonios (March 7, 1913) who died on
April 7, 1913 from childhood epilepsy, Margitsa (September
18, 1914) who died on March 17, 1917 from bronchitis, Grazia (February 14, 1918), Rosa (April 25, 1925), Anargyros-
Kosmas-Damianos (November 17, 1927) who died on February 9, 1930 and Anargyros-Leontas-Maria (October 18,
1930).

The last three were born after the Vamvakaris family
moved to Piraeus in 1920. Leonardos died in 1941 without
building his own family. Frangiskos or Tzekos married Fran-
giska Ioanni Vamvakari on May 12, 1935 and died on April
3, 1963. Grazia was married to Michalis Vassiliou Pavlopou-
los on March 10, 1935 and died on February 14, 1987. Rosa
was married to Manolis Ioanni Palaiologos on August 1, 1943
and died on August 29, 1988. Anargyros or Argyris married
Kyparissia Nikolaou Kantari on June 9, 1952 and died on August 3, 1983.

Markos's descendants

In 1920, at the age of 15, Markos Vamvakaris left Syros
and went to Piraeus, where, on December 7, 1923, at the age
of 18, he married Eleni Dimitriou Mavroudi, 18 years old,
Orthodox, from the region of Mani in the Peloponnese.[107]The wedding was held in the Catholic parish church
of Saint Paul in Piraeus.

After divorcing Eleni, Markos had a second marriage on
July 11, 1943, with Evangelia Eleftheriou Vergiou (1918-
2014). He had six children: Domenikos who died on February 23, 1945, Vassilis (April 10, 1944), Varvara (May 30,
1945) who died on March 12, 1946, Stelios (March 2, 1947)

---

[107] Eleni D. Mavroudi died on March 17, 1998.

who died on June 17, 2019, Elpida (February 2, 1948) who died on May 19, 1949 and Domenikos (January 8, 1949).

Markos Vamvakaris died on February 8, 1972 at the age of 67.[108] Beforehand, on December 22, 1971 he had confessed and received communion. His funeral service took place on the February 9, 1972. He was buried in the 12th section, tomb no. 70 of the Third Cemetery of Athens, in Nikaia.

---

[108] Chronic nephritis, diabetes mellitus and heart failure were reported as the cause of his death at the Registry Office of the Municipality of Nikaia.

FAMILY TREES
OF

MARKOS DOMENIKOU VAMVAKARIS

ELPIDA LEONARDOU PROVELENGIOU
(Markos's mother)

Data collection and study
MICHAIL M. ROUSSOS

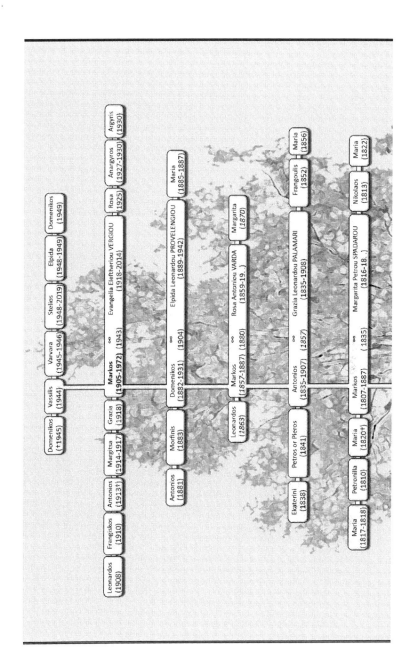

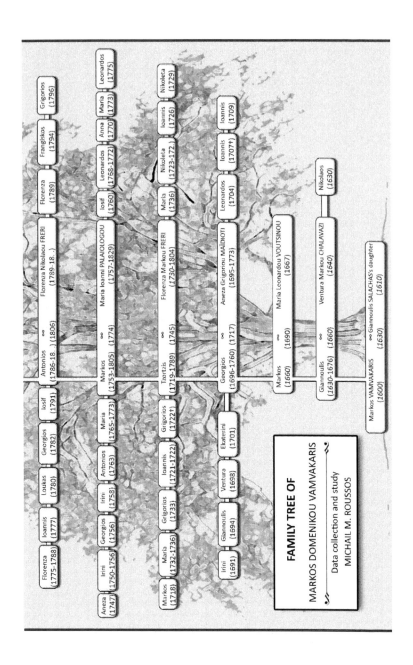

FAMILY TREE OF

MARKOS DOMENIKOU VAMVAKARIS

Data collection and study
MICHAIL M. ROUSSOS

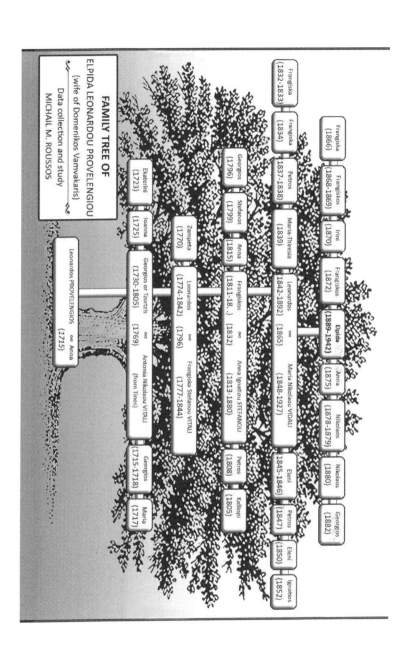

6

SAINT PAUL'S FRENCH SCHOOL OF PIRAEUS AND THE "VAMVAKAREIO FOUNDATION-AROGI"

I

Frère Marios I. Kapellas, a professor of French who was the general director of the frères' Saint George's School in Syros, as well as of the Saint Paul's School in Piraeus, told me the following: "The Saint George's School of Syros and the Saint Paul's School of Piraeus occupy a prominent position in the society of Syros and Piraeus respectively. Markos Vamvakaris had a relation with both of them for many years. With the first, it was when Markos was still just like any other child; he would go and play in its backyards. With the second, it was when as a parent he sent all three of his children to get educated.

When the frères arrived in Syra in 1914, they first settled in a dwelling in Apano Chora, very close to the house the family of the great bouzouki player was renting, across from Saint Sebastian. In the surrounding poor neighborhoods, the kids – including Markos – used to hang out in the frères' school during their spare time because they felt safe under their paternal supervision. This is where he first met the frères. Their image was imprinted in his memory.

Many years later, Markos had children. Without further reflection, he decided to send them to the school of his well-known frères, confident that they would receive the best Greek-French education."

Vassilis Vamvakaris was born in 1944. He finished the

12th elementary school of the First District of Piraeus. He enrolled in the seventh grade of the Saint Paul's French School of Piraeus on September 21, 1955. Markos Vamvakaris declared himself as an instrumentalist during the enrollment of Vassilis. Vassilis distinguished himself in the first quarter of 1957 in French and graduated during the 1960-1961 school year. Domenikos told me about Vassilis: "After graduating from Saint Paul's French School of Piraeus, he became a sailor at the urging of our mother's brothers, because they too were sailors. He was born for this job. He was also led by good fortune. Now he's a shipowner. He married an English teacher. He speaks French and English. He has two children. Andreas, his son, also attended the French School of Piraeus. He's a naval architect and lives in Ekali[109]. His daughter Evangelia is a lawyer."

Markos Vamvakaris's second son, Stelios Vamvakaris, was born in 1947. He graduated from Saint Paul's French School of Piraeus on June 24, 1959. After finishing the eighth grade, he attended another high school. Stelios too has fond memories of his school years at Saint Paul's French School of Piraeus: "I went to Saint Paul's of Piraeus, at the frères' school. I was quite a rascal. I went there when I was five years old. I learned all the prayers. We were taking the bus with my older brother Vassilis from Palia Kokkinia. Different times... They were also giving us food at the school."

Markos Vamvakaris's third son, Domenikos Vamvakaris, was born in 1949. He finished the 45th elementary school of Piraeus. He enrolled in the seventh grade of the Saint Paul's French School of Piraeus on September 6, 1961. This is what

---

[109] Ekali is an affluent suburb of Athens located to the north of the city. It is a lush area, home to many of the country's most powerful business and shipping families.

Domenikos told me: "I was going to school by bus. I was leaving from Nikaia, from Aspra Chomata, at seven o'clock in the morning. I was arriving at school at eight o'clock. I was back home at three o'clock, again by bus. What I particularly remember from school was the food they were giving us. All us Catholic children were gathering and eating regular food every day. Whatever the frères were eating, we were eating too. Delicious, fragrant foods. I was taught French by Petros Roussos and frère Leonard. We weren't studying English back then. Every Sunday, Stelios and I used to go to the church of Saint Paul in Piraeus with the frères. I loved basketball and volleyball. But where I stood out was at running. I was running like the wind since I was a kid. When I was 16 years old, I came out first and got a medal in a panhellenic running competition that took place at the ancient stadium of Piraeus in the presence of my parents. Both of them were really proud."

II

On February 11, 2010, the foundation ceremony of the shelter for orphaned and destitute children with disabilities from the "Arogi"[110] Foundation took place by the Archbishop of Athens and All Greece Ieronymos II at Armatolon Street, in the area of Avliza[111], with a total project budget of 1,600,000 euros for its construction and equipment.

The first major donation was made by the 2006 Telethon organized by the ANTENNA group and raised € 303,740. The rest of the money was donated by the shipowner Vassilis Vamvakaris, son of Markos Vamvakaris. The foundation was named "Vamvakareio foundation – Arogi" in memory of

---

[110] Arogi means "succor".

[111] A suburb of northwest Athens.

Markos Vamvakaris, because of the abovementioned donation.

All credit to his generous son, the shipowner Vassilis Vamvakaris, who accomplished – 38 years after the death of Markos Vamvakaris – his great wish.[112]

Dimitris. V. Varthalitis

Vassilis Vamvakaris.

---

[112] "If it had been me and I'd got that much money [...] I'd have fixed up a retirement home and put all the poor old people in it" (op. cit., p. 244).

7

MARKOS'S DANAKOS

I was born in Apano Chora in 1905, in Portara. I love this place. When I was a kid Danakos had many residents. The old families of Danakos were the Germanoses, the Laftises, the Vitoriases and the Vamvakarises.

The Vamvakarises were three brothers: the first one was Antonis, the second was Domenikos, who was Markos's father, and the third was Morfinis. They had some plots. Markos's father Domenikos lived with his family in the canyon. He knew how to weave baskets and I remember one day he'd come here, to our house, and he was weaving some of those. Markos and I were helping him too. When there were no jobs here, everyone used to do what Markos's father Domenikos did. Markos used to help him. They all had a donkey or a mule and cut branches and uprooted thyme from the mountains. They used to make parcels and bring them down to the bakeries.

Do you know what else the Vamvakarises used to do in order to get by? They gathered some woods from the mountain, lit a fire, burnt them and collected the ash in a sack; then, they sold it to some wealthy women in Kato Chora[113] and they, in turn, did the laundry. They boiled water, washed their clothes a little, and then laid them out on some baskets. After that, they poured all that ash. They used to put some lemon leaves inside and cut some lemons so that the clothes would smell good, as they used to say. Then they would pour hot water on top and the clothes soaked up the

---

[113] The lower ("kato") Chora, i.e. Ermoupoli.

ash from inside the baskets and get clean.

Markos Vamvakaris lived in Danakos, in the houses of barba Pieros Rokos, in Tsygros. He was born and lived there in his early childhood. I was born in Apano Chora, not Markos. Those who say that Markos was born in Skali are lying. We used to play together occasionally because we worked all the time. God rest his soul; he was a good guy... When I was a kid, I remember myself and my family, as well as Markos and his family, going to Malia, at the festival of Amaliani.

Here in Danakos, During Christmas and when we were young, we used to slaughter roosters or chickens. On New Year's Day we used to make some psathouria, some koulouria[114] with sesame seeds and bake them. We had an oven back then.

One year, us boys had gathered and we went down to the market just after the sun had set to sing the carols. Markos had a drum. He had a nice voice, a little loud. He used to remember the lyrics. He was having fun. Women were staring at him in the eyes as he was singing the carols. He used to say to us: "With my share I'll buy a pair of sandals to wear to school, so that my feet don't bleed and that my dear teacher Nikos Printezis won't scold me." He was talking with affection about school.

In a carnival party in Galissas I remember Markos playing the drum and sitting next to his father, who was playing the gaida[115]. Although he was young, he knew the lyrics and sang them. He wasn't shy. He knew them by heart. When Markos was a little older, he went down to Ermoupoli to work. He must have worked in the factories as well. Then we lost touch. I learned he went to Piraeus.

We had around fifty sheep and some goats. They were all

---

[114] Psathouria and koulouria are ring shaped buns with sesame seeds.
[115] Bagpipe made from upturned goat or sheep skin.

wearing bells. My father would send me to graze them. Markos sometimes came with me. He was going crazy when he was hearing the bells. He loved their sound. When he was alive, Danakos's animal life was as it is today. Nothing's changed.

My late father was a merchant. During Easter, he was collecting animals – goats, sheep, lambs, he had his own too. He obtained a license from the mayor and he would go to slaughter them. He recruited Markos's father Domenikos as a butcher. They would throw them in a barge, slaughter them and sell them for five drachmas; it was cheaper than the rest of the market, so people were gathering to buy them. Back then, a day's wage was a taliro[116]. He was selling about sixty animals. Markos and I were there too. One night we slept in the barge. We never forgot that night. We wandered around Kato Chora; we went to the square. Our fathers gave us some pocket money because we had helped them. Markos ate a baklava and I had a kadayif[117]. Then we went to Vangelistra[118] and attended the Compline[119].

I saw Markos again in the army. We were soldiers together in Goudi[120] in 1926. The officer we had was a saint.

---

[116] A note or coin worth 5 drachmas.

[117] A dessert made with roughly chopped walnuts (and sometimes other nuts), scented with ground clove and cinnamon, wrapped into buttered crispy kadayif dough and bathed in lemon scented syrup.

[118] The church of the Catholics of the island was built in 1829 in the place of an older church.

[119] The night prayer and final service of the day in monasteries before the great silence till morning.

[120] Goudi is a neighborhood of Athens. It became famous following a military coup in August 1909, as well as by the "Trial of the Six", the trial for treason, in late 1922, of the officials held responsible for the

He wanted from Markos to go on Friday mornings and just say "good morning" to him, and then he would let him leave and return on Monday mornings. Markos was going to the slaughterhouse on Fridays and Saturdays. He had a bouzouki there and he was playing. I met Markos again in Danakos when he came to Syros in 1955. We went to Giakoumis Vamvakaris's kafeneion and remembered our childhood...

Giorgos Palaiologos or Ralias

Markos Vamvakaris at the age of 10 in Lazareta, Syros. Clean Monday 1915.

Greek military defeat in Asia Minor. The trial culminated in the death sentence and execution of six of the nine defendants.

8

MARKOS WAS BORN IN TSYGROS

The place where we're standing is called Tsygros. This is the house where Markos Vamvakaris was born and spent his childhood. It must've gradually been built until 1860. The house is built in a sheltered, windless, sunny, dry, moisture-free place. It's an east-facing house so there's sunlight in the morning. The trees that surrounded it protected it from heavy rain or flood. This spot was acting as a windbreak. The beds, however, where they were sleeping, were north-south-facing so as not to resemble the graves. Graves have been east-facing for thousands of years. So thought it was bad luck. The Vamvakarises property reached up to the sea. The back has been subjected to sedimentation and, from what people say, this sedimentation was due to the Santorini volcano. There's also some water in the back. When barba Pieros got angry because of Markos's mother Elpida – she was a little bit frisky – they moved further down the road. The stove, the fireplace, the lockers of the house are still there. They used to bake bread and sometimes they were preparing chicken and potatoes in that oven. Ever since he was a young child, Markos had been uprooting thyme and sage twigs to fire up the stove; the place was smelling so good.

When he was a kid, Markos had put three German steel wires on a forty inches long and eight inches wide piece of wood. He used to sit under a fig tree, near his house, and pluck at the wires for hours, striking and singing, wearing a cap like a small beret with a button on it. He was born with music. When I asked my father where Markos had seen and how he was inspired by all this stuff, he replied: "At festivals, weddings and during the Carnival he used to sit and watch the players. He was listening and watching them through the window. He also liked going to both of Galissas's cafés with his father."

It was around Markos's time to go to school and his mother didn't get along with barba Pieros, so Domenikos took his wife Elpida and his son Markos, when he was about five years old, as well as Leonardos, when he was two years old, and left and rented a house in Skali, in Apano Chora. He tried to find a job in Ermoupoli to support his family and he sent Markos to school.

Grigoris Iosif Voutsinos

The ruins of the house of barba Pieros in Tsygros, where Markos was born and spent the first five years of his life.

9

MARKOS BY NIKOS METAXOTOS

I was four years older than him and I watched him work in my father's warehouses as a basket maker with the rods he was collecting from the gullies of Galissas and Della Grazia as the only material. His father was the tutor and the reward for Markos's carelessness and clumsiness were slaps.

The grand finale to a quarrel was for Markos to leave and find shelter in the grocery store of my uncle Stamatis Paramanis.[121] He stayed there for a long time and, loaded with a basket on his back, he was bringing the groceries to the Syran mansions.

I didn't have any relation with Markos. We had an age difference, a different character and occupation, so the distance between us was determined. And that was his complaint, that I systematically avoided him. And despite the fact that I was publishing songs, as well as op-eds, in the Syran newspaper "Avgi"[122] published by P. Stefanou, Markos was unknown to me.

But sometimes luck comes persistently knocking at your door. The German Occupation had come with its daily dramas, and I was wandering around the streets with a sack on my shoulder in order to feed my family; even with the stalks

---

[121] "Someone called Paramanis Stamatis had a grocery shop in the central marketplace of Syros and offered to hire me as assistant since I was smart and knew loads of people through my work as a newsboy" (op. cit., p. 72).

[122] Avgi means "dawn".

of cauliflowers.

As I was returning one morning from Athinas Street loaded with... fresh air, I stopped at Omonoia[123] ready to collapse from disappointment. I heard a voice calling me but I didn't pay much attention: "Mr. Nikolakis... Mr. Nikos." I turned around and outside the music joint of Ionos Street[124] I noticed a sign from Syros that reminded me of something. "Maybe my luck's changing", I thought to myself and I read the sign: "Marios Dalezios". And below the sign, like a faithful watchman, Markos Vamvakaris with his band, rehearsing with the bouzoukia.

Markos approached me full of curiosity.

"Mr. Nikos, what brings you here? I see you're carrying a sack on your shoulder."

"It's full", I replied.

"Full of what? Full of fresh air or of lamentations for our times?"

I took a braid of garlics out of the sack and showed it to him.

"Here's my grocery shopping, Mr. Markos."

"Don't 'gentleman' me and wait. I'll be back in a sec."

He was back in a bit and his jacket was inflated; he was cautious. He pulled out an Italian pagnotta[125] and gave it to me. "Take this and off you go... And, hey, let's not be strangers..."[126]

I was amazed by this Christian and human act.

---

[123] Omonoia is a neighborhood in downtown Athens, centered on the square of the same name.

[124] "I spent the Occupation at Marios [Dalezios]" (op. cit., p. 190).

[125] Italian for round loaf.

[126] "Plus other poor souls who were starving [during the Occupation] and I'd see them and say: 'Take a piece of bread to eat.' [...] I gave them whatever I had" (op. cit., p. 191).

"What do I owe you, Mr. Markos?"
"Shame on you", he said. "Nothing."
"But..."
"No ifs or buts!"

Nikos G. Metaxotos

Nikos G. Metaxotos standing outside the grocery store that belonged to his uncle Stamatis Paramanis in 1918. It is in this grocery store that Markos worked as a grocer's boy.

10

VAFEAS, MARKOS'S FIRST TEACHER

I

My dad was Antonis Michail Vafeas[127]. He was born in 1889 in Apano Chora. My father was a barber. His barber shop was located inside the market. In addition, my father was also good at playing the bouzouki. When closing up shop in the evening, he would definitely go to the tavern of barba Gavrilis. They were really good friends. He was playing his bouzouki, drinking and coming home stuffed, ready to sleep. On Sundays, he used to take his bouzouki and his tools and go to Kini, to Tzekos's kafeneio, in order to barber, shave and play.

But I'm telling the truth when I say that Markos learned to love the bouzouki next to my dad, the barber Antonis Vafeas. It was him who gave him some courses when he was a young kid, before leaving from Syros. When I asked my mother, who had taught my father to play the bouzouki, she replied that it was in his DNA.

Elpida Vlachou

---

[127] "As I said, when I was a kid, I heard Stravogiorgis the blind man, Maoutsos, Manolakis Trisimisis from Apano Chora, Vafeas. These guys were playing the bouzouki" (op. cit., p. 107).

Antonis Michail Vafeas

II

The house that we're standing in right now belonged to Marigo Altouva. Maria Vafea, my wife, who is the daughter of Isidoros Vafeas, son of the barber Antonis Michail Vafeas, who gave bouzouki lessons to Markos Vamvakaris and became what he became, got it as dowry.

This was the house on whose roof the boulder fell and forced Markos to leave Syros. [128] Right next to the house

---

[128] "From high up on a slope, just for kicks, I set a boulder that weighed several tons rolling downhill. As it rolled it fell on the roof of a house. [...] It smashed through the roof tiles and dropped inside the house. [...] I was scared they'd catch me [the police]. I stowed away on a boat and ran away to Piraeus. The high place from which I rolled the rock

where Markos had thrown the boulder is a big rock. This place is called the "Balkonaki"[129] of Portara.[130] Markos went to that place with a friend of his who loved him very much[131] and finished the lyrics of "Frangosyriani".

Antonis Dalezios and Maria Daleziou

---

was called Persinos and the place where the boulder landed was called Portara" (op. cit., p. 79).

[129] Balkonaki means "small balcony".

[130] "Kids used to go and play over there, in Portara, they were hitting, stoning each other. [...] The kids higher up rolled rocks onto those below, in Portara. But the result was just some bandaged heads or hands with gauzes, nothing much worse than that from all the rock fighting" (op. cit., p. 51).

[131] Nikos Chalavazis had four children. One of them was Iosif, who was born in 1901. A fraternal friendship was gradually formed between Markos and Iosif. They left together from Syros in order to go to Piraeus in 1920. Iosif went to work with his brothers in Piraeus and soon served in the military. They came back to Syros in 1935 and sat in the "Balkonaki" of Portara; this is where Markos finished the lyrics of "Frangosyriani". This fraternal friendship would last until 1937, a key year in Markos Vamvakaris's life.

11

THREE BOYS RAN AWAY FROM SYRA

A group of three boys ran away from Syra in 1920 and went to Piraeus. Two of them were Markos Vamvakaris and my uncle Nikos Gavriil Maragos, who was born on May 19, 1903 and was my father's brother and two years older than Markos. I do not know who the third boy was. In Piraeus, at first, they both became skinners. My uncle stayed in Athens until the 1970s and then returned to Syra. Markos never came back permanently.

Father Gavriil Maragos, Societas Iesu

Markos traveled to Piraeus with the boat "Pelops" in 1920. The search for the whereabouts of the ticket and the exact date he traveled to the port of Piraeus is in full swing!

12

IN PIRAEUS

In order to assess the degree of influence of the tradition of Syros on the personality of Markos Vamvakaris, we will try to determine the timing of his departure from Syros. This effort will only be made through his autobiography and documents from registry offices in order to confirm the conclusion that will follow. Thus, we will be able to approximate at what age Markos was the recipient of the intellectual tradition of Syros and of the island's lifestyle in general.

Markos Vamvakaris states the following: "The blockade ended in 1917. I was a thirteen-year-old lad by now [...] One day, I did a dumb thing. I stowed away on a boat and ran away to Piraeus" (p. 80). "When I left Syros and came to Piraeus, I stayed with an aunt of mine called Irini Altouva [...] Over there I met some fellow Frankosyrans [...] they were also stevedores [...] They took me on as one of the team even though I was young [...] I was carrying huge sacks of coal on my back and I was just a boy of fifteen" (p. 81). "[...] I worked four years on the coal [...]" (p. 87). "Nine months after I got to Piraeus, my whole family arrived in Piraeus and we all lived together in Tabouria[132]. My father got a job straight away carrying coal in the same place as me" (p. 82). "I had to go with my father [...] I was feeling sorry for him [...] I was only a kid after all, a seventeen, eighteen-year-old kid" (p. 83) "It was round this time, when I was working on the coal, that I began my relationship with the woman who became my first wife" (p. 86). "From the very first days, love took

---

[132] A neighborhood of Piraeus.

hold of us and a year passed without the flame dying down. One day I eloped with her and we ran away" (p. 87) After I'd worked four years on the coal, I managed to go to Zea[133], to the customs [...]" (p. 87). "By the time I was working at the customs I was already married to [...] my first wife. I stayed there for two or three years" (p. 89). "Before going to the army, I left off being a docker and went to work as a skinner in the Piraeus slaughterhouse [...] From 1923 to 1929-1930" (p. 96-97).

The reality is this: First of all, Markos's father Domenikos declared on March 6, 1917 the death of his two-and-a-half-year-old daughter Margitsa Vamvakari. Consequently, Markos's father was already in Syros in 1917. And secondly, on January 30, 1918, that is, 9 months and 23 days after the above incident, Domenikos Vamvakaris declared the birth of his daughter Grazia Vamvakari. On March 3, 1918, the girl was baptized in Saint Sebastian, so it appears that the Vamvakaris family was definitely in Syros until March 3, 1918.

Markos Vamvakaris, based on the aforementioned excerpts, left Syros in 1920. In Piraeus, at first, he got a job in a grocery store and then worked as a stevedore, probably for three years. In the meantime, his family also came from Syros. After their arrival, Markos met Eleni, and a year later he eloped with her and got married. Indeed, if we add the number 3 to 1920, that is, the years that he worked as a stevedore, we arrive at the year 1923. On December 7, 1923, Markos Domenikou Vamvakaris married Eleni Dimitriou Mavroudi. They met at the age of 17, given that they got married a year later, when Markos was still working on coal.

On February 10, 1926, at the age of 21, Markos Vamvakaris was called to serve. Based on his draft and in order to work as a slaughterer, he must have worked at the customs

[133] See page 110 for more information.

from 1923 to 1925 and then as a skinner until his departure for the army, that is, in 1926.

Markos Vamvakaris, taking into account the documents of the registry office, his marriage and the duration of his military service, indeed must have left Syros in 1920 when he was 15 years old.

Dimitris. V. Varthalitis

Piraeus, as Markos saw it for the first time in 1920.

13

MARKOS'S FIRST MARRIAGE

Markos Vamvakaris describes his first marriage as follows in the pages 86, 87 and 105 of his autobiography: "I used to go pretty often over there, in Tabouria, at the house of a cousin of mine, Koula Rigoustou. The girl I was in love with was living in the same courtyard. She was Orthodox, from the Peloponnese and she was called Zingoala [...] A year passed without the flame dying down. One day I eloped with her and we ran away. We stole off at ten o'clock at night and I took her home. She was a pretty, spirited woman, dark, wonderful eyes and a beauty.

Mark, after his elopement with Eleni, went to the Catholic church of Saint Paul in Piraeus and asked the priest to marry them. From research conducted, it was found that the marriage ceremony of Markos Vamvakaris, son of Domenikos, with Eleni Mavroudi (not Zingoala), daughter of Dimitrios and Theodora, also born in 1905, took place in the Catholic church of Piraeus on December 7, 1923.

Markos Vamvakaris and Eleni moved to her mother's house in Nikaia, 40 Nikis Street, after 1933. Markos Vamvakaris created the most beautiful rebetiko songs ever written in that house and, of course, "Frangosyriani". Fortunately, it has not been demolished. If only it could be turned into a museum in honor of Markos Vamvakaris. The mayor of Nikaia has first claim, in consultation with Theodora Chalavazi.

Slowly, living with Eleni Mavroudi became overwhelming, bickering became part of everyday life and the couple could no longer coexist. After Markos Vamvakaris got divorced from Eleni in 1937, he left and stayed in his family house, which was next to Eleni's house. In that house, Markos Vamvakaris wrote, among others, the painful songs referring to his separation.

Dimitris. V. Varthalitis

Markos lived with Eleni Mavroudi in this house, 42 Nikis Street, in Aspra Chomata, from 1933 to 1937. This house is the cradle of rebetiko music.

14

WITH YOUR BIG HEAD YOU'LL ASK FOR XERXES

Dimitris, I'll tell you now who Xerxes and Eleni are. The song "Ithela na'mai o Iraklis"[134] (1937) is relevant:

I was a mangas once,	*Ήμουνα μάγκας μια φορά*
with blue blood in my veins,	*με φλέβα αριστοκράτη·*
now a master I shall be	*τώρα θα γίνω δάσκαλος,*
like Socrates the sage.	*σαν τον σοφό Σωκράτη.*
I'd become like Paris	*Ο Πάρις θα γινόμουνα,*
and steal fair Helen away,	*να 'κλεβα την Ελένη·*
I'd leave poor Menelaus	*ν' άφηνα τον Μενέλαο*
heartbroken all the way!	*με την καρδιά καμένη!*
I wanted to be Hercules	*Ήθελα να 'μαι ο Ηρακλής*
that first time I saw ya;	*όταν σε πρωτοείδα·*
I'd cut off your head	*να σου 'κοβα την κεφαλή*
like the Lernaean Hydra.	*σαν τη Λερναία Ύδρα.*
What else d'you want me to be-	*Τι άλλο θέλεις να γινώ,*
come	*για να με αγαπήσεις;*
in order to say "I love you"?	*Εσύ με το κεφάλι σου*
With your stubbornness,	*τον Ξέρξη θα ζητήσεις.*
you'll ask Xerxes to marry you.	

My father Iosif Chalavazis, son of Nikos and Florentia, was born in 1901 in Parakopi, Syros. This is where he met with Markos, when the latter was an apprentice, and slowly

---

[134] "I wanted to be Hercules".

became best friends. Markos worked here and there, in Ermoupoli and in the villages. However, he never forgot Parakopi. In the early 1920s, when my father was about to go to the army, he left with Markos and a third guy and they came to Piraeus with the boat "Pelops", if I remember correctly. Markos threw a boulder at a house on purpose; he wanted an excuse to leave Syros. In Piraeus, my father's two older brothers, Zannes and Tzekos, transported the islands' agricultural products by boat to the port. At first, my father and Markos were both living in a rowboat. Then, Markos went to his aunt Irini Altouva in Tabouria. He worked initially in a grocery store. He never worked with my brothers, they had other workers. Markos was married to Eleni Mavroudi when he was young, at the age of 18; Eleni was the same age as him.

We had never slept in their house because they were coming all the time to Agia Sofia, to Lipasmata, to Anastasi[135], generally to Piraeus, where there were taverns, and they used to go and drink. I was always with them. Markos wasn't playing the bouzouki in those taverns back then. He was only playing in his own joint[136] in the evening and, in the morning, he was operating it as a kafeneion. This was a corner kafeneion, just across the street from his house in Aspra Chomata. He had barrels of wine inside. Many people were coming. I used to go there often with my parents because they would take me along. Markos used to tell me: "Come, Nikolakis, dance zeibekiko." He was playing his bouzouki and I was dancing. You have no idea how much I liked to dance when I was eleven years old. Markos, who was thirty-

---

[135] Neighborhoods of Piraeus.

[136] "Later I set up the other joint at Aspra Chomata with my own funds" (op. cit., p. 155).

two at that time, was playing the bouzouki for me. Unforgettable childhood memories. I loved uncle Markos very much. I used to call him uncle out of respect.

It was the summer of 1937. Markos had come with his wife Eleni and we went to a tavern and had fun. It was late and they slept at our house, 59 Vitolion Street, near Agia Sofia, in Piraeus. In the morning, Markos left in order to go and open his coffee shop, but Eleni stayed at our house. The houses back then were built around each other and had a small courtyard in the middle. The lady who was living in the house across from ours passed in front of our kitchen and saw my father[137] and Eleni... "together". And she went and told to my mother when she woke up. She shouldn't have! Everything got all messed up. That same night my mom took me and we went to Markos's tavern in Aspra Chomata and said to me: "Go get your uncle Markos." So, I said to him: "Uncle Markos, my mom wants to talk to you." Markos broke up with Eleni that night. But my parents didn't. Markos wrote the song "M'ekanes kai chorisa"[138] (1937):

You made me break up	*Μ' έκανες και χώρισα*
and you were the cause;	*κι εσύ 'σουν η αιτία·*
and now I'm shooed out	*και τώρα μένω*
into the street.	*μες στους πέντε δρόμους.*
You vexed me a lot,	*Πολύ με αγανάκτησες,*
I'm in such despair,	*σε τέτοια απελπισία,*

---

[137] "He was a friend of mine, also from Syros, a distant relative, and he helped me, but he had something else in mind. He wasn't a man of honor. He was a scoundrel, as it became clear from what happened later. My treacherous wife fell in love with him. Don't even ask... There's no need to spell out the obvious" (op. cit., p. 143).

[138] "You made me break up".

there's no one anymore
that I want to meet.

δεν θέλω για να βλέπω
πια ανθρώπους.

Then there were huge fights between my father and Markos's family. One day, in 1937, he came home covered in blood and all tattered. They'd thrown him off the bridge of Amfiali[139]... I remember that my mother made me a pair of short pants out of his pants. Three months later, my father grabbed a sword, wrapped it up in a coat and went to take down Markos. He alerted the police and they found the sword. My father was sentenced to six months in prison. When he got out of jail, he came home, but continued to have an affair with Markos's wife. I grew up and went after them. They had gone to Pasalimani[140] and rented a house. I don't know how I discovered this. So, I went there and made a fuss in front of the neighbors. They packed up and left. But my father was coming home, he wasn't living with Eleni. He kept working in the port and feeding us. He had also undertaken to support Eleni, who had gone live in her old house, where she was staying with Markos before they split up.

From then on, about eight years later, in 1945, my father brought a little girl to my mother, secretly from me, and said to her: "I want to adopt her. Let's keep and raise her." I was married and my mom said to him: "Soon our daughter-in-law will give birth, our finances don't allow us to raise a second child." My father took the little girl and gave it to a friend of his. She baptized her and raised her as her daughter

---

[139] A neighborhood of Piraeus.

[140] The bay of Zea, since Ottoman times and until recently known as Pasalimani, is a broad bay located at the eastern coast of the Piraeus peninsula. During the ancient times, it was the biggest Athenian military harbor.

with the financial help of my father; I wasn't aware of anything at all regarding that matter.

One day, I was walking in Piraeus and I was headed to the kafeneion where my relatives used to hang out. A nice young lady came up to me and said:

"Did you see my dad?"

I replied: "Who's your dad?"

And when she told me his name, I was speechless. I didn't know anything. This was when I first met her. Then I understood who had sent her in order to see how I would react...

I saw Markos again in 1947, when I was 21 years old. I had gone with my brother-in-law and a friend of his to have some wine at a tavern near "Faliriko", where Markos was playing. I gave him a drachma and a half and told him to play "Syros" (1936). He said:

"Will you dance it, manga?"

"No. I'll just listen to it and, when you're done, come to my table so I can tell you who I am."

After he finished, he came to the table and told me:

"Who are you, manga?"

"I'm the son of Iosif, your former best friend."

"Damn, Nikolakis", he said and hugged and kissed me.

I never stopped loving "uncle" Markos and my beloved sister Theodora.

Nikos Iosif Chalavazis

15

"OH MARKOS, I HAVE A SWELLING, A FLAMING BURST OF HEAT"

I

My mother, Eleni, who was from the village of Mavrovouni, Mani, told me that after her marriage to Markos in 1923, his mother Elpida had two more children[141]: Rosa in 1925 and Argyris in 1930. My mother raised these two children and loved them very much because she didn't have children of her own. Rosa once said: "Even if I receive a slap from Eleni, I'll accept it." She was that close with her. She also invited her to the wedding of her son Palaiologos. I was there too.

My mother was a smart woman. She didn't take flak from anybody. She was fair, reasonable and good-hearted. She loved me very much. She passed away in 1998.

I remember Markos Vamvakaris sitting on a stool or on a chair outside his house and playing his bouzouki. I was kind of scared of him, but I had realized from his behavior that he was a mensch.

My mother told me about "Frangosyriani" that in the spring of 1935, while sitting in the courtyard and holding her chest because she was feeling pain, she told Markos: "Oh Markos, I have a swelling, a flaming burst of heat." And then

---

[141] On Sunday, October 20, 2013, at 11 o'clock in the morning, I visited Theodora Chalavazis, daughter of Iosif Chalavazis and Eleni Mavroudi, at her house in Aspra Chomata, which is exactly where Eleni lived with Markos until their breakup in 1937.

again: "Oh Markos, I don't know. I have a swelling, a flaming burst of heat, here, in my heart." And a third time: "I feel a swelling, a tightening, a flaming burst of heat in my heart." So, Markos grabbed a piece of paper and wrote it at that very moment. My mother has told me this and we have to tell the truth. We may not know it. But, when we do, we have to tell it. That's how "Frangosyriani" started.

Theodora I. Chalavazi

II

In 1935, when Markos was thirty years old and came to Syros and composed "Frangosyriani", he went to Apano Chora. He also passed by our house, which was in Skali, as well as Bantikos's kafeneion; he sat outside and drank coffee. He was beautiful. A palikari[142], a tall man.

From there, he went to Kamara, opposite Nichori, which had only one house and above that house was the gunpowder factory where they used to make gunpowder and bullets before the war, when I was unborn. So, he went and sat there, on a rock, across from Nichori, with another guy. He was inspired to compose "Frangosyriani", then he wrote it down and soon we heard it on a record.

Tereza Roussou

III

My name's Kasounios. I was born in 1925. One time,

---

[142] A brave young man who illustrates the qualities of the palikaria: courage, fighting spirit and boldness.

when I was ten years old, I grazed some sheep on the beach of Galissas.

There was no one at the beach. I saw someone sitting on a mound of pebbles right on the beach and I didn't know him at all. He was all alone. I fell down and crawled on my belly in order to hear what he was saying. He was playing "Frangosyriani". After matching the lyrics, he sang it and I was able to listen to it because I was about thirty meters away. The sea was a little bit stormy. He sat there the entire afternoon and was playing and singing until nightfall. When the sun set, I took the sheep and left.

The next day I heard from my father that Markos Vamvakaris sang "Frangosyriani" for the first time in Tabakas's kafeneion in Galissas. This testimony is true. I swear.

He had also come in Syros in 1955 and had brought a woman with him. At that time, I was a milkman and I was distributing milk every day.

After selling off, around 9-9:30 a.m., I used to go and drink coffee with Markos Vamvakaris. We were sitting and discussing. He was deeply moved when I told him that I had seen him when he first played "Frangosyriani" on Galissas beach in 1935.

When I was in Athens for work in 1956, I went with some friends of mine from Galissas to "Kipos tou Allah"[143] where Markos was playing. He played "Frangosyriani" when he saw me. After that I lost him, I never saw him again...

Giorgos Ioannou Voutsinos or Kasounios

---

[143] "Garden of Allah".

16

THE SS AND THE PRISONS
BELONG TO THE PAST

My father, Giorgos Markou Maragos (1901-1984) or Markoulios, from Syra, was a childhood friend of Markos Vamvakaris. My mother, Louisa Vakontiou, was an aristocrat, from Apano Chora, from Saint Sebastian. She used to say that she was related to Markos. When my father came to Athens, he opened a store in the vegetable market and, wherever Markos was singing, he would go and have fun. Sometimes he also accompanied him on his trips to Syra.

In 1935, Markos was sitting on the patio of Saint Sebastian's courtyard with my father. Don Almansis passed by and hit Markos's shoulder with his walking stick. So, Markos said to him: "Don Almansis, why did you hold out on me like this?" And he replied: "Can you see the window above the entrance door of the church? You broke it with your slingshot when you were a kid and it's still cracked." They both smiled and Markos pulled a coin out of his pocket and gave it to Don Almansis to replace the glass.

In 1939, Markos was playing in the tavern "Dasos"[144] in Votanikos[145]. They used to say:

"Where will we go today?"

"Let's go to Markos, by the railway lines."

---

[144] Dasos means "forest".

[145] A neighborhood west of central Athens that takes its name from the nearby botanical garden. At that time, there were large wooded areas and an industrial zone near the railway.

The train was passing by close to there. Four or five people were playing on stage and the koutsavakia[146] were dancing zeibekiko.

I was born on 4 Efpatridon Street. A wedding was held next to our house during the Occupation in 1942. The Germans had entered Athens. So, a black marketeer from Mytilini was getting married and having a feast next to our house. Of course, my family was invited too. At some point my father said to a kid: "Go to 'Dasos' and wake up Markos Vamvakaris, the bouzouki player. He's sleeping in the bouzouki joint, which is currently closed. Tell him to take his bouzouki and come to the wedding celebration. He'll eat well and he'll make some money." Markos came and, after drinking two to three drinks, he said to my father: "I wrote a new song. I was struggling two whole nights. I'll play and sing it." So, he started playing and singing:

When the British come,	*Όταν θα 'ρθουν οι Εγγλέζοι,*
they'll bring us suits to wear,	*θα μας φέρουνε κουστουμάκια*
they'll be new ones;	*να φορέσουμε καινούργια,*
chocolates, jams and scones	*σοκολάτες, μαρμελάδες και*
they'll bring for us to eat,	*βουτήματα για να τρώμε,*
when we're stoned as shit.	*όταν θα 'μαστε μαστούρια.*
The SS and the prisons	*Πάνε τα Ες Ες*
belong to the past,	*και οι φυλακές,*
inflation billions didn't last.	*σβήσανε τα δις και τα τετράκις.*
All this money is now gone,	*Πάνε όλα αυτά τα παλιολεφτά*

---

[146] Koutsavaki(s) (pl. koutsavakia) = a tough guy who usually carried a knife, spoke a particular slang and walked with a characteristic insolent air. A koutsavaki used to wear distinctive clothing (often a jacket over one shoulder only and a cummerbund hanging and touching the ground) and have a twirling mustache. In general, these were the most dangerous types of manghes.

and every rascal
is going back to work alone.

και ο κάθε κατεργάρης (του)
στον πάγκο του θα πα'.

When Markos mentioned the SS, my father said to him: "Shut up, Markos, the Germans are right outside!" Behind the house where we were having fun was a bakery that had been commandeered by the Germans in order to produce their kommissbrot[147] and the Italians their pagnotte. And every day the Germans were doing raids with bicycles. Markos laughed and said to my father: "Don't be afraid." And he played it again. I was close to him and immediately memorized it. I even accompanied him the second time because Markos had written it on a piece of paper and gave it to me. I wonder where could this paper be now...

I cannot forget these lyrics and melody. Markos left after the party. He was sleeping in the tavern and made his living from the saltadoroi[148].

Markos and my father knew each other since they were kids. My father used to say to my mother: "Let's go have a night out with Markos." She would always reply to him: "No, I don't want this kind of fun." My mother Louisa Vakontiou (1906-1963) was beautiful and classy. In any case, my mother was also present at that wedding. And I remember well that when Markos was singing "Frangosyriani" he was looking at her in the eyes. When he finished, he said to me: "You little rascal, I was also thinking of your mother when I wrote

---

[147] Kommissbrot is a dark type of German bread, baked from rye and other flours, historically used for military provisions. It has a firm but not hard crust, and because it is normally baked in a loaf pan, it develops a crust only on the top. It is noted for its long shelf life.

[148] Saltadoros (pl. saltadoroi) = "van-dragger". A saltadoros was someone who jumped on the vehicles of the German occupiers in order to steal various useful items (food, tires, etc.)

Giannis G. Maragos

Giorgos Maragos, Markos's childhood friend, with his
wife Louisa Vakontiou.
(Giannis G. Maragos's archive)

17

HE WROTE "FRANGOSYRIANI" ON A PIECE OF FISH-WRAP

Antonis Vamvakaris, my grandfather, was the brother of Domenikos, Markos's father. He married Elpida Xanthaki. He was a fisherman. They were a very poor family and they had only daughters: Anneta, Rosa, Santina, Eleni and Speranza.

In 1972, I went with my mother Santina at a clinic in Piraeus to visit Markos shortly before he died. Markos said to my mother: "Santina, look what I've become! I'm all alone, abandoned and poor..." He was crying with my mother. I could see they were really fond of each other. Markos loved his family very much. After a while we learned that he had died. What I learned was that they didn't have any money to bury him. He was that poor...

It strikes me that after all this poverty, after his death, he has become big and famous. But I remember well what he said to my mother: "You know, Santina, it may seem like people don't give me any importance now. But, when I die, you'll see who I really am."

Regarding "Frangosyriani", my aunt Eleni used to say that Markos went to her house in Apano Syros in 1935 and asked for a piece of paper. She didn't have any so he went to the grocer and borrowed a piece of fish-wrap and wrote it. She remembered it well, because it was the first time he visited her.

Katerina Foteinia

18

THE BEGINNING OF THE DISASTER

"That's when I wrote 'Ziliara'[149]. A tortured song; I was in a terrible state when I wrote it. It was 1936 and I was on a boat heading for Syra. [...] I put in the music after I got back to Piraeus." (p. 282)

Markos wrote the song "Ziliara" (1936) on a boat during a trip of his to Syros. The creative mood that the aquatic environment procured him should not come as a surprise to us, given that Markos came from an island and had a fond habit of playing his bouzouki on board the boat.

Ah, you wicked woman,	*Αχ, κακούργα,*
you break my heart;	*πόσο με πληγώνεις,*
these games of yours,	*με τα σκέρτσα σου,*
they tear me apart.	*πώς με σκλαβώνεις!*
You made me wander	*Μ' έκανες και σαν*
like a screwball,	*τρελός γυρίζω,*
my heart is now	*την καρδιά μου, πια,*
out of control.	*δεν την ορίζω.*
Ah, you wicked woman,	*Αχ, κακούργα,*
put away this jealousy	*πάψ' αυτή τη ζήλια,*
and with your sweet lips kiss me.	*φίλα με τα γλυκά σου χείλια.*
You oughta know, you wither me,	*Αχ, να ξέρεις πώς με μαραζώνεις,*
you jealous woman;	*ζηλιάρα,*
why do you want to hurt me?	*γιατί θες να με πληγώνεις;*
My lady, since the day	*Σαν σε πρωτογνώρισα,*
you first met with me,	*κυρά μου,*
you burnt me deeply,	*μου 'καψες βαθιά*
my guts are fiery.	*τα σωθικά μου.*

---

[149] "Jealous woman".

The smallest things,	Ζηλιάρα, που όλο θες
they put you in a rage;	να με θυμώνεις,
what you want is to upset me.	γιατί με το παραμικρό κακιώνεις;
You oughta know, you wither me,	Αχ, να ξέρεις πως με μαραζώνεις,
you jealous woman;	ζηλιάρα,
why do you want to hurt me?	γιατί θες να με πληγώνεις;

Markos Vamvakaris admitted that his great distress was the reason for his inspiration. "If I'm in a state, a little bit worried, things turn out better both in the lyrics and the music." (p. 258) During that period, he was married to Eleni, but we do not know what happened between them in 1936. The title "Ziliara" is enough for us to assume the situation Markos was experiencing when writing it. Moreover, if we read the lyrics carefully, the pain that he was feeling from the jealousy of his beloved one is evident.

In his autobiography, Markos Vamvakaris admitted that his marital problems began with the coming of his recognition and glory: "As long as I kept her poor she was fine, she wasn't looking for more. When they called me to make records and I began to make money I dressed her up [...] in all kinds of things. [...] I was getting tons of money, I was up to the mark with 2-3 thousand a month [...] I was very pleased." (p. 276) What Markos said reasonably lead us to conclude that she was deeply jealous of his success and great impact. "Couldn't she see that our life had changed and we'd raked in the big bucks? I'd accustomed her to thousands. [...] "Was I to blame? I did everything I could to make her a lady." (p. 277)

Eleni, with the financial comfort that Markos was providing her, should have been grateful to her man and support him. But the feeling of jealousy and bitterness gripped her soul and led her on a path of no return. "Sometimes I'd say to her: 'Quit the down-hill path you're on, let's try to live happily'." (p. 160) Perhaps she was thinking less of herself next to Markos and wanted to get back at him. Eleni, blinded by jealousy, hurt him in the most despicable way possible: she established a relationship with his best friend. "He was a friend of mine, a fellow Syran and a distant relative. [...] I mean, it was the first time a friend took advantage of my misery. He handed me a glass of water and it turned out to be poison." (p. 144)

Dimitris. V. Varthalitis

Eleni Mavroudi seated.
(Dionysis Maniatis's and Giorgos Thanopoulos's archive)

19

MARKOS, JUST WALK AWAY

Petros Nikolaou Provelengios's[150] mother was Maria and his father "Pseftonikolas"[151], as they used to call him. He was born on December 27, 1905 in Skali, in Apano Syros, and he knew Markos since they were children. They were living next door to each other in Skali, in the parish of Saint Sebastian. They ran away together and came to Piraeus in 1920. Petros never returned to Syra. He left and never looked back. He left once and for all, unlike Markos. He went to Piraeus and directly worked at the slaughterhouse, where Markos also worked with him for several years.

Eventually, Petros opened a butcher shop in the market of Piraeus with his son Dimitris. Markos often used to go there and have a chat. Because Petros was friends with Markos, Dimitris's godmother was Eleni, Markos's wife. I married him on July 26, 1970. My husband used to tell me that up to the age of thirteen his godmother Eleni was shopping clothes and toys for him and giving him pocket money. However, his father was biased and didn't want her because she had done played that dirty trick on Markos. We went and visited her for the first time when my first child, my sweet Irini, who was born in 1970, was four months old; it

---

[150] "We used to make little toy boats out of paper or tin. There were some hollows where the water got deeper and we used to go and play there in the river, me, a certain Petros Delasoudas, another one called Petros Provelengios, and Dimitrios Delasoudas, a whole bunch of kids from the neighborhood of Skali" (op. cit., p. 53).

[151] A nickname meaning "Nikolas the liar".

was a sign. My husband told me: "Let's go see my god-mother." She hugged and kissed me when we entered her house. I put my little baby on a bed. Eleni went over to her and put fifty drachmas in her clothes because she hadn't gotten anything for her.

Let me describe you Eleni: a little bit chubby, around seventy kilos. She was of average height. Her hair was styled into a bun, like they did in those days. She had nice legs. She was a beautiful woman, even in 1971, when she was 66 years old and I met her for the first time. She was wearing some clothes for older people. She was talking really well. She was a really nice woman, very polite. She kept telling me: "I love your husband very much because he comes and sees how I am."

My husband kept going back to visit her because he wanted to. He was drawn to her, even though his father was getting angry, grumbling, and was telling him not to go. Dimitris, unintentionally, continued to be the only communication channel between Markos, Petros, Iosif and Eleni after Markos's break up with Eleni, his godmother. One time, my father-in-law was with my mother-in-law near the church of Saint Paul in Piraeus and stumbled across Eleni. My father-in-law said to his wife:

"Let's go, let's go, don't talk to her."

And she said: "Why not talk to her?"

"Because she did that thing to Markos."

From that bad day she never spoke to Eleni again. That's how much she loved Markos. Sometimes, when we listened to some of Markos's songs, my husband used to say: "He wrote this song for Eleni, after they split up."

— *Elpida, did you know Iosif?*

Yes, I did. He was the same age as Markos and my father-

125

in-law. One time we met him and my husband addressed him as "uncle" because of the age difference. He was Markos's childhood friend and they were in and out of each other's houses. I mean, Iosif and his wife used to go to Markos's house in Aspra Chomata and stayed for the night. And Markos used to go with Eleni to Iosif's house in Agia Sofia, in Piraeus. But Markos could never have imagined that his childhood friend would wrong him like that.

Markos, however, loved Eleni very much and used to go outside the window of her house and talk to her and tell her to open the door. And she was saying: "Markos, just walk away", and was turning him away. And his brother Tzekos was telling him: "Brother, why don't you divorce her after what she did to you?" He had a passion for her.

— *Did you know Markos?*

Yes. I used to see him during Easter and Christmas in the church of Saint Paul, where my father Michalis Vafeas also used to go. They met outside the church during the Easter of 1969 and went and had a chat in a kafeneion. I was there too. Markos was handsome, tall, a burly man, but overwhelmed by fatigue, illnesses and sufferings...

— *Did you know Domenikos and Stelios?*

Yes. Domenikos would come to church every Sunday in 1980 and go up to the gallery where the harmonium was. A foreign girl, Miluška, was playing, and Domenikos would observe her because he too is a musician. He wasn't playing, just watching.

In 1971, Stelios married Maria Töl, a Dutch woman, who spoke Greek really well; they had three daughters. I often

126

saw Stelios at church with his family and when he was sometimes coming to pick up his children from school.

One day, my father-in-law said to Markos Vamvakaris: "Hey, Markos, what's with all that glory of yours? People are talking about you all over Greece. How did you learn to play the bouzouki like that? Your songs are all about passion and lamentation. Where did you find the muse that inspires you?" He used to tell us that Markos would listen to the birds chirping, since he had many cages with different birds in the basement of his house in Aspra Chomata, and register their music and then play it with his bouzouki.

Elpida Vafea-Provelengiou

Dimitris Provelengios, wearing a cap, with his parents.
(Elpida Vafea-Provelengiou's archive)

20

BIRDS TAUGHT ME MUSIC...

"He had a lame donkey. And eighty little birds in cages. As soon as he was sitting down and rolling a cigarette, he used to say to me: 'Listen to them...' And all of them were starting to sing. He would listen carefully and his soul would rejoice. 'Eh, now, after their performance, what could I possibly play?' And as he was listening to them for a long time, he would sigh sadly and grab the bouzouki. With the first stroke of the pick and the sound produced from the instrument, all of them were getting quiet; they were listening to him..."[152]

The passion of Syran erudite teacher and researcher Dimitris Varthalitis for his townsman, the great Markos Vamvakaris, and for the promotion of his contribution to the Greek and world music heritage prompted me to write this text, where I refer to the relationship of Markos Vamvakaris with birds and nature.

After many hours of discussions with Dimitris Varthalitis about the origins of Markos's music, his relation with Syros, the folklore expression of his songs about social inequalities and injustice, the futility of life, the hybrid modality of his songs – due to the music he had heard during his childhood from the Catholic church – and many more, I was enormously impressed. One issue, however, that I was particularly concerned with was Markos's constant reference to

---

[152] This story is from Giorgis Christofilakis's book "Mythos rebetikos – Markos Vamvakaris" ("Rebetiko myth – Markos Vamvakaris"), published by Tegopoulos-Maniateas publications, Athens, 1997.

birds and nature.

His naturalistic mood is evident in all of his interviews, but also in his songs. The stimuli from the environment he lived in during his childhood in Syros and later when he came to Piraeus – an environment that he gradually built as he had about eighty bird cages – are variously conveyed through his songs with hints, allegories and musical improvisations.

Markos, a bird expert, an avid ornithologist, expressed his folk wisdom by continuing the tradition of the great composers of classical music. He was inspired by the melodic lines of his goldfinches and canaries, unaware that masterpieces of classical music were written based on birds' melodic motifs. He did not know that Beethoven wrote the theme of the famous "Fifth Symphony" after being inspired by the buntings and that Vivaldi composed "El Carduelis" for goldfinches, or that the basic motif of Mozart's "Magic Flute" is based on the mimicry of the chirping of a nightingale by flutes, oboes and pipes.

Another paradox about the influence of birds on his inspiration and mood is that the famous French modern music composer Olivier Messiaen (1908-1992), who was active during the exact same period as Markos in Paris, stands in contrast to Vamvakaris's folklore expression. Reading Markos's thoughts regarding the influence of birds on his music, I ponder, through Plutarch's "Parallel Lives"[153], over the duo Markos Vamvakaris - Olivier Messiaen. They were both or-

---

[153] My metaphor relates to the work "Parallel Lives" of historian Plutarch, which is a series of biographies of famous Greeks and Romans, arranged in pairs, in order to emphasize their common moral values or failures (written around 100 AD).

nithologists and naturalists; Markos influenced the folk culture of his homeland and Messiaen music. The folk culture of naturalist Markos Vamvakaris met, during the same period, with the pursuits of Olivier Messiaen[154], who was fascinated to hear and record birds on the other side of Europe[155]. Their quests converge in a common place: that of birds, of God's messengers and of nature; in the ideal state of Aristophanes's "Birds", Nephelokokkygia[156], where birds become the regulators of the relationship between gods and humans.

---

[154] Messiaen (1908-1992), a great composer of modern music and a teacher of the sacred cows of contemporary music of the 20th century (Xenakis, Boulez, Stockhausen), had a deep love for songbirds and studied their singing as well as their voice production system in a scientific manner. He believed that birds are the best musicians and he considered himself to be both an ornithologist and a composer. He had recorded bird songs around the world and incorporated these recordings into several of his works.

[155] Bird singing was something exciting for Messiaen from an early age. Messiaen used bird tweets recorded by himself in some of his early works. Gradually, this use was incorporated into his compositional techniques and, along with the use of modes and the timbre of the chords, this became his musical style. In the work "The awakening of the birds" ("Le réveil des oiseaux"), his technique reached its most mature stage, as the entire song is based on cheeps. As an acoustic result, what we hear is basically a chorus of birds that are waking up, transcribed for an orchestra. The same applies to the work "Epode" ("Épode"), where there are no fewer than eighteen violins each playing a specific tweet. The score refers to which bird each tweet belongs to. However, we should not consider these works merely transcriptions of tweets. On the contrary, these are audio poems that represent a place with its colors, sounds and general atmosphere.

[156] The "cloud-cuckoo-land", that is, the city of birds.

Markos, in his autobiography and in many interviews, remembered his childhood in Syros and accurately described the birds of every season, analyzed their characteristic tweet or squawk and the effect on his mood. He essentially created descriptive soundscapes.

Markos described the soundscape of a midday autumnal equinox at Syros with great longing and admiration, and he also analyzed the characteristic sound as well as the physiognomy and behavior of each bird. This empirical analysis is not far from the analysis of an ornithologist-scientist who studies the behavior of birds.

And as his son Domenikos says, Markos was writing notes while listening to the birds: "I was a high school student back then and Markos had around eighty cages with various birds. So, Markos was listening to the birds and through their singing he was writing down the notes. He was writing notes even after being inspired by frogs."[157]

So, let's travel into the world of birds through folk ornithologist Markos Vamvakaris in order to understand the magic of bird music. In a world where we can all find refuge, and as Markos used to say: "Birds offered music to my soul; and humans offered sufferings." Let's plunge into Markos's deep ecological knowledge of birds and nature. Let's learn from the acoustic ecological consciousness of a man of the people who mentally met – in a modern parallel life – Olivier Messiaen!

Anastasia Georgaki

---

[157] Unpublished interview to Dimitris Varthalitis (Piraeus, 2013).

21

MARKOS'S SECOND MARRIAGE

"I'd had that disaster with my first wife and under no circumstances did I want to marry." (p. 195) But his older sister set him up with Vangelio, who was a neighbor, and their mother loved her when she was alive. Evangelia Vergiou was the daughter of Maria or Marianthi Katri and Eleftherios Vergiou. Markos took the decision "one Sunday in 1942 [...]" (p. 196) "to marry this decent girl." (p. 195) The second marriage took place on July 11, 1943, not in 1942. The wedding service was held by priest M. Manolakakis, pastor of the church of Saint Nikolaos.

After the wedding, the couple stayed at 35 Ofryniou Street, in Aspra Chomata. Markos had his children in that house. But many musicians also went down to the basement to visit him. This is where Markos Vamvakaris had the inspiration to write the original and timeless musical compositions of the period commencing after his second marriage with Evangelia. This is also where he held meetings – besides rebetiko musicians – with the students with who he began writing his autobiography. This house has now been demolished and turned into a corner shop.

When Domenikos served in the air force, the family moved and settled in 24 Dedalou Street, in Korydallos. Markos lived the last years of his life in 24 Dedalou Street. In the same year that Markos Vamvakaris died (1972), Evangelia and Domenikos bought an apartment in Korydallos, 24 Dimitrakopoulou Street, where they moved after his death.

Dimitris. V. Varthalitis

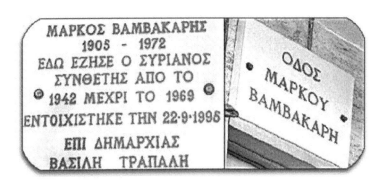

35 Ofryniou Street.
A commemorative plaque is attached
to the front of the building.

24 Dedalou Street,
on the day of his funeral.
(Giorgis Christofilakis's archive)

22

THE CELLAR WAS CREAKING

In 1955, I heard that Markos came to Syra, so I said to my friends: "Why don't we go drink some wine at the joint where Markos plays? Maybe I'll be able to bring him to my joint too."

We went and the place was full, fully packed! I nodded at him and he came over. I said:

"Welcome, Markos. How are you?"

"Where are you from?"

"I'm from Ano Syros."

"And what do you want?"

"When you're done from here, come to Ano Syra; I have a tavern that's more to your liking."

"I'll let you know."

I left, but I wanted to bring him up to Ano Syros. So, I went there again with the same group of friends. As soon as we arrived, he approached us on his own. He said to me:

"I'm ready now."

"Here, climb up."

The people who came were Giorgos Rovertakis, playing the accordion, Lefteris Naoumidis, playing the bouzouki, Mary Kokkinou, singer, and Markos.

He took a look when we entered into the "Katoga"[158].

"Hey", he said, "if I knew I'd find such a place, I wouldn't have gone anywhere else. And I recommend that you keep it like that until you die. This place is unbelievable."

"Markos, how could I have known?"

---

[158] Katoga means "cellar".

"Anyway..."

"There's no stage though."

"Hey man, what I want is a dance floor!"

He took four chairs and they went to the corner of the tavern. What can I say, what happened was something else! People were forming a queue the next day. The cellar was creaking when the singer was singing "I'll dive deep into the sea so the water covers me". People were coming to see Markos as well as Mary. Leonardos Xanthakis, a guy from Ano Syros, sold his donkey in order to have money and come to the "Katoga" to dance. His wife asked him:

"Where's the donkey?"

"The donkey died."

Markos stayed for quite some time. He was playing in the joint. At one point he said to me:

"Lilis, I'm gonna go because I've been away from my home for a long time."

"Hey, my dear Markos, whatever you think. Are you satisfied?"

"I'm glad because I saw this tavern."

The bouzouki and the accordion players left with him too. The woman didn't leave because the business was going well. The tavern was full as long as Markos was there. Only people from Apano Syros were filling up the place.

I remember one time when we were eating what he said to me: "Now my wife's waiting for me to send her money so she can heat up a cauldron and feed the kids. Here, I received twenty drachmas today. I'll send them over to her so that she can cook." He was being paid on commission. I know that this is how Markos raised his children; he was always on the move. He was feeling sorry about the situation with his children, but what could he do? He was always away from home.

Markos was a good man, a quiet man. He didn't object to anything. He wasn't a blasphemer either. He also had a good friend, Artemis. He liked Markos since they first met. They met when he was a grown up. Artemis was taking care of Markos like no one else in the world. He didn't smoke, but he used to drink a lot of wine. He's now dead too... And Vikentios, your father, loved Markos very much. He came to the "Katoga" many times. One time, a woman came to the tavern. She entered, kneeled and started praying to Markos. I said to her: "Is he a saint? Did you come to worship Markos or to have fun?"

Leonardos D. Roussos or Lilis

Markos Vamvakaris (bouzouki), Mary Kokkinou (guitar and singing). Giorgos Rovertakis (accordion) and Lefteris Naoumidis (bouzouki) in Lilis's "Katoga" in 1955.

23

LIKE TWO PEAS IN A POD

My grandfather Artemis "Neroulas"[159] Katevatis lived in Vrontado. He was born on January 19, 1917 in the same area. We were living very close, 12 Averof Street, a hundred meters further.

In 1965, I was a kid and one day, early in the morning, I went to get my grandmother Evangelia to go shopping and I saw grandpa drinking coffee with Markos Vamvakaris. So, I said to him:

"Grandpa Markos", that's how I used to call him, «what brings you here?"

"I slept in Artemis's bed for the night."

"Grandma, did you sleep on the divan?"

"Yes, my child."

Stelios came a week later.

Outside the house, where there were sloping steps and stairs, they used to spread out rags in the evening; Markos was playing his bouzouki and us neighborhood kids were gathering around and listening to him. A little further up was the tavern of Tebelis Nomikos, grandma's brother, and the people coming up used to stop and enjoy Markos Vamvakaris. I was sitting on my grandfather's lap. He was so happy and, when Markos was leaving from Syros, he was so unhappy. And then grandpa would take out of the gramophone and listen to Markos's records waiting for his return... We last saw him in 1968.

---

159 Neroulas means "waterseller".

When Markos was leaving from Syros, grandpa was escorting him up to the boat's boarding ladder; you couldn't get a word out of him for a week.

In the first week of February 1972 I saw grandpa Artemis cry inconsolably:

"Paw paw, why are you crying?"

"We won't be seeing grandpa Markos again..."

My grandfather had a photo of King Constantine I[160] above the bed and, next to it, a photo of his best friend Markos Vamvakaris. He was keeping his icons elsewhere.

When his children Stelios and Domenikos would come to Syros they used to say: "We're going to visit grandfather Artemis." Stelios was even closer with him; he would call grandpa Artemis once a week. He considered our family to be a part of Markos's family. He greatly appreciated the love and support our family had for Markos's family. I know very

---

[160] Constantine I (1868-1923) was King of Greece from 1913 to 1917 and from 1920 to 1922. He was commander-in-chief of the Hellenic Army during the unsuccessful Greco-Turkish War of 1897 and led the Greek forces during the successful Balkan Wars of 1912–1913, in which Greece expanded to include Thessaloniki, doubling in area and population. He succeeded to the throne of Greece on 18 March 1913, following his father's assassination. His disagreement with Eleftherios Venizelos over whether Greece should enter World War I led to the National Schism. Constantine forced Venizelos to resign twice, but in 1917 he left Greece, after threats by the Entente forces to bombard Athens; his second son, Alexander, became king. After Alexander's death, Venizelos's defeat in the 1920 legislative elections, and a plebiscite in favor of his return, Constantine was reinstated. He abdicated the throne for the second and last time in 1922, when Greece lost the Greco-Turkish War of 1919-1922, and was succeeded by his eldest son, George II. Constantine died in exile four months later, in Sicily.

well that Artemis supported Markos both morally and financially during difficult times.

When my grandfather talked about Markos, the stories were tragic. He used to say: "Markos will be vindicated as a man and as a musician after his death. His character doesn't allow him to rise high as long as he's alive. He's a maverick, a man who doesn't bow his head, a folk of the nightlife, someone who doesn't mind taking out a coin tray in front of him on the sidewalk. He lives in poverty. He lives a life of misery. He never ever steps on people to get ahead. He avoids this path and instead follows a true, a real one."

This was my grandfather's Artemis Katevatis description of Markos Vamvakaris. These two people were like two peas in a pod.

Maritsa M. Markynioti

Artemis Katevatis, the waterseller.

24

DON'T TEAR MY HEART TO PIECES

I

My uncle Markos lost his first boy Domenikos and believed that the name was to blame. So, my father Frangiskos named my brother Domenikos and then me Elpida.

I was born in Nikaia in 1936. I was going to church every Sunday in Aspra Chomata because my uncle Argyris, his brother, was giving me pocket money. I was also going to my uncle Markos to eat. Then I was going to visit my aunt Grazia and my aunt Rosa. My uncle Markos was treating me very well. He was a good man. He was writing songs and was playing the bouzouki. He was writing songs even when he was going to the toilet to pee. I've heard people say this. When I listen to his songs, I'm focused. I don't want nobody talking to me. I listen to my uncle.

My uncle had rented a pen near his house in Aspra Chomata and had animals that he liked. I've heard people say that his children were even drinking donkey milk.

As a young man, Markos was working in the slaughterhouse with my dad. They were butchers. After that, he was into music; he was writing songs, playing the bouzouki. My dad stayed there, in the slaughterhouse.

When Markos got sick, he confessed and received communion. He was very religious. I remember him saying: "I'll be dead, but my name will be heard. I've written and sang songs. You'll hear me for the rest of your lives."

Elpida Palaiologou

Frangiskos or Tzekos, Markos's brother.
(Elpida Palaiologou's archive)

II

I was born in Athens. My mother Grazia[161], Markos Vamvakaris's sister, was born in Syra in 1918 and came here when she was two years old, very young.

— *Did you know Markos?*

Very well. And I mean it. He was living opposite our house.

---

[161] "There was Grazia, seventeen years old, who worked at the factory and brought something home. [...] A good and decent girl" (op. cit., p. 143).

— Tell me some facts that associate your life with your uncle Markos.

In 1933, my grandfather Domenikos, my grandmother Elpida and their children were all living in sheds at the port of Drapetsona[162]. Because the Port Authority needed this place in order to build the Port, the state created the settlement of Aspra Chomata. They built roughly similar houses, each with a basement and a large hallway room, a kitchenette and a bathroom above as well as a garden in the back, and were allotted to the families who were living in these sheds.

The house where my uncle Markos lived with his first wife Eleni Mavroudi for some years without having a child was at 42 Nikis Street.

During the Occupation, Markos was working in Athens, where he had moved with his mother and his brothers. In 1943, he married his second wife Vangelio, a native of Symi[163]. Vangelio's family was also living in Drapetsona, in the sheds, from where they knew each other. After the wedding, he took her with him to Athens. He had his first two children there, the ones he lost. At one point he lost his mother too. Then they came back to Aspra Chomata.

---

[162] Drapetsona is situated on the north side of the inlet to the port of Piraeus. Its built-up area is continuous with those of neighboring cities of Piraeus and Keratsini. After the 1922 Asia Minor Disaster, there was a notable population increase. Since the 19th century, Drapetsona has become an important part of the Piraeus industrial area. The first major port facility was the Vassiliadis Shipyard, founded in 1898. Subsequently, other industries were established: a fertilizer factory, a plaster factory, a cement factory, a tannery and more recently installations of petroleum companies (Shell, Mobil, BP).

[163] Symi is an island, part of the Dodecanese island group.

My uncle Markos loved animals very much. A little further from that house was the pen where he'd put his animals. He also had a peacock and a donkey.

I got married when I was 19 years old, in 1968. My husband, who was a sailor, immediately sailed out.

He had to travel because we were building our apartment building. The same day I went and sat in my uncle's house, where his mother-in-law, his sister-in-law and some other neighbors were sitting. As I was sitting down, I was thinking of my husband who had left and, without wanting it, I began to cry. Everyone was looking at me, but they didn't tell me anything. When I left, they went to talk to Markos and who knows what they told him. The following day my uncle said to me: "Come here. Did I understand correctly? Why are you crying, my dear? Don't be sad. Don't tear my heart to pieces. Your husband is crazy about you. What are you afraid of?" "Uncle, I'm not afraid", I replied. "I'm just sad because he left. That's all." "Don't tear my heart to pieces..." He told me that because he loved me from the bottom of his heart. When I was pregnant with my first child, I was mopping in my house one day and, even though Markos couldn't climb the stairs because he had a respiratory problem, he saw me from downstairs and suddenly I saw him in front of me. "Uncle, what brings you here?" "I came to tell you to be careful, because if something happens to you, a first-time pregnant woman, then..." I mean, he loved me so much that despite the fact that he couldn't climb the stairs, he came to advise me. I was moved.

— *How would you characterize your uncle Markos?*

He was a loving father, uncle and a good man and I'm proud of him. I can say that I, too, have followed Markos's example and am affectionate with my children. My uncle taught me the most beautiful thing.

I'm the daughter of Grazia, Markos's sister. Markos loved me and I loved him a lot. I'll always remember his words: "Don't tear my heart to pieces."

Athanasia Pavlopoulou

Grazia, Markos's sister, with her three children Elpida, Athanasia and Vangelis.
(Athanasia Pavlopoulou's archive)

III

Markos loved me very much. He even set me up with someone. He said to me:

"Hey, Margitsa, come here. I'll set you up with that guy, who's a Catholic. You'll be swimming in gravy."

I said to him: "Uncle, I don't want to swim in gravy."

"Ah, you don't get it... When you'll get older, you'll understand."

My uncle Markos loved animals very much. He had a donkey and a cart. When I was a kid I used to go and hide under the cart and he would act like he was trying to find me. He used to park the cart in the corner of his house. Next to it there was a plot and my uncle had put animals inside. He also had goats. My grandmother, my uncle's mother, had a goat of her own too. During that time, my uncle was in the process of breaking up with Eleni. My grandma used to say: "My child should drive her away so he can break free and I'll slaughter the goat." At some point the uncle broke up with her and said to his mother: "Mother, I got divorced." But grandma didn't slaughter the goat. She found it all swollen up the next morning. Markos's sister Rosa, my mother, used to tell me this story.

My uncle Markos loved the bouzouki, he was longing for it, he was living through it. My father Manolis was also playing the bouzouki with him. I remember the musicians who were coming here and going down to the basement and doing rehearsals. Many of them became famous. My uncle was in the basement which he had turned into a bouzouki school.

Margitsa Palaiologou

IV

I got married to Argyris (1930-1983), Markos's brother, in 1952, in the Catholic Church of Piraeus, where I have also baptized my children. A party ensued at Tzekos's house, Markos's brother.

Markos loved me very much. My husband grew up with

Markos. He was always close to him. He taught him the bou-zouki[164]. But he also went to the conservatory. They were children of the war, they had to scramble for footholds, stand on their own feet. They, as well as their families, had to sur-vive.

Kyparissia Vamvakari

Argyris, Markos's brother.
(Kyparissia Vamvakari's archive)

---

[164] "I began to train Argyris in my own line of work. He was about ten years old when he first held the bouzouki in his hands and, within one year, he got to be ace. It looked like he'd end up a famous player and he did. I looked after his education and sent him to the Piraeus Conservatory" (op. cit., p. 194).

V

We too had a small house in the settlement of Aspra Chomata. Next to it was the house of uncle Markos, aunt Rosa and aunt Grazia.

I would often go visit him in the basement, where he was playing the bouzouki and writing new songs. He used to stop playing when I was arriving and he was greeting and hugging me. It had struck me that, while he was sitting on the sidewalk and playing and people were passing by, he was focused. He wasn't distracted at all.

He was a sweet man. He wasn't bothering anyone. He was looking after his family, his children and his bouzouki. He wasn't someone who would get into trouble. Everyone loved him.

Aunt Vangelio, the wife of uncle Markos, also loved me very much. She was a decent lady. We always talked to each other. She was a slim and beautiful woman. She was taking great care of her husband and children.

I knew uncle Markos's three children well. Vassilis, Stelios and Domenikos. However, I didn't happen to mingle with Vassilis, nor did I see him a lot. He was older. On the contrary, I was often meeting with Stelios and Domenikos.

The night uncle Markos died, I went to his house to mourn for him and the next day I went to his funeral. We took him to the cemetery on foot.

Georgia L. Palaiologou

VI

In 1964, I married one of Rosa's daughters; Rosa was the sister of Markos Vamvakaris. Markos was older than me and

I respected him.

What impressed me most about Markos was that, while ten people were discussing, for example, he would hear one phrase from someone and another one from someone else and he would write them on his pack of cigarettes and then he would write a song. Markos was charismatic, he was a genius.

I've heard that he included the toponym Della Grazia in "Frangosyriani" to please his sister Grazia.

Spyros Christakos

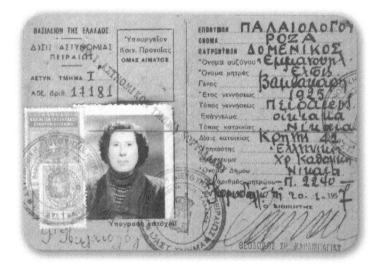

Rosa, Markos's sister.
(Margitsa Palaiologou's archive)

25

MARKOS, THE PRIDE OF
ASPRA CHOMATA

I

Markos's second wife Evangelia was from Symi. She had six siblings: three brothers and three sisters.

Evangelia was much younger than him, but she married Markos, the pride of Aspra Chomata. The wedding took place at Vangelio's house and the party at the adjacent house operated as a grocery store by Nikos Persiadis, a man of Russian origin. I'm also from Russia, born in 1922, but I'm a Pontian Greek. We danced outside, in the street, because it was a corner shop. The entire neighborhood was dancing very happily and Markos was also happy.

— *What do you think was the thing that made Markos a bouzouki player?*

Everyone is born and then does whatever is in his or her DNA. OK, the environment has also an impact. But it was in Markos's DNA. Everybody in his family were singing and Markos also became the same.

— *How did he become great and famous?*

Markos was playing the bouzouki day and night. All the time his thought was on the bouzouki, even during the little time he was sleeping[165]. The bouzouki was the first companion of his life. That is why he became Greece's finest player.

— *What kind of man was Markos?*

He was very social, very polite. A very good man. He didn't harm anyone; he didn't argue with anyone. The whole neighborhood loved him and talked about him. There were two kafeneia in our neighborhood and Markos used to go to both of them. Markos was extremely fond of animals. First and foremost, I remember his donkey. He would feed his donkey first and then he would eat. He adored it. He had chickens, turkeys, goats, rabbits, whatever.

— *What are your memories from Vangelio?*

I remember Mrs. Vangelio cooking. Back then, we used to always cook outside the house, under a sheet metal protecting us from the rain and the sun. When the food was a little late, Markos was getting worried. He liked to grill herrings and the entire neighborhood smelled good.

— *Did you go to his funeral?*

There wouldn't be a funeral if I wouldn't go. Catholic

---

[165] "Sometimes I do the music even in my sleep, and I get up straight away and pick up the instrument, the bouzouki, and play it. I hear it like a song in my sleep. I sleep and I dream this song. And then I wake up and start mouthing the words" (op. cit., p. 258).

priests held a funeral for him at the Third Cemetery[166]. Stelios and Domenikos played "Frangosyriani" and all the people who were there sang it. The funeral was conducted in a very dignified manner.

Liza Karakatsidi

II

So many years separate us from his death and I still remember his kindness. I got a taste of his kindness when I was just a little kid and I make mention of him for it. Do you understand what kind of praise is that for a rebetis bouzouki player? I can taste his kindness when I talk about him; I don't have anything bad to say. When we were little children, we used to pass by and he would talk to us politely and kindly.

Music gives a man peace. This man was with his bouzouki all day long. What he was receiving from music he was offering to the little kids, his friends and neighbors. We never heard in the kafeneion across from his house that Markos had had a quarrel with someone or that he had scolded a kid in the neighborhood.

Here was my corner, over there was his. We lived together since I was born and until he died.

Dimitris Stratis

III

In 1961, I was working at the Harbour Master's Office.

---

[166] The Third Cemetery of Athens is located in Aspra Chomata, in Nikaia. It is the largest cemetery in the Balkans, with more than 27,000 tombs.

When I was out patrolling, I used to finish at about half past two in the morning. The office car was dropping me off at Thivon Avenue, where my home was. I was stumbling upon Markos on the way, who had his bouzouki tucked under his arm. He was playing in the basements of Argyrokastrou Street in Kokkinia. He used to sing two songs and take out a coin tray. He was alone in the beginning and then he would take Stelios with him.

When I came across Markos, I would put him in the office car and take him home. I was living closely. Markos was laconic in the car. These events happened during his unfortunate times. Markos was born poor and died poor...

Michalis Xenakis

Painting by Stavros Pasparakis, 2013.

26

I AM NOW A MUSIC GENRE

My grandfather from my mother's side Nikos Persiadis, a Russian, was an officer in the Russian Navy. He met my grandmother Maria Persiadou in Batumi[167], and they got married. They left for political reasons and settled in Constantinople.

They boarded a ship for America in 1924. Off the coast of Piraeus, however, my grandmother had some pains that had to do with her pregnancy and they disembarked in Piraeus, where my mother Victoria was born. The rest of our relatives continued their journey to America. My grandfather settled in Drapetsona and opened a small café in a shack, which he set up on his own.

In 1933, the houses in Aspra Chomata for the refugees in Drapetsona were given by drawing lots and my grandfather got a house in 97 Krinis Street, next to Markos Vamvakaris's house. He turned half the house into a grocery store, the other half into a coffee shop and the basement into a tavern. In 1943, Markos and Vangelio had their wedding feast in this kafeneion.

My grandfather from my father's side Nikos Krousthianakis was from a village near Heraklion, Crete. However, my father Manolis was born in Palia Kokkinia, where he had started a bakery. He wanted to buy a bouzouki and his father used to say to him: "Should you buy a bouzouki, I'll smash your head." At that time, the bouzouki was being hounded.

---

[167] Batumi is the third-largest city of Georgia, located on the coast of the Black Sea in the country's southwest.

So, when my father grew up, he bought one and I learned from that one too. He was also a fan of Markos and was playing his songs. He was following in his footsteps.

Outside our store was the only water fountain in Aspra Chomata by Ulen[168]. The entire neighborhood was getting water from us. The only phone that existed was inside of a booth in front of our grocery store. Markos was making his calls from that phone.

One of our good customers was Eleni Mavroudi, Markos's first wife, whom I used to bring ice to. Around 1950 she was a simple, plump woman. She was a bit standoffish and I was surprised by that. But she like me, in any case.

She had a peacock and some chickens in her garden. A nice girl, Theodora, was living in her house. Us kids used to call her Ritsa. She was my peer. I was intrigued by the peacock me and I was going to Mrs. Eleni's house regularly to play with Ritsa. Eleni's mother, Mrs. Theodora, an old woman with a mole on her face, and her sister Anna, lived in her house. I also remember a man coming and going; his name was Iosif Chalavazis. He was chubby and had a mustache.

My mother Victoria remembers Markos smoking the narghile in the yard of his house, but never on the sidewalk.

In 1951, Markos had set up a stage in the middle of a vacant lot and had put tables all around. He was playing there with his orchestra. He had also distributed flyers. Us kids used to collect the lids from the bottles and play. The shop of my grandfather, the Russian, who was supplying them, was across the street.

One day, in the summer of 1952, I heard a familiar voice shouting: "I'm the grocer! I'm selling tomatoes, eggplants, cucumbers, watermelons!" I went out and saw Markos riding

---

[168] Ulen & Co., an American water company.

155

a donkey with a cart. I jumped and climbed up to the back of the cart. "Hey, Nikolakis, you'll get killed, you'll fall and break your neck! Come here." So, I went and sat next to him. He was shouting, I was shouting too and he was selling his merchandise.

In 1953, I saw a guy leaving his bike next to Markos's house. He was wearing work clothes, whitewashed trousers and carrying ceilings paintbrushes. At some point, I heard the sound of the bouzouki and singing. I took my stool and sat next to the apprentice artist. I loved the way he was singing. I remember Markos saying to him: "Well done, Bithikotsis, you're doing well! You have a nice voice." During a break, he told me: "Hey, kid, what are you looking at? How are we doing? Go get me a pack of cigarettes." He came back many times, for several years, and rehearsed various songs.

In 1955, I was in third grade. One day, when I was coming home from school, Markos told me: "Nikolakis, since you told me that you learned your times tables, how much is 7 times 7?" I bowed my head and left. I wasn't expecting him to set me up the following day too: "Nikolakis, how much is 7 times 7?" I was really embarrassed. The day after that, coming home from school, I was saying to myself on the road: "7 times 7 equals 49." I arrived where Markos was sitting. "Hey, Nikolakis, how much is 7 times 8?" I just wanted to fall off the face of the earth! I went home and learned by heart all the multiplication tables on that same night.

In 1970, I visited Markos at his house with my fiancé Popi Tsikoura. Among other things, he said to her: "My young girl, I am now a music genre. People have proposed me to put a divan in a tavern so that people can have a look at me."

Nikos Krousthianakis

27

MARKOS'S HAIRDRESSER

During the bombing of Piraeus in 1943, three bombs were dropped onto our house and we came to Aspra Chomata, 97 Krinis Street and Patriarchou Ioakim Street. I was seven years old. The first thing I remember after settling in Aspra Chomata was Markos Vamvakaris's marriage to Evangelia and the feast that took place in Nikos Persiadis's kafeneion, across from his house.

Next to the kafeneion there was a grocery store and us children used to go in and take a handful of chickpeas and beans, put them in our pockets and run back home. His assistants were our pals and he himself turned a blind eye. He had turned the basement into a tavern with wine barrels. Outside the joint he had a box that looked like a room and he was selling ice by the column. He used to cut a quarter of or half a column with a pitchfork and we were all standing in line to get ice.

In Thivon Avenue was the orchard of Michalis Malikoutis, in which we lived. We were waiting for the guys with the carts to come and throw the cabbages and cauliflowers they didn't need to the cows and sheep behind Malikoutis's fences. We would collect the best of them and bring them to our homes; our mothers would cook them and we would eat. Markos used to go to the orchard and Malikoutis, who loved him very much, was giving him cabbages, cauliflowers, onions, carrots, tomatoes, potatoes and artichokes. Markos had put up a stall outside his house and was selling the vegetables. When it was noon and he hadn't sold them, he was harnessing a donkey with a two-wheeled cart, he was riding it and passing in front of our houses. I remember him shouting with his husky, heavy voice: "I'm selling sprouts, cauliflowers, onions, cauliflower sprouts, parsley, carrots!" He was going up to "Kritika" and coming back and he was setting up his stall again. He was going out all bundled up during the winter.

He was crazy and passionate about wild birds

Markos used to tell me: "Nikos, did you get me anything?" And I would answer to him: "I'll go tomorrow. I'll bring you whatever I catch in a cage." I was going with old man Papadeas, who had hunting nets, and we were catching birds: small greenfinches, goldfinches and siskins in Malikoutis's orchard. We were catching them and I would go to Markos's place and he would say: "Well done, Nikolas!" He was looking at them in admiration and saying: "Are any of them female? That's all right, I'll have a look and tell them apart." He was sitting down and distinguish them. He was setting free the females and keeping the males in cages. "Nikolakis, only the male ones sing, not the females."

When it was sunny, he used to hang the cages outside. He was playing his bouzouki as they were singing. They affected him very much. I was a 10-year-old kid and I admired him because he liked listening to birds singing and he was trying to imitate them with his bouzouki and his voice. Dimitris, as you may understand, I formed a bond with Markos during my entire life since I was a young kid thanks to birds.

Once, his beloved goldfinch got sick and he was asking me anxiously what to do: "I'll ask barba Papadeas", I told him. He also had many birds in cages. It was his passion. Papadeas told me: "He needs to put a finely chopped piece of garlic into a jar with some water and leave it for a day. He'll change it the next day. The bird will drink as much as it wants in a day." Three days later, the goldfinch was feeling well and Markos was glad to hear it sing, so he took off and started playing his bouzouki. He hadn't touched it for three days.

"Markos" tavern

In 1947, Markos opened the first bouzouki joint after the Occupation at the corner of 31 Patriarchou Ioakim Street and 97 Krinis Street in Aspra Chomata, in an elevated basement owned by Nikos Persiadis, the Russian. Our house was right next to it. We had a chicken coop in our garden and across the street was an unbuilt plot. Markos made some good earthworks and I still remember the – originally – earthen dance floor. He had set three rows of tables with red tablecloths, for four persons each. He couldn't put any other color here; the area was politically painted. Markos surrounded the whole plot with a rope. Us kids named the tavern: "Markos".

Markos, Batis[169], Papaioannou and Tsitsanis played there. It's as if I see them now. The youngest of them all was Tsitsanis. Papaioannou was the least handsome. Batis was so short, with very little hair, a scarf, a cummerbund and heeled shoes. He was a badass, the wild animal of the gang. So, there

---

[169] Giorgos Batis (1885-1967) was one of the first rebetes influential to rebetiko music. His real name was Giorgos Tsoros, although he was also known as Giorgos Abatis. In 1931, he opened a kafeneio in Piraeus and formed the most important hub of rebetiko. In the 1930s, he dedicated himself solely to music. He died on March 10, 1967, and was buried with his beloved baglama, as he had requested.

was a dance floor and people were dancing. They were play-ing zeibekika, chasapika, but also syrta[170].

People with animals from Aspropyrgos and Elefsina[171] used to come here. The rich folks were eating at the tables while the poor and the children were staying on their feet and still, on the other side of the rope. Anyone who was dis-turbing was kicked out. All the neighbors were sitting on the rooftops listening to the world's top bouzouki player. I re-member that us kids used to step into the dance floor the day after, just before going to school; we were picking up strings and putting them on some board and pretending to play the bouzouki and singing whatever we remembered from the songs we'd heard. We also used to find pennies, which were falling from the people who were dancing, buy a koulouri and share it between us. So, I was young, and by listening to these great bouzouki players, I became acquainted with re-betiko music. The tavern operated for a few summers. Then the police shut it down. I was really lucky. It's funny how things work out...

The red notebook

Ever since I was a little kid, I was an assistant at the bar-bershop of barba Petros in Palia Kokkinia and I was receiving

---

[170] Syrto(s) (pl. syrta) = a folk dance in which the dancers link hands to form a chain or circle, headed by a leader who intermittently breaks away to perform improvised steps. Syrto, along with its relative kalamatiano(s), are the most popular dances throughout Greece and Cyprus, and are frequently danced by the Greek diaspora worldwide. They are very popular in social gatherings, weddings and religious fes-tivals.

[171] Aspropyrgos and Elefsina are suburbs of Athens, in the West Attica regional unit.

pocket money. Back then, barbershops were inside the cafés and were separated with a folding screen. I was among the first to start changing things. I worked hard and thrived. The first thing I did was to open a barbershop in 1961, 97 Krinis Street and 32 Patriarchou Ioakim Street. From then on, Markos would come every day and spend endless hours sitting on a small chair. He was drinking his coffee, smoking and writing his songs on papers and packs of cigarettes.

Dimitris, now is a good time to tell you how he was writing them: Markos had a notebook. He was "stealing" words from my conversations and the ones of my clients, from the manghes and the koutsavakia, who were coming in for a haircut. He would arrange these words the way he wanted in order to form a new song and then he would whistle a tune. He would then sit outside his house and compose it with his bouzouki. He was playing endless hours.

Once, he came here with a red notebook and wrote down whatever he was writing. Who knows where he had found it! Back then, it was much sought after to have such a notebook, and especially a red one. So, he left and forgot it on the coffee table. I took it and hid it. He came back the next day; he looked for it, searched for it, but didn't ask me anything about it. I understood that he was frustrated. Ten days later I put it back on the coffee table. "Oh! Nikos, it was you who hid it from me? I nearly went out of my mind." Markos was a man of few words. I had hidden the notebook for ten days and he didn't ask me if I had seen it. I'll be honest, I didn't imagine then that I had such a treasure in my hands. A hundred songs could maybe had been written in it...

One morning, Markos was in my barbershop and the mangas Dimaras, who lived in our neighborhood, came in. He was wearing a white shirt, black trousers, patent leather shoes and he was carrying a velvet handkerchief in his back pocket in order to polish his shoes if they were dusty, because the streets were dirt roads. He also had a really big American car. He was doing some shady business in Trouba[172], in Piraeus, and he'd made a lot of money which he was spending. It was the time when cigarettes had just come out in individual packs and this guy had the pack in his shirt pocket and half of it was sticking out. Markos winked at me and said: "Hey, Dimaras, give Markos a cigarette." Markos took it and told him: "Mangas, why don't you give me another one so I can put behind my ear?" So, he gave him another cigarette and Markos put it behind his ear in order to smoke it later. But Markos didn't like these manghes who made money the dirty way; he didn't like them.

If someone like that was stumbling across him in the street and saying: "Hello, Markos", Markos would waive his hand and say in a low voice: "Hello, jackass..." So, I asked him:

"Why are you answering him like that?"

"Because he's a jackass and he has the nerve to talk to me! How should I answer him?"

— *What was the color of his hair?*

I was cutting his hair until the end of his life, as well as of his three children. He didn't have a lot of hair and it was gray, not very white. He didn't part his hair, he combed it back. He had hair on the side. He was shaving himself.

— *And what about his eyes?*

His eyes were kind of light. They weren't blue, they were

---

[172] One of the shadiest areas of Piraeus renowned for its bars, cabarets and brothels.

a bit green. If you see him in some photos, you can see that his eyes are a bit greenish. He had light eyes, but not blue.

— *Did he read newspapers?*

Yes, he was always having a look at the newspapers. Back then I used to buy "Avgi"[173], because down here, if you didn't buy "Avgi", you'd get punched in the face. Markos used to sit and read it. He never made any comments. When my clients were discussing politics, Markos was acting as if he didn't care.

The Whopper

A peer of Markos was also barba Kyriakos, the so-called "Whopper". We called him like that because he was such a liar.

He used to work in the port. When he was getting up to dance, no one else had the guts to dance. There was nothing like the zeibekiko he was dancing! Markos tried some of his songs based on his dance steps. He was living here, in the house next door. When Markos was stumbling upon him, he was greeting and having a chat with him. Barba Kyriakos was following Markos wherever he was playing. They were pals. He was dancing correctly; he was using his few steps by harmoniously moving his body. Markos applauded only him.

Grigoris Bithikotsis

Around 1960, Bithikotsis, when no one knew him yet,

---

[173] Avgi ("Dawn") is a daily newspaper leaning to the left wing of the political spectrum published in Athens. It was first published in 1952.

used to ride a black bicycle with a big back rack and his trousers legs were fastened with pegs so as not to interfere with the chain. He would walk into my shop, sit next to Markos and tantalize him: "Teacher, what did you say to me? Two months have passed..." And Markos would reply: "I'll let you know. Go now." "When shall I come back?" "Come whenever you want." He wouldn't give him any specific date. I had realized that Bithikotsis was expecting to sing one of Markos's songs.

So, time passed. Outside Markos's house there was a chair and I saw Grigoris Bithikotsis sitting on a stool, right next to him, and talking. Then, they went down to the basement of his house. When they came out, Markos had changed. Bithikotsis had achieved what he wanted. What I can say is that both of their lives changed after that.

Eleni and her family

When I first met Eleni, Markos's first wife, she was a plump and burly woman. She was kind, she was living in her own bubble. She also had a little girl, Theodora. She was younger than me. We used to call her Ritsa; she's still alive. An old woman was living in her house too. It must've been her mother. She had a black mole on her face. She must have lived to be a hundred years old. We knew that Markos hadn't had a child with Eleni. The older ones used to say that Eleni was the prettiest woman in the neighborhood.

I also remember her sister Anna. She would put on fabrics and clothes inside a tablecloth, make a knot, put it on her shoulder, go for a walk and sell them. She was going to villages too; she was a peddler. The same man was always coming in and out of Eleni's house. I never found out who he was, nor his name. She was a little older than her.

Rebetiko has a lot to do with philosophy... I know that Markos wrote his songs thanks to Eleni. Homer achieved greatness thanks to Helen. Markos achieved greatness thanks to Eleni, his first wife.

The incurable rebetis

He would see something and say: "Hey, can I take that?" "Take it." Someone would have many cages and Markos would say to him: "Hey, mangas, can I take one?" And he was taking it. He was a simple man and, well, if he wanted something, he was just asking for it.

He was a very nice person; someone sweet, if you were close to him. He was always calm and quiet. He wasn't a chatterbox; he was a man of few words. He was sentimental. He wasn't bothering anyone. He was an incurable rebetis. He was, he is and he will be the soul of rebetiko. He was a Catholic and a Syran, we all knew that.

Dimitris, Markos was someone who we didn't know who he really was. If we had known who Markos was, people from all over the world would have come here to learn the whys and wherefores. I would have understood him through his eyes, I would have asked him everything and I would have recorded it. His story and so forth. There was just a good man near us who didn't seem to have anything special because we were neighbors and we had gotten used to him. That's why he was so poor. If we had really known him, we would have done everything to keep him from dying.

Markos's death

I supported both Markos and his children. I used to cut their hair when they were young and that's why Mrs.

Vangelio always held me in high regard. It was winter. Although they had moved out, one morning, Mrs. Vangelio passed by my barbershop and told me: "You know, Nikos, they took Markos to Saporta Hospital." In the old days, when people were saying that someone was taken to Saporta Hospital, it was bad. At lunchtime, I went to the hospital and saw Markos bedridden. As soon as he saw me, he smiled at me. I stroked his cheek a little and said to him: "Markos, don't worry. It's nothing. We'll overcome it; the doctors told me so." I went to visit him one more time. He wasn't feeling good; he was talking weakly... I stroked him a little on his face. He looked me straight in the eye and I said to him: "Don't worry. You're a mangas. It's nothing. You'll be all right." He died in February 1972.

Nikos P. Kallitsis

Markos's skillful hairdresser.

28

I AM THE ACCLAIMED ARTIST

During the Occupation, Marios Dalezios, who was originally from Syros, had opened a bar in Omonoia, 6 Ionos
Street.[174] Later, in 1947, Marios Dalezios opened up a tavern
in Tzitzifies.[175]

Dalezios and Konstantinos Deligiorgis also created an artists' agency in Athens, 35 Acharnon Street. At this agency,
Babis Papadimas, a personal friend of Marios Dalezios, who
owned a restaurant in Chicago named Athenian Corner Restaurant & Cocktail Lounge Grecian & American Cuisine
(338-340 South Halsted St. Chicago 6, III) sent him a letter
on June 18, 1963 and asked him to send him "good, well-
known and talented artists, as well as young and beautiful
girls because this is what is huge today; beauty plays a leading role", in order to work in various venues. The letter was
posted June 18, 1963, from Chicago, and arrived in Athens
on June 20, 1963.

Markos Vamvakaris met with Marios Dalezios who read
the letter to him. Markos Vamvakaris was longing to go to

---

[174] "In the meantime, my fellow Syran Marios Dalezios had opened a
new music dive in Omonoia, 6 Ionos Street. I agreed to go and play
there in the evenings and set up a band again. It was me, Keromytis,
Papaioannou, Peristeris, Karipis" (op. cit., p. 190).

[175] "Later, Marios Dalezios opened up a joint too. He was a fellow Syran, also a Catholic. From Ionos Street he came down to Tzitzifies. [...]
And it was me and Papaioannou" (op. cit., p. 211).

America – where his uncle Morfinis[176] and his brother Argyris, who was at his peak during that time, had gone – and told Marios: "I am the acclaimed artist they are looking for.[177] Write them back so they can call me." So, he wrote his name and his phone number on the envelope: 492755, Markos Vamvakaris.

Markos Vamvakaris was already dreaming of the moment he would travel to America since his childhood.[178] The following song entitled "Sto Hollywood"[179] (1938) describes the longing of the great rebetis for this journey:

I'll go to America	Θα πάω στην Αμερική
and acquire riches;	και πλούτη θ' αποχτήσω,
Americans and Greeks,	Αμερικάνους και Ρωμιούς
I'll please them with my pitches.	να τους ευχαριστήσω.
I'll go to Hollywood as well,	Ακόμα και στο Χόλυγουντ
I'll set my foot right there,	θα βάλω το ποδάρι,

---

[176] "Morfinis, who died in America, also played the bouzouki a little. He left in 1912 and didn't come back. His children are in New York. There's another Markos Vamvakaris over there, same name. His name is Markos Morfini Vamvakaris, while mine is Markos Domenikou Vamvakaris" (op. cit., p. 35).

[177] "If I were going to America it would be even better because I'd earn more money there. Not from the university, but I'd make appearances, I'd do recitals. [...] They'd know that this guy singing is the head of laika, [...] For as long as I'd be there I'd write five or ten songs [...] American inspiration. [...] Even now I have faith, I believe God will make me well and I'll get to America" (op. cit., p. 239).

[178] "I'm a big name. I never thought I'd arrive at such a point. I never expected it with the bouzouki. The bouzouki! I had a black mark on my name and they didn't let me go to America to make dough. Not that I'm in love with money though" (op. cit., p. 256).

[179] "To Hollywood".

where it's paved with gold,	*που 'ναι στρωμένο μάλαμα*
a very swell affair.	*κι όλο μαργαριτάρι.*
The big-eyed movie stars,	*Τ' άστρα θα ιδώ του σινεμά*
I'll get to see them all;	*με τα μεγάλα μάτια,*
I'll visit Anny Ondra	*στης Άννης Όντρας*
up in her golden hall.	*θ' ανεβώ τα ολόχρυσα παλάτια.*
And if anybody wants to send	*Κι αν θέλει χαιρετίσματα*
some greetings on their part,	*κανένας να της στείλει,*
I'll put knots in my scarf	*έγνοια θα τα 'χω μες στο νου*
and learn them off by heart.	*και κόμπο στο μαντήλι.*

Dimitris. V. Varthalitis

Markos Vamvakaris's envelope with his signature and
phone number.

29

I WAS HOOKED ON MARKOS'S SONGS

I first met Markos Vamvakaris when I was working with the Myrogiannis Orchestra in "Kava"[180], Stadiou Street, and singing European songs. But as European songs began declining, I was left without a job. Myrogiannis told me: "A band is looking for a singer to sing laika and European songs. You should go." I replied that I wasn't willing to go work in bouzouki joints.

After a few days, he took me to "Attikon". There I met Giannis Laoutaris[181], Christakis[182] and Akis Panou[183]. Akis

---

[180] Kava means "liquor store".

[181] Giannis Laoutaris was a bouzouki player.

[182] Christos Syrpos, best known as Christakis (1924-1981), was a singer and songwriter. He was born in Constantinople but grew up in Drama, where he worked as a plumber. He entered the music scene with the help and encouragement of rebetis Kostas Kaplanis. During the period 1950-1967, he sang second voice and played the guitar and the baglama next to the stars of laiko. He got his success after the mid-1960s.

[183] Akis Panou (1933-2000) was one of Greece's most important composers and songwriters. He grew up in Kallithea, an Athenian neighborhood with many refugees, and from the age of 9 he started playing the mandolin and the guitar. He appeared on stage for the first time in 1947 and, for about a decade, he appeared alongside many famous artists of the time in various music joints. He composed his first song in 1958 and many great hits followed. On August 1, 1997, Akis Panou killed 30-year-old Sotiris Gialamas, the boyfriend of his then 19-year-

told me one day: "Come with me to the bar of Marios Dalezios, in Ionos Street. You'll meet Markos Vamvakaris, Vassilis Tsitsanis, Papaioannou, Daralas[184], etc." I was listening to Markos's songs on the radio and I was hooked on them. But I had never seen him. So, I was excited when I met him.

One day, in the bar of Marios Dalezios, Markos told me: "Katy, will you come with me to Larissa?" I was overjoyed. I considered it a great honor and opportunity for me.

So, Markos, Keromytis[185], a dancer and I went by train to Larissa a day earlier and the hotel owner wasn't expecting us and had only a triple room available. Us two women entered first, put on our pyjamas and then the men came in. Markos fell immediately asleep and started snoring and Keromytis was pissed off. He went out, found a string and tied Markos's leg and pulled it every time he snored. There was a festival and we worked really well. This is how I got to know Markos very well and how I was introduced to rebetiko.

---

old daughter Eleftheria, following a fight at his home. For this act he was sentenced to life imprisonment. He was transferred from Komotini's prisons to Athens' Korydallos prisons, and shortly afterwards he was diagnosed with cancer. He was released on account of his poor health in 1999 and died a few months later in Athens.

[184] Loukas Daralas (1927-1977) was born in Athens and is perhaps best known as the father of singer Giorgos Dalaras. He was a performer of rebetiko during the 1950s and early 1960s and is famous for composing the well-known song "To vouno" ("The mountain").

[185] Stelios Keromytis (or Kiromytis) was born in Piraeus in 1908. He came from a wealthy family and began to be interested in rebetiko from an early age. He started learning bouzouki by listening to his father Charilaos, who was playing as an amateur, even if the latter prevented him from doing so. In 1935 he began his professional career. He died in 1979.

— Where did you meet Markos again for professional reasons?

When he told me to sing "Angelokamomeni mou" [186] (1960) with him I was thrilled. When I sang the song "Kale mana den boro"[187] (1961), Markos kissed me and said: "You have the voice of an angel!"

Markos, this very honest man, who wrote thousands of hits, died a pauper. He was spending all day in his basement, accompanied by his bouzouki, his birds and his memories.

Katy Grey

Katy Grey behind bouzouki player Giannis Palaiologou.
(Katy Grey's archive)

---

[186] "My angel-made beauty".

[187] "Mother, I cannot". The song was first recorded in 1931 by bouzouki player Giorgos Manetas.

30

"MARKOS VAMVAKARIS" CHAIR

My father was friends with Markos and his brother Argyris. I got to know Argyris very well. He was the one who taught me some special songs on the bouzouki, not Greek. I also got to know Markos's nephew Giannis Palaiologou[188], who had great talent, he was a great bouzouki player. We had only a four-year age gap. Both of his parents were from Syros. We played on stage and in recordings together.

When I was fourteen years old, my father Theodoros took me with him – he was then head of the band at "Madhubala" – and when he finished his job at five o'clock in the morning, as we were heading to our house, we passed by Markos Vamvakaris's house. Someone nearby was playing the bouzouki: it was Giannis Palaiologou, Markos Vamvakaris's nephew. My father told me: "Listen to him, he was playing with me all night and now he's studying at five in the morning." Giannis wanted to surpass his uncle as well as everyone.

---

[188] Giannis Palaiologou was born in 1944. He was the son of Markos Vamvakaris's sister Rosa, and grew up in the same neighborhood where Markos lived, in Aspra Chomata. He was very fond of his uncle Argyris. His father Manolis also played the bouzouki. He made his first appearances next to Argyris when he was 16, singing songs by Kazantzidis; he later started playing the bouzouki. His first appearance was in the tavern "Madhubala". He worked with Tolis Voskopoulos, Poly Panou, Stratos Dionysiou and others. He became Stelios Kazantzidis's indispensable collaborator since 1990. He died on July 11, 2008.

To some extent he managed to do it. Unfortunately, his health failed him and he passed away early.

Stelios and Domenikos, whom I know very well, are two brothers who stood out.[189] Stelios followed Markos's path, while Domenikos focused on music theory.

— *Thanasis, tell me a little bit about Markos Vamvakaris.*

Markos was sent by God. He was sent by a great force; he was not of Earth. I believe that. Why didn't anyone else do what Markos did? Some people, including Markos, are sent by another force and are more than mortals. A French philosopher says that "an artist is a man plus something". This "plus something" means a lot as regards Markos Vamvakaris. Beethoven wrote his last symphony while not being able to hear. This is something staggering.

— *How was he inspired in order to write his songs?*

I believe that Markos's inspiration is not like ours: we are commissioned to write a song, for example for Kazantzidis[190]

---

[189] "I'm quite confident the youngest one [Domenikos] will become a great musician. [...] He writes and reads European music, the great music, he goes to the Conservatory. He's on the way to becoming a maestro this one. The other one [Stelios] is following my path and he also writes very nice songs like nobody else has written. [...] He is following my path" (op. cit., p. 240).

[190] Stelios Kazantzidis (1931-2001) was a leading singer of laiko. He was orphaned at the age of 13 when his father, a member of the Greek Resistance, was tortured to death. This forced Kazantzidis into employment, working as a baggage-carrier, then for an interstate bus

or for Stratos Dionysiou[191]. Markos was writing only for himself, for his soul. His soul was his inspiration and, of course,

---

company, as a seller of roasted chestnuts at open markets and as a laborer in textile mills. His life changed when the owner of a factory gave him a guitar. In 1952, he made his first studio recording and with his newfound popularity he began to make appearances in some of the biggest clubs of the time. A hallmark in his career – and an event of great importance for the musical scene of post-war Greece – was his cooperation with composer Vassilis Tsitsanis. Starting in 1956, it resulted in several new songs as well as reinterpretations of Tsitsanis's older songs. Kazantzidis, thus, sung and popularized such rebetiko classics. Songs previously unknown to the wide public suddenly became cherished and sought-after. A few years later Kazantzidis started to develop his own musical style, a style with influences ranging from rebetiko to Indian music. This new turn met with considerable success and became a template for later developments in Greek popular music. Kazantzidis's death was an emotional event for Greece, as attested to by the many obituaries in appreciation of his life and works. He was given a state funeral. His music was also beloved by the Greek diaspora all over the world, capturing their feelings in the difficult post-war period.

[191] Stratos Dionysiou (1935-1990) was a singer who featured predominantly in the 1960s, 1970s, and 1980s. At age 13, he lost his father. These early childhood experiences had a deep impact on the style of his music and were a great influence to him. He went to work as a tailor and was married, at age 20. While still working as a tailor, he also appeared in night clubs in Thessaloniki. Dionysiou left Thessaloniki for Athens to further his singing career. Success, however did not come until the late 1960s, when he turned several of Akis Panos's songs into hits. He was rising to stardom, when his career was abruptly halted by his arrest due to a gun and cannabis possession. He was sentenced to two years' imprisonment. Dionysiou recorded even

the socio-political problems of his day influenced him. But above all, he had passion, passion to play. That was what he wanted, though it was forbidden at the time.[192] So, when something is forbidden and you want to do it, it means that you are expressing your pain anyway, you are protesting.

— *What's the relation between Byzantine music and Markos?*

Byzantine music and church hymns are directly related to our tradition. When we listen to "Frangosyriani" we can easily sing "Christ is Risen".

— *How was he inspired to write "Frangosyriani"?*

He surely saw some Frankosyran girl and fell in love with her. All musicians-composers had this habit, because love coexists with music. They all had their muse. Everyone sings and plays for love, for women, for their beloved one.

"Frangosyriani" has evolved into thousands of forms. The

---

in prison and continued after his release in 1976. He successfully switched from laika to a more western form of the laiko genre and enjoyed great popularity even with the younger crowd into the 1980s.
[192] "It wasn't just that my poor bouzouki was the only thing that had the power to sweeten my life but I was also remembering that time when the bouzouki was being hounded. I told you they were chasing us in the tekedes. They were giving us a hard time and they didn't want to hear about the bouzouki in any way. But it had such power since then and it went all over the place; look where it's at today" (op. cit., p. 185).

best one for me is Chatzidakis's[193] version, who has turned it into a work of art.[194] I keep "Frangosyriani" in me. I keep it in me because I love it. And I say to my students: "I don't want you to become rebetes. I want you to read Markos Vamvakaris's story first, and then I'll teach you how to play 'Frangosyriani'."

— *What was Markos's relation with the bouzouki?*

It was what my relation with the instrument is too: if someone takes the bouzouki away from me, it's like he's cutting my hands off. They were one and the same. I mean, I can't imagine Markos not playing and singing. The bouzouki was an extension of himself. Markos considered his bouzouki more important than the gods of Olympus.

— *What particular techniques did he use?*

Everything was empirical. But tradition has shown that

---

[193] Manos Chatzidakis (1925-1994) was a composer. In 1961 he received the Academy Award for Best Original Song for his song from Jules Dassin's film "Never on Sunday". He is, like Mikis Theodorakis, extremely popular in Greece and is credited with the introduction of bouzouki into classical culture. In 1949, he gave a speech on rebetiko which has remained famous and which shook the official Greek music world. Chatzidakis emphasized the simplicity of expression and the sincerity of emotion in rebetiko, and praised composers like Markos Vamvakaris (who even participated in this speech) and Vassilis Tsitsanis.

[194] "Later on Chatzidakis recorded it ["Frangosyriani"] too and sent it abroad and is sold until this moment. Everyone ran to congratulate me on this big hit I'd pulled off" (op. cit., p. 157).

experience is of great value. Markos had no teachers, no techniques. He was playing with the first thought he was having. If he were to search for a technique, he would lose his first thought.

— *Markos and Chiotis?*[195]

One gave birth to the instrument and the other made us proud with its evolution. He turned the three-stringed bouzouki into a four-stringed bouzouki. Both of them are great, but Markos is the number one.

— *Markos Vamvakaris and Mikis Theodorakis?*

I believe that Mikis followed in Markos's footsteps. And not only Theodorakis. Many followed in Markos's footsteps. I can say that I too have elements from Markos in my repertoire. We all come from Markos. We all followed in Markos's footsteps. This is the beauty of music and its evolution.

— *Markos Vamvakaris and Chatzidakis?*

When Chatzidakis, with whom I was fortunate enough to

---

[195] "The one who goes down his own path is Chiotis from Anapli. He brought out a more refined bouzouki. This guy doesn't really play the bouzouki, more like the mandola. But he's an ace player, I mean he's out of reach" (op. cit., p. 186).
Manolis Chiotis (1920- 1970) was a Greek rebetiko and laiko composer, singer and bouzouki player. He is considered one of the greatest bouzouki soloists of all time. He popularized the four-stringed bouzouki and introduced the guitar-like tuning.

play in the album "O skliros Aprilis tou '45"[196], brought me the 1945 covers on tape, I said to him: "Master, these songs must be placed in the era of Vamvakaris, Papazoglou[197], Mitsakis and of all of those." He replied: "This is exactly what I want you to do."

For all Greek bouzouki players, Markos Vamvakaris is what the people say: the "Patriarch". It was he who gave rise to the recognition of the bouzouki. 150 years after its foundation, the Athens Conservatory will create a "Thanasis Polykandriotis" chair in bouzouki this year. Markos was dreaming of the Greek bouzouki to travel to Vienna.[198] He was a great prophet. I wish that the Greek Parliament would vote to establish of an Academy of Folk Art. I wish he were alive to see how we are trying to include him in UNESCO's List of Intangible Cultural Heritage. There should be a "Markos Vamvakaris" chair in the University. We owe it to him.

Thanasis Polykandriotis

---

[196] "The cruel April of 1945".

[197] Vangelis Papazoglou (1896-1943) was a self-taught musician. He played the mandolin from a young age and, later, he learned how to play the guitar, the violin and the banjo. He was one of the most distinguished composers and songwriters and one of the leading pre-war rebetes.

[198] "And if it's the bouzouki we're talking about, do you know what it would mean if they invited him [Domenikos] abroad now, to Vienna for instance, to Germany? [...] Suppose they invite him and he picks up the instrument, the bouzouki and performs some songs on the bouzouki" (op. cit., p. 240).

31

WE ARE FOLLOWING
IN HIS FOOTSTEPS

Markos Vamvakaris is the leader[199] of rebetiko. As a composer, he was excellent. As a musician, he was authentic.

— *How is Markos's music perceived today?*

It's considered timeless. It's fully accepted and it's inescapably played in every venue – in the big ones and mostly in the smaller ones – where good music is played.

— *What particularities did Markos bring to rebetiko?*

Markos is the one who established rebetiko and the first who started shaping this genre. Until then, various timbres were dominant, mainly from Asia Minor.

— *What are his similarities and differences compared to other musicians, performers, composers of rebetiko and laiko?*

I don't think he has any similarities. On the contrary, the others got elements from Markos. Markos is considered as the most authentic representative of this genre.

— *How can Markos's music survive and, generally*

---

[199] "And they announced me as 'Markos Vamvakaris, the leader of laiko music'" (op. cit., p. 249).

speaking, how can his personality inspire nowadays?

There's no need for his music to survive, it has already survived. There's no way for Markos to not exist; no one can reject him. He's in the classical folk repertoire.

—   *Did Markos influence the later artists of rebetiko and laiko?*

He clearly influenced them.[200] He offered them the basics and introduced a new form of rebetiko.

—   *Who was Markos's successor?*

Markos's successor was Tsitsanis.

—   *What did Markos mean for Syros and Piraeus in his time, but also for Greece today?*

He symbolizes an era when one did what he did because he liked it and not because he had to.

—   *With which instrumentalists did Markos collaborate throughout his musical career?*

I'll only refer to the "Famous Quartet of Piraeus", which

---

[200] "Whatever you do, whatever you say, I'm your teacher. I was the first to lead the way. I'm your teacher. Didn't we say that these guys who came after learned from my dromoi?" (op. cit., p. 243).

was composed of – apart from Markos himself – Stratos Pagioumtzis[201], Giorgos Batis and Anestis Delias[202].

—   *Who do you think Markos's music was addressed to?*

---

[201] Stratos Pagioumtzis (1904-1971) was a rebetiko singer. He was born in Asia Minor and migrated to Greece before the Greco-Turkish war. He settled in the port city of Piraeus and supported himself by working as a fisherman and later as a supplier of provisions to moored ships. He started to sing professionally in the late 1920s and his first recordings appeared in 1933. He is considered as one of the greatest singers of the classical rebetiko era. Pagioumtzis recorded over 400 songs with his voice and worked with many well-known composers. He died of a stroke in New York, after completing a concert in a Greek nightclub.

[202] Anestis Delias (1912-1944) was a bouzouki player, composer and singer of rebetiko, also known with the nicknames "Anestaki" or "Artemis". His real surname was Delios. He was born in Smyrna and his father, who was a noted santouri player, taught him how to play the guitar. After the end of the Greco-Turkish war, Delias and his family moved to Greece and settled in Piraeus. Having lost his father during the destruction of Smyrna, Delias worked in many different jobs in order to support his family. He was a very talented musician and by the early 1930s he had moved on to play the bouzouki and the baglama. In 1937, he was introduced to heroin by a prostitute and became addicted. He was later convicted of drug use and was expelled to the island of Ios. When he returned to Athens, his friends tried to help him abstain from drugs but without success. Eventually, he increased his daily heroin dose and was unable to perform or work. He was found dead from a heroin overdose on the morning of July 31, 1944. Despite his short life, Delias is an important figure in rebetiko.

Back then it was addressed to the petty bourgeoisie, that is, to the common people. Later, of course, his music was also "adopted" by people of other social classes.

— *What do Greeks abroad think of him?*

They have great respect for him, because he's a classic Greek artist.

— *Did he consider music as fun, entertainment, art, profession or something more?*

He didn't consider it as art. What Markos Vamvakaris was doing was spontaneous. He was a pioneer and he didn't even consider what he was doing as a profession. It was something that just occurred to him and, in order to survive, he pursued it as a profession.

— *What does the bouzouki mean to Markos?*

Everything. It was with the bouzouki that he proved himself and it was with the bouzouki that he made songs.

— *Did you personally meet Markos?*

Yes, I met him towards the end of his life. In fact, I played two songs with him in a studio in Kypseli[203], probably in 1968. One was "Ta omorfa ta galana sou matia"[204] (1966) and

---

[203] Kypseli (meaning "hive") is a densely populated neighborhood in central Athens.

[204] "Your beautiful blue eyes". The music was composed by Stelios Vamvakaris. The song was recorded in 1963 but released in 1966.

the other song I had played with Markos was "I atakti"[205] (1966).

— *Did you love Markos?*

Yes, very much! And I love all of these guys, because I believe that it was them who paved the way and we are now following in their footsteps.

Christos Nikolopoulos

Lefteris Papadopoulos[206] on the left and Christos Nikolopoulos on the right.

---

[205] "The wild girl." The music was composed by Stelios Vamvakaris. This song was recorded in 1963 but released in 1966.
[206] Lefteris Papadopoulos (born November 14, 1935) is a famous lyricist, writer and journalist.

32

MASTER, YOU LEFT YOUR MARK ON ME...

—   *My dear Mario, when and where were you born?*

My mother came as a child refugee from Asia Minor, and when she got married she got a house in Platy, Imathia[207]. I was born in 1945. My father was a drummer and I played the accordion with him for many years, mostly at festivals. At some point, Christos Nikolopoulos, who is from the neighboring village of Kapsochori, worked with us and played the bouzouki. He was two years younger than me. We would travel all over the plain of Imathia. We used to go to all the festivals of the region. We made a pretty good living.

—   *When did you meet Markos Vamvakaris?*

In early December 1967, I went to play the accordion and sing at the tavern "Ximeromata"[208], in Neapoli, Thessaloniki, next to a river, where Markos Vamvakaris was also working at the time. When I met him I told him:

"Master, would you like me to help you? Could I sing the backup vocals?"

---

[207] Imathia is one of the regional units of Greece, part of the region of Central Macedonia. The Imathia region is characterized by its fertile plain crossed by river Aliakmonas and by its verdurous mountains Vermio and Pieria. The capital of the prefecture is the city of Veria, built amphitheatrically at the foothill of mount Vermio.

[208] Ximeromata means "at daybreak".

185

"Sure, my daughter", he answered.

— *What hours was the tavern open?*

The place was open from 10:30 pm until dawn. Markos appeared for half an hour in between that time. Before going up on stage, he used to sit at a small table and drink a glass of retsina[209]. He didn't drink whiskey. When he would finish playing, he would leave to go to sleep. When Markos was on stage, I used to sit in a chair, in front of me was the microphone and to my right was the master with his bouzouki, and, when it was time for him to sing, he would say to me:

"Mario, should we play 'Frangosyriani' and 'Atakti'? Will you do the back up vocals?"

And I would reply: "Of course, master."

Then, he used to sing the following songs on his own: "Charamata i ora treis", "Psila ti chtizeis ti folia", "Arrostisa sta xena makria sou", "Ti pathos ateleioto"[210], "Antilaloun oi fylakes", "Ta matoklada sou laboun".

— *How was he on stage? Describe him.*

He played his bouzouki with virtuosity. He was very generous. A proud man, a gentleman. He would sing his songs, greet and leave. People loved him very much. He would grab the bouzouki in order to play and sing and this was an entire ritual for me. He was amazing!

---

[209] Retsina is a Greek white or rosé resinated wine which has been made for at least 2,000 years. Its flavor is said to have originated from the practice of sealing wine vessels, particularly amphorae, with Aleppo Pine resin in ancient times.

[210] "At three, at dawn", "You build the nest up high", "I got sick in foreign lands away from you", "What endless passion".

Markos was a simple man. He respected the entire team that played on stage. He didn't single anyone out. He considered all the instrumentalists and the musicians as his own children.

— *Did you ever seek his guidance?*

At one point, when we were alone, I said to him:
"Master, I want to go to Athens to work".
His reply was: "My dear daughter, why would you want to go there? He, who has the gold, makes the rules. You have a good thing going here in Thessaloniki. Don't leave your hometown. Everyone will eat you up alive."
That was it. I'll never forget his words and, of course, I followed his advice.

— *Did he ask you for any favor?*

Before leaving Thessaloniki he told me: "Maria?"
"What is it, master?"
"I want to give a present to my wife Vangelio in Athens."
"What kind of gift?"
"A shawl."
"OK, master, I'll go to Tsimiski Street[211] tomorrow and find one for her."
So I went to Tsimiski Street, got her a nice watermelon-colored scarf and gave it to him.
"How much?"
"It's a gift from me, Master."
"But you paid five hundred drachmas for it and you only

---

[211] Tsimiski Street is a major street in Thessaloniki. Tsimiski Street was named after the Byzantine Emperor, Ioannis Tsimiskis (c. 925-976) and is nowadays one of the busiest streets in Thessaloniki's city center.

get a hundred drachmas..."

"I'm not poor. Just the fact that I met you, master, makes me very rich."

"God bless you, my daughter..."

I'm still proud because at the age of twenty-two I sang with the "Patriarch" of rebetiko. Isn't that the dream? What I experienced then was greatness. It was like winning the lottery.

— *What did you say to him before saying goodbye?*

Master, you left your mark on me...

— *Will Markos be remembered?*

Rebetiko, thanks to Markos, has already been inscribed to UNESCO's list of the intangible cultural heritage of humanity. As time goes by, he will become increasingly popular... Besides, today's youth sings Markos's songs.

— *If Markos appeared in front of you, what would you say to him?*

Well done master, you have left a great legacy for Greece and for the world: rebetiko music. We're very grateful to you.

— *Mario, please compare him with the other rebetiko musicians.*

Look, Markos is the "Patriarch". He's the number one. The others followed him. Markos is the founder of rebetiko. He was the one who paved the way.

— *What did you like about Markos?*

His authenticity, his honesty and his simplicity.

— *Where did he find the inspiration for his songs?*

All the songs he wrote were spontaneous and drawn from his own life, his own experiences. He set to music the story of his life and his sufferings. The years he lived were harsh, difficult, dark and faceless. Markos lived through a very difficult time. The path he went through was full of thorns. He trampled them and he made songs out of the pain they caused him. He had this talent. People generously listen to these songs because they are a sort of medicine and a consolation to them.

— *Have you ever been to Syros?*

Two years ago, in 2018, the municipality invited me and I sang at the Syros Rebetiko Festival. I thought I was in paradise during my stay in Syros. The night I sang, Miaouli Square[212] was full of people, and behind me the steps of the city hall were crowded all the way up. When I finished I, said to the people: "I, Mario, am proud to have met and worked with Markos Vamvakaris in 1967. You should be proud, you and all the residents of the island, that Markos is the founder of rebetiko!"

Mario

---

[212] Miaouli Square is the main square of Ermoupoli. The square was designed by the Bavarian architect Wilhelm von Weiler in the early 19th century. It took its current name in 1889 from the admiral Andreas Miaoulis, hero of the Greek Revolution.

33

"THE DIASPORA OF REMBETIKO"

In the summer of 2014, during a trip to the French capital, I visited a record shop and found, to my surprise, a collection of rebetiko music, produced in Germany in 2004, entitled "The Diaspora of Rembetiko". The collection includes a thirty-five-page introduction in three languages (English, German and French) by Christos Scholzakis, Nikos Valkanos, Jannis Karis and Jean Trouillet, and two CDs of a total duration of approximately two and a half hours, with fifteen and eighteen tracks respectively.

"This first international anthology to present the most outstanding representatives of 'Greek blues', with 31 ensembles from 13 countries illustrating how rembetiko spread throughout the world and continued to develop in a wide variety of forms all around the globe."

It is really great to discover the name of Markos Vamvakaris and his son Stelios in a collection of rebetiko songs abroad. In the "Greek taverns of Amsterdam, Berlin and Stockholm, even in Toronto, New York and Melbourne", rebetiko, with Markos Vamvakaris as its representative, is heard.

On the first CD I found a song by Markos Vamvakaris entitled "Bouzouki mou diplochordo"[213] (1937) performed by Christos Pantelis, who was singing at a tavern in Munich in 1986:

---

[213] "Double stringed bouzouki o'mine".

Double stringed bouzouki o'mine,	*Μπουζούκι μου διπλόχορδο,*
you're the only thing that can	*μπουζούκι μου καημένο,*
soothe the hefty pain	*μονάχα εσύ παρηγορείς*
of every wretched man.	*κάθε φαρμακωμένο.*

Double stringed bouzouki o'mine,
you're the only thing that can
soothe the hefty pain
of every wretched man.

The ache I've in my heart,
you know it and despair.
Minx, you remember who I was
before you stripped me bare.

Now people are avoiding me,
"drifter" is what they say.
This kind of life is not for me,
Charos²¹⁴, just take me away.

If I'm a drifter and a wretch,
I'm not to blame, I say;
for two lying little eyes
I weep for, night and day.

Bouzouki, faithful mate,
you're the only one that's left
to let the bright light shine
into that phony life of mine.

Μπουζούκι μου διπλόχορδο,
μπουζούκι μου καημένο,
μονάχα εσύ παρηγορείς
κάθε φαρμακωμένο.

Το ντέρτι που 'χω στην καρδιά
το ξέρεις και λυπάσαι,
πριν να με κάψεις, άπιστη,
ποιος ήμουν, το θυμάσαι.

Τώρα με αποστρέφονται,
με λένε αλανιάρη,
τι θέλω τέτοια πια ζωή;
Ο Χάρος ας με πάρει.

Κι αν είμαι αλάνης, φουκαράς,
δε φταίω, σας το λέω,
για δυο ματάκια ψεύτικα
μέρα και νύχτα κλαίω.

Μπουζούκι, σύντροφε πιστέ,
εσύ μονάχα μένεις
αυτή την ψεύτικη ζωή
να μου την εγλυκαίνεις.

"Bouzouki mou diplochordo' is an ode by Markos Vamvakaris to the instrument. Markos Vamvakaris was one of the leading proponents of the Piraeus style. In the early 1930s he was one of the very first to make recordings with this instrument."

On the second CD I found the song "I fantasia stin exousia"²¹⁵ (1994) performed by Stelios Vamvakaris and Louisiana

---

[214] "Grim Reaper".

[215] "Imagination in power".

191

Red[216]:

The baglamades are playing Dylan,	Οι μπαγλαμάδες να παίζουν Ντύλαν
Peter Hammill is plucking the strings,	κι ο Πίτερ Χάμιλ διπλοπενιές,
Tom Waits is playing the clarinet	ο Τομ Γουέιτς με τα κλαρίνα
and the drums are playing yé-yé,	και τα νταούλια να παίζουν γιες,
they're playing yé-yé.	να παίζουν γιες.

Put the window in the socket,	Βάλ' το παράθυρο στην πρίζα,
call the radiator,	κάλεσε το καλοριφέρ,
give the laundry to the tax office,	δώσ' τη μπουγάδα στην εφορία,
write a slogan in the elevator,	γράψ' ένα σύνθημα στο ασανσέρ,
in the elevator.	στο ασανσέρ.

Step on it with your mind,	Άνοιξε γκάζι με το μυαλό σου,
speed up with the heart,	βάλε ταχύτητα με την καρδιά,
imagination in power,	η φαντασία στην εξουσία,
give what you got for a night,	δώσε τα ρέστα σου για μια βραδιά,
for a night.	για μια βραδιά.

"In 1988, Louisiana Red came to Athens for a concert. On-stage, without any previous rehearsing, he met Stelios Vamvakaris and they played together for four hours. Some time later, they would record in the studio, in the same way. [...] Stelios Vamvakaris – son of Markos the great rebetis – with his father's historic three-stringed bouzouki improvises as he follows the traditional Eastern modes."

I was thrilled to see the name of Markos Vamvakaris and of his son Stelios written in three languages. The titles and

---

[216] Iverson Minter (1932-2012), known as Louisiana Red, was an African-American blues guitarist, harmonica player and singer, who recorded more than 50 albums. In 1994, Louisiana Red fused the blues with rebetiko with Stelios Vamvakaris on the album "Blues Meets Rembetika".

first lyrics of the songs "Plimyra" and "Bouzouki mou diplo-chordo" of the great rebetis were translated into English, French and German in the introduction of the musical anthology. The collection also includes songs by: Stavros Xarchakos[217], Pavlos Sidiropoulos[218], Mikis Theodorakis, Grigoris Bithikotsis, Nikos Xydakis[219], Manolis Rasoulis[220], Nikos Papazoglou[221], Dionysis Savvopoulos[222] and others. In the introduction of the anthology there is a commendable reference to Panagiotis Kounadis and to his contribution to the study and promotion of rebetiko: "Probably the most comprehensive study to date is Panagiotis Kounadis' two volume anthology 'Is anamnisin stigmon elkystikon'. Kounadis is also the driving force behind a painstakingly edited re-release of old Rembetika on more than 100 CDs (published by Minos-EMI)."

Dimitris. V. Varthalitis

---

[217] Stavros Xarchakos (born March 14, 1939) is a composer and conductor. He is one of the most famous contemporary musicians in Greece.

[218] Pavlos Sidiropoulos (1948-1990) was a prominent rock musician.

[219] Nikos Xydakis (born March 17, 1952) is a composer, pianist and singer.

[220] Manolis Rasoulis (1945-2011), best known as the lyricist of famous songs, was a music composer, singer, writer and journalist.

[221] Nikos Papazoglou (1948-2011) was a Thessaloniki-born singer, songwriter, musician and producer.

[222] Dionysis Savvopoulos (born December 2, 1944) is a Greek singer-songwriter.

34

REBETIKO IS IN MY BLOOD AFTER BEING PASSED DOWN IN THE FAMILY FOR GENERATIONS

I was listening to Markos's songs from the get-go because my uncle Andreas was a professional instrumentalist, he was playing the bouzouki. He had a Grundig tape recorder and was recording the records of Markos which he didn't have. He was playing and listening to those records. I was listening to him and I loved rebetiko and Markos very much. I was humming his songs from a young age. I still adore Markos and rebetiko. When I happen to come across a rebetiko song, I stop everything I do and listen to it.

Three years ago, at my first daughter's wedding reception, I danced to a song by Markos Vamvakaris. It was the first time my wife and daughters saw me dance zeibekiko; and I have been a married man for forty years...

The place where we are now, "Cheers" brewery, 60 Papanastasiou Street, in Kastella[223], was a bouzouki joint called "Kalyva"[224] and Markos was singing with Bellou. When I bought it, it was decorated with many photos of Markos Vamvakaris. But I left for America in 1971 on a scholarship to a university in Washington for my Master's degree and the photos and furniture of "Kalyva" unfortunately disappeared. I'm really sad about that.

In 1961-1967, when I was a student at the Saint Paul

---

[223] A neighborhood of Piraeus.
[224] Kalyva means "hut".

Greek-French School in Piraeus, I was lucky enough to have Domenikos, the youngest son of Markos Vamvakaris, as my classmate. At a school event, Domenikos introduced me: "This is my father, Markos Vamvakaris." I knew him very well from what I had heard from my uncle Andreas, and as soon as I saw him, I froze. He was a tall and handsome man. He shook my hand. I felt proud to be standing in front of the renowned Markos. In fact, I remember that I sang "Frangosyriani" to him and he looked at me with great affection. "Be good students and good friends", he told us. And so it happened.

Markos was so discreet that for six years I was only seeing him as a guardian who was very interested in the progress and conduct of his son and my friend Domenikos. He was not like the people who were waiting for their drivers outside the school to pick them up. Usually, he would come to the school on a three-wheeled motorcycle. He was just a poor breadwinner... But he was "Markos".

Right now, rebetiko is on the rise and I can see that from here, in America. Markos Vamvakaris is not confined to Syros or Greece or only to the Greek people who are scattered all over the world. Everyone loves rebetiko. Markos is famous all over Europe, in France, Germany, the Netherlands, England, in the Scandinavian countries, but now also in America. When Greek artists come to America and play and sing Markos's songs, first, second and even third generation Greek-Americans dance chasapiko and zeibekiko.

I do not know if you are aware of the value of your project. You are a gold-digger; not from California, but from Syros. Your book will be very successful in Greece, Europe, America, Australia, New Zealand and South Africa. I promise that we will invite you in order to a give a speech on Markos Vamvakaris in Washington.

I am prepared to do something in Syros, from where I

come from my grandmother's side, in order to honor Markos Vamvakaris. What would you recommend me?

I wish that the construction of a statue of Markos, which would be erected in the port of Syros, where he was playing, could be financed.

Mr. Dimitris, I believe that rebetiko is a valuable part of Greek history and Markos Vamvakaris is its founder. This is now where I must stop.

Anastastios E. Vasilas

Second from the right is AHEPA's President Anastasios Vasilas, to his right Ioannis Freris, former Director at Saint Paul, and in the center of the photo is Eleni Vasila.

35

HIS SONGS... EUPHORIA OF THE SOUL

The events that came to me are those I heard from my father, who lived the same time as Markos, as well as the other Greek musicians who offered us rebetiko.

My father was the child of his mother, who came from Syros, and of his father, who came from Mykonos. A native of Piraeus, at a time when it was the main port and when all goods were coming from Russia. This was also the place where the ships, after the destruction of Smyrna, brought the first Greeks after the persecutions by the Turks.

It was the city that smelled salep [225] in the morning, soutzouki [226] and mackerel from the kafeneia and the ou-zeri [227] during lunchtime and all the wonderful smells of foods from Poli [228] at night. It was the city that looked like a neighborhood's patio door. To get in, you had to go through there first. The charcoal from the ships of the time was filling the air and, along with the smell of the sea, it always made you think of the port as a place with beauties to offer for its time.

---

[225] Salep is a flour made from the tubers of the orchid genus Orchis. Salep flour is consumed in beverages and desserts, especially in the cuisines of the former Ottoman Empire.

[226] Soutzouki ("sujuk" in Turkish) is a dry, spicy sausage which is eaten from the Balkans to the Middle East and Central Asia.

[227] An ouzeri is a type of Greek tavern which serves ouzo (a Greek liquor) and mezedes (small finger foods).

[228] Poli, meaning "city", is how many Greeks refer to Constantinople.

Growing up in a city like Piraeus, poverty, hard work, the search for something better and, of course, lawlessness was bound to exist. It was the center of Greece, the place where when most people were going to bed, another kind of people were waking up and going outside. Men and not just people were raised with this way of life. Markos, my father and so many others of their time were not just people. They were men of courage, filotimo[229], honor and, of course, dignity.

As a child coming from a poor family, my father started working at a young age. First at a barber shop, then at a shoe repair store, after that he was a glassmaker and, finally, he worked in barges and tugboats in the port. The house was always full of food.

After a day's hard work and the abundance of money that went through his hands, it was time for the quest for fun. Here comes his contact with the musicians of the time, such as Markos.

It wasn't unusual to go to work early in the morning straight from the musical joints of the time. But not everybody was like that. Poverty, diseases, misery among the people were also conditions for rebetiko to prevail. It was all the above conditions that made musicians write and people listen. The more the rebetes were writing about their lives, the more people wanted to hear their songs.

---

[229] Filotimo is a Greek noun translating to "love of honor". However, filotimo is almost impossible to translate sufficiently as it essentially describes a complex array of virtues. It is considered to be the highest of all Greek virtues, the standards for family and social living; the core concept is that of respect and walking in right paths. In its simplest form, the term means "doing good", actions that ensure that one's behavior be exemplary and demonstrate one's personality and the manner in which one was raised. Filotimo to a Greek is essentially a way of life.

My father knew Markos as a regular customer in the beginning and he always had the best impression of his "compatriot", as he used to call him, because of his origin from Syros.

Markos was a man of his era; he was someone who you could go to listen to and not think about the hardships you were going through in your daily life. The various joints where he was singing were social gathering spots. These were places where you could go and forget your sorrows, where they could give you hope that the next day something different would come. But these were also places where quarrels, knife fights and of course all sorts of transactions were occurring. There were no other ways and no other places to... show off.

It was the place where the "word of honor" was an unwritten contract and a handshake the stamp of that contract. Everything was done in a time without the need for lawyers.

From what my father used to tell me, Markos's life was very tormented and nothing was handed to him; he earned everything by himself. He was a serious, honest person and there's no way he would trick anyone. His songs were music pieces that spoke to the heart of every person of the day.

After the war, Markos began to feel the effects, that is, he had to work more and gain less.

It was the time when one could find him in the big orchards of Aspra Chomata walking on foot in the morning in order to hear the birds' songs. Markos had told my father that he wasn't eating from the game animal and that he was feeling disgusted with those who were killing birds.

People stopped going to the joints where Markos was playing. People like my father were starting families and money was tight. Everything had changed. Markos died, but my father always listened to his songs until deep old age. We, from our side, perceive that era through his songs.

Vamvakaris didn't appear in my life during my time in America. When I came to America, I just brought Markos with me in my luggage. His presence was in the form of a tape and I was always making sure that the car I was driving had a tape player.

Markos is not something that you have or that can put somewhere forever. He's not a statue, he's not a monument, he's not a hill. He represents the songs that were sung by the workers who were going at work in the mornings. He represents the songs coming from the open windows of the houses and the songs one could listen to in the taverns in the evenings, the songs that were sung by word of mouth.

Markos's songs are not enclosed in stone walls. They are the air that passes through the cracks of the door, they are the breeze that caresses your face at noon and the smell of the garden on a spring day. His songs are the euphoria of the soul. They are childhood memories, the melody that makes you think about where you were and who you were with when you listened to his song, and in addition, they are songs that remain deeply rooted in you.

The songs of the soul have no expiration date. They don't have specific hours or days in order for you to listen to them. There are songs like "Oh, my sweet spring"[230] that, when you listen to them, thousands of images, faces, situations and descriptions come to your mind. Markos's songs are not just songs. They are chants of melodic greatness, images of the soul and life conveyed in sounds. That's who Markos is.

Andreas Vasilas

---

[230] "Oh, my sweet spring" is one of the most famous Byzantine hymns, a part of the lamentations before the Holy Sepulchre.

Sketch by Spyros Ornerakis, 2016.

36

HOMER, THE THREE TRAGIC POETS, MARKOS

A rebetiko nest was created 7,000 years BC between Syros and the surrounding islands.

Markos positioned himself on this nest. He was enlightened by tradition, like Homer and the three tragic poets. He didn't owe anything to anyone but tradition, which either accepts you or doesn't let you be a part of it. Markos had all this divine wisdom that Greece has. A people who doesn't follow its tradition is standing just on one leg. Markos owed no one anything but his homeland and is a continuum of a fine tradition.

We have such a tradition that we have left if behind us and buried it. All of our great personalities were judged by unscrupulous men; even Socrates. It's our curse, but history is written in the backstage. Markos found himself into poverty, into misery, he was chased. He didn't budge, he didn't kneel. He remained unperturbed. Although Markos was illiterate, just like the painter Theophilos[231], Makrygiannis[232]

---

[231] Theophilos Chatzimichail (c. 1870-1934), known simply as Theophilos, was a major folk painter of modern Greek art. The main subject of his works are Greek characters and the illustration of Greek traditional folklife and history.

[232] Giannis Makrygiannis (1797-1864, born Giannis Triantaphyllou), was a Greek merchant, military officer, politician and author who joined the Greek struggle for independence, achieving the rank of general and leading his men to notable victories.

and Sisyphus[233], he carried the entire Greek civilization on his shoulders. Markos inherited his fate. When Troy fell, they learned the news in Athens within an hour from the phryctoriae[234]. Music traveled to the phryctoriae in the same way and found Markos. Markos was at the top, like Homer and the three tragic poets.

But there was an access point: his father played the gaida, and the first instrument Markos played was the drum, the most difficult instrument. This means that he learned all the rhythms. The drum played a key role in ancient tragedies as well. Then, with this heritage, he began to become "Markos". In Syra there were great bouzouki players. He heard those bouzouki players. He was also a great dancer; he was dancing zeibebiko since his childhood.

In 1948, when I was nine years old, I was sent to Athens to learn my letters. We had no teacher in the village. A priest was giving us lessons. I met Stavros Tzouanakos[235], started

---

[233] In Greek mythology Sisyphus was the king of Ephyra (now known as Korinthos). He was punished for his self-aggrandizing craftiness and deceitfulness by being forced to roll an immense boulder up a hill only for it to roll down when it nears the top, repeating this action for eternity.

[234] Phryctoriae were a means of communication used in Ancient Greece that consisted of towers built on selected mountaintops so that one tower (phryctoria) would be visible to the next tower. The towers were used for the transmission of a specific prearranged message. Flames were lit on one tower and then the next tower in succession also lit flames.

[235] Stavros Tzouanakos (1925-1974) was a bouzouki and guitar player, composer and singer.

listening to classical music from the Third Programme[236] and collecting records and information about Markos Vamvakaris. When I was a little older, in 1959, I went to Aigaleo[237]: Kolokotronis[238] was playing on one side of the street and Markos with Stratos were playing on the other. I jumped over the fence because I didn't have the money to see Markos for the first time.

One day, in 1960, I walked from Kypseli to Aspra Chomata.[239] I knocked on the door and Vangelitsa opened. After we got acquainted, she accompanied me downstairs and I said to Markos:

"My dear Markos, I came to meet you."

He said to me: "Sit down."

He needed to talk to someone. "You're not bothering me by sitting here, I don't have anything to do", he said. I stayed for an hour and I feasted my eyes on him. I said to him:

"Markos, I'm collecting your records, I have this one and I have that one..."

"I don't have this one and that one", he replied.

I must admit that, at first, he was reserved. Step by step, though, he opened his heart to me and I became his confidant. Markos was reticent, like all the geniuses I met. Kostas

---

[236] The Third Programme is the third public radio station of Greece's state broadcaster, ERT. The station's main program broadcasts focus on culture and classical music, and enjoyed great prosperity during the period when it was headed by Manos Chatzidakis.

[237] Aigaleo is a municipality in the western part of Athens. It takes its name from Mount Aigaleo.

[238] Christos Kolokotronis (1922-1999) is considered one of Greece's most important lyricists, but also produced a very important work as a composer. He was also a singer.

[239] A distance of about 8 km (4.97 miles).

Varnalis[240], Vassilis Rotas[241], Kazantzakis[242], whose hand I kissed and gave me his pencil as a gift.

— *What was Markos's relation with birds?*

Markos learned music from birds. He couldn't live without birds. When he was a pauper and people were giving him pennies, instead of buying food for his household, he was buying birds. He had 80 different birds in the house where I met him. He was going to the farmers' market on a lame donkey and the sellers there were worshiping him as a god. They were giving him goodies for the birds, such as birdseed. Markos was spending three hours cleaning the birds, feeding them water and feeding them. I would sit next to him and ask him: "Markos, why did they stop singing?" "They know now that I came to talk to them and to take care of them so they're waiting. All 80 of them have shut up." And he would tell me a little bit later: "Listen to them now!" They would start singing. And he would tell me again: "Giorgis, this one

---

[240] Kostas Varnalis (1884-1974) was a poet.

[241] Vassilis Rotas (1889-1977) was a writer, critic and translator.

[242] Nikos Kazantzakis (1883-1957) was a writer. Widely considered a giant of modern Greek literature, he was nominated for the Nobel Prize in Literature in nine different years. Kazantzakis's novels included Zorba the Greek (published 1946 as Life and Times of Alexis Zorbas), Christ Recrucified (1948), Captain Michalis (1950, translated Freedom and Death), and The Last Temptation of Christ (1955). He also wrote plays, travel books, memoirs and philosophical essays. His fame spread in the English-speaking world due to cinematic adaptations of Zorba the Greek (1964) and The Last Temptation of Christ (1988).

205

sings niaventi[243], that other one sings a douzeni; it's singing my douzeni. That one's singing a Syran douzeni." He could distinguish the makams[244] and the tunings. He had a stringed instrument in his ear. "That one, in the back, the calandra lark, I don't know which makam it's singing. It's Persian. The Arabs have 90 makams..." Markos would say: What could I possibly play now?" But he had to express his passion. He would timidly take the bouzouki and, as soon as he would pluck a string, all of them would stop in order to listen to him.

Once, I went to his house at three in the afternoon and he said to me: "Have a loukoumi from Syros." He grabbed his red bouzouki which was made of mulberry wood and started playing a taximi[245] at three o'clock. When I looked at my watch, it was nine o'clock in the evening. He had played only one taximi! I said to myself: "God, why am I poor? Why don't I have the means to buy a device and record this?"

— *What was Markos's relation with flowers?*

I had heard that if someone would offer him carnations,

---

[243] A musical scale.

[244] The Turkish makam is a system of melody types used in Turkish classical music and Turkish folk music. It provides a complex set of rules for composing and performance. The Arabic maqam is the system of melodic modes used in traditional Arabic music, which is mainly melodic. The word maqam in Arabic means place, location or position. The Arabic maqam is a melody type. It is an improvisation technique that defines the pitches, patterns, and development of a piece of music.

[245] A melodic musical improvisation that usually precedes the performance of a traditional Arabic, Greek, Middle Eastern, or Turkish musical composition.

his eyes would become wet with tears. Before going to Markos's house for the third time, I turned left at the Third Cemetery of Athens. It was winter, I was wearing a big reefer jacket, I met a priest and I asked him where the expensive tombs were. He showed me. I found a tomb where there were some carnations. I collected them from the vase, I put them under my jacket and took them to Markos. As soon as I arrived, I told him: "My dear Markos, I brought you some carnations!" He said to me: "Giorgakis, I don't have a vase, where will I put them? I have a coffee pot over there." He had a pocketknife; he pulled it out, he cut the stems, put water in the coffee pot, put them in and started crying... He took out his ring to give it to me. I didn't take it, of course.

— *Describe Markos in one word.*

Jules Dassin[246] said that Markos was the Bach of Greece. Nearchos Georgiadis[247] wrote that Markos was the last rhapsode[248] of the Greeks. I have a friend in called Spyros Lappas,

---

[246] Jules Dassin (1911-2008) was an American film director, producer, writer and actor. At the Cannes Film Festival in May 1955 he met Melina Mercouri, prominent Greek actress and politician, and the two of them married in 1966. Dassin was considered a major philhellene.

[247] Born in 1944 in Morphou, Cyprus, Nearchos Georgiadis was a researcher, musicologist, director and rebetiko scholar. He studied law at the University of Athens. From 1973 to 1999 he worked as a director and television producer at the Cyprus Broadcasting Company and from 1999 to 2012 as a music producer at the radio station "Astra". He systematically studied popular Greek song, while writing reviews of books and films in newspapers and magazines. He died in Nicosia on July 31, 2013.

[248] A person who recites epic poems, especially one of a group in ancient Greece whose profession it was to recite the Homeric poems.

an agronomist, who calls Markos the "Universe Man". He was writing the lyrics, the music, he was playing the bouzouki, he was singing and he was dancing.

He was also proud. I'll tell you this: Markos used to go to Kostas Nitsos, the news director of the newspaper "Ta Nea", who, although a young man at the time, was very much respected. There, Markos wasn't even interested in drinking a single cup of coffee. He was sitting on a chair in Nitsos's office.

— *And what was he doing?*

He was sitting, just like that, without talking. He was getting up, saying goodbye and leaving!

— *What was Markos Vamvakaris's greatness?*

Markos's greatness in comparison with other musicians was that he was profoundly proficient in our language. When he would choose to write a song from his tumultuous life, he was focusing on the subject with a magnifying glass. Markos was distilling his subject with the magnifying glass of his soul and he was accurate. He was doing this with his own magnifying glass and with his mind. He was gleaning with love, patience, discipline and precision and, within three minutes, he had supreme lyrics and supreme music, which he added later. When he had a song ready, he was playing it to the flower salesman Spyros Garizas, who was dancing to it. If he was feeling it, all was well. If not, Markos was either working on it again or throwing it away. When Markos was writing a single word, it was coming from his soul. He was writing with his heart, not with his mind.

— *When did he give you his amulet?*

I went to see Markos one last time. He was very sad. I said to him at some point: "Markos, I'm gonna go." Markos stretched out his hand and pulled out his amulet. He put it in my hand and I said: "So long, Markos." He said to me: "So long, Giorgis." I never saw him again. My story with Markos ended with a "so long".

Giorgis Christofilakis

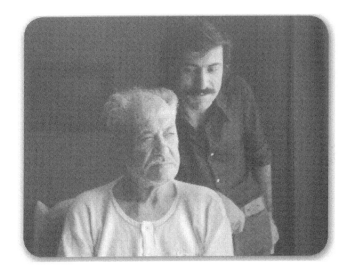

Markos Vamvakaris and Giorgis Christofilakis.
(Giorgis Christofilakis's archive)

37

MARKOS VAMVAKARIS
IN THE FISH STORES
OF THE PORT OF ERMOUPOLI

I grew up on the beach of the port of Ermoupoli. The year 1848 was engraved on the balcony of our house, but also on the transom at the entrance; it was probably the year of completion of the floor that united older ground floor buildings. In the corner there was Michalis Lemonis's large fish and grocery store, where I grew up.

Lemonis was a very good friend of Markos Vamvakaris. They had the same way of communicating, the same behaviors, even the same way of expressing themselves and speaking. Lemonis knew things about Markos that no one else knew. The two of them used to talk about stuff they never mentioned in front of others, most likely about politicians and political developments at local or national level. Lemonis was into everything, he was a big fisherman, a man of the market, a reveler brought up with the wine culture, but also a spiritual man.

As I grew up in the fish store, I developed an obsessive interest in fish from a very early age, which Lemonis and other fishermen, such as "Arapis", encouraged by bringing me sharks, swordfish and tuna to see.

After "Arapis's" fish store, the fishermen's stalls began. Markos Vamvakaris frequented there observing the big fish. The area of the fish stores was where the initiates in the hookah, rebetiko and wine culture socialized. Michalis Lemonis was a well-known reveler and boozer and was by far the dominant figure in the area. When Markos used to pass by, he would shout to him from afar.

— *It seems that he had a great friendship with Lemonis.*

Lemonis, apart from spending time together with Markos, also supported him, in general. He took care of him, he used to bring him food. He would ask him: "Did you eat? What did you eat?" And Markos would reply: "Skourantzos." I will never forget this word coming out from Markos's mouth; it's Old Syran. "Skourantzos" was the salted cod, known in Syros also under the name "koklanos" – another Syran word which no one uses anymore. Markos mentioned all these words in his daily communication because he remembered them from his childhood. Today, no one would understand these Old Syran words...

— *What about your mother?*

My mother was deeply and exclusively immersed in classical music. She taught singing for seventeen years in every school of Syros, where she was extremely popular, played and taught the piano and had a wonderful voice. I would say that my mother didn't have the time to take a step back, listen and understand the dimensions of laiko music. But every afternoon around five, as soon as she came back from school without even eating, she would take me for a walk... Can you guess where? Well, at the fish stores, of course!

— *So, would she listen to "Frangosyriani"?*

She would definitely listen to "Frangosyriani", and in fact with some indefinite pride, because my mother loved Syros, so, consequently, she loved anything Syran. She would listen to almost everything: Greek, French, Italian, German and Russian songs, and of course operas; she sang and played them on the piano. When someone is so devoted to a branch of learning, like she was to classical music, for example, there's no "space" and no time to think about anything else.

However, she had a deep respect for musicians, and, in this sense, she also respected Markos Vamvakaris. For my mother, being a musician took precedence over nationality, ideology or any other identity.

Once, in the middle of the dictatorship, my mother played a record from "Melodiya", the state-owned major record company of the Soviet Union. My father, a Greek-Romanian refugee, said: "But, they're communists..." And my mother replied: "They are musicians above all." She had the same idea about rebetiko and the rebetes.

— *What's your personal relation with rebetiko?*

I have no prejudice. English is the last language I learned to speak, at the age of 30. So I had no influence. Neither from the Beatles, nor from the music we used to hear at parties in general. I never bought a Tom Jones record. I grew up with Theophrastos Sakellaridis[249], Neo Kyma[250] and other music

---

[249] Theophrastos Sakellaridis (1883-1950), was a Greek composer, conductor, and basic creator of Greek operetta.

[250] Neo Kyma ("New Wave") was a movement in Greek music that started in the mid-1960s and lasted about a decade. It was a mixture of entechno (music with elements from Greek folk rhythm and melody. Its lyrical themes are often based on the work of famous Greek poets) and French songs; it was so named after the French Nouvelle Vague (French art film movement which emerged in the late 1950s). See also footnote ? for more information.

genres that some considered "soft". So I grew up with all that, with French and Italian music...

— *Have you ever danced zeibekiko?*

No, I've never danced in my life. I'm stiff as a board. I can only sing. I sang several times; I have also done vocal exercises to have a correct voice. I can sing you any Greek or foreign song of that time. Rebetika songs too. There's no song that I don't know. Now, as far as rebetiko is concerned, as much as I was influenced by the rest of the range of Greek music and by music in general, I was just as much influenced by rebetiko. I can say that I know rebetiko just as well. I usually don't remember the singers or the lyricists very well, but I know all the melodies and songs.

— *If I asked you to describe Markos, what would you tell me?*

After much thought and after having talked a lot about Markos, I have one thing to say: Markos was a rhapsode, a poet and a musician. He was a rhapsode because he had a million things running through his mind. Markos was the carrier, the host. He appropriated and used lyrics from dimotiko music because he belonged to the people. His songs are ingenious to me, especially if you think the time period that he wrote them.

What was Greece then? What was Greece like when these songs were written? It was an act of resistance to write such songs. They were at the same time revolutionary and subversive, in the good sense. They were also erotic; I would say very erotic. I would even call them "sexy" today. They dare to speak in a way that no one has spoken before, at least no one of the... downtrodden. No man in contempt will

213

stand tall to express such things. So Markos spoke out on his behalf. He got up and said what an oppressed person would say. And what would an oppressed person talk about? He would talk about love, about the misery of unrequited love. Alas if some poor guy in the 1920s expressed his desire for a girl; he would do it secretly. But Markos expressed it for him. It's a bit like Márquez[251]. In his novel "Love in the Time of Cholera", Gabriel García Márquez presents us the protagonist of the story as a writer of love letters. The couple – or the deprived and illiterate young man who wants to get the girl on the hook or the girl who wants to get the young man on the hook – goes and tells him: "write for me". And the writer... writes. This is what Markos does too. He is the mediator because, in those years, man was res, that is, he was a thing. Alas if that... "thing" also needed love or was in love! He wouldn't express that, he wouldn't dare. So Markos set it to music. It's what we often say, that we fell in love with these songs. By that I mean that sometimes we identified with the words of these songs as if they were our own words. It's what many say: "I wish I'd written this book", when they identify themselves with the author of a book they're reading. The same goes for songs.

It's unfair to compare Markos with anyone after World War II. Markos's Greece stops at the beginning of the German Occupation. Those who appear after the World War II, after the civil war essentially – because the civil war was of great importance for rebetiko – are something different. Tsitsanis and others are something else. They're awesome,

---

[251] Gabriel García Márquez (1927-2014) was a Colombian novelist, short-story writer, screenwriter, and journalist. Considered one of the most significant authors of the 20th century, particularly in the Spanish language, he was awarded the 1972 Neustadt International Prize for Literature and the 1982 Nobel Prize in Literature.

they're great, but they're from a different world. They don't come from the same Greece as the one that was under the rule of Metaxas, under the Occupation, the same Greece as the one that was in 1922, in 1912, in 1917 or as the one during the Balkan Wars, that is, when Markos grew up.

— *Fair enough. You also said that he was a poet.*

Yes. A poet is interested in collecting words. He gets ideas from everywhere. A poet has a good time even in prison. He can hear even a vulgar word, "knit" it and create a masterpiece. But when I say "vulgar" I don't mean a swear word, but a word that would not or could not be written. Markos was crazy about words. Onassis[252] once said: "Always have a piece of paper and a pencil with you so you can write everything down, even your dreams." So, what I want to say is that Markos was a poet. He would hear a word, use it, and create masterpieces in the end. He was also a poet in a narrow sense, because his grandfather Rokos wrote verses. So they were poets, they had the talent of a poet; they would sit in the corner, listen to words and sounds and start composing.

— *You gave him a third attribute, that of a musician.*

Of course he was a musician. But I can't elaborate on that because I'm not a musician. Nevertheless, musicality was his main feature. He may have been a rhapsode and a poet, but he produced all of this out of music. Just as a painter expresses himself through painting, so did Markos through mu-

---

[252] Aristotle Socrates Onassis (1906-1975) was a shipping magnate who amassed the world's largest privately owned shipping fleet and was one of the world's richest and most famous men.

sic. And he had a genius for that because each song was different from the others. The important thing with Markos was his relationship with dimotiko, with what Greeks have always been. The Greeks have always been people of the countryside, sailors, farmers, stockbreeders. They didn't live in cities. People in Syros were locking themselves in their houses to avoid being caught by pirates, and during the day they were in the fields. That's how the Greeks were at that time. That's why I say that it's unfair to compare Markos's music with that after World War II. What was released after World War II was not exactly rebetiko. Also, rebetiko is not only about smoking hashish nor a marginal music genre...

— *Tsitsanis once said: "I wish I'd written the song 'Antilaloun oi fylakes'."*

Tsitsanis was a genius musician. He was "self-luminous" and he "bloomed" on his own. But Tsitsanis's Greece is another Greece. Tsitsanis never got beaten up, never went to jail and was no stoner. He didn't have regrets about anything. Markos had regrets all his life; regrets for his father, for what he did, for his brother... Regrets for a lot of things. Why would Tsitsanis have regrets? He definitely had his passions. I'm not trying to belittle him. He's great. But Greece was no longer like it was when he stepped into the spotlight, it was another Greece and it's about that Greece that he wrote. His spiritual strength and genius helped him write these masterpieces. I can't say whether he's better or not than Markos. They're two different things, they can't be compared. Each of them had different experiences. It's just that Tsitsanis was never under persecution.

— *I want you to comment on Markos as a poet.*

216

What ultimately differentiates a poet from a great musician? What generally makes someone exceptional? Humans become exceptional because they have a passion for something, for which they either have or have not an aptitude; they transform when they deal with that passion. A while ago, Mouthoukis, an elderly hunter, died here in Syros. He was nothing more than a hunter during all his life. Well, I can tell you that this man was a source of inspiration. When he would talk about hunting, he would become a predator, a leopard. Do you know why? Because he was passionate about it. It doesn't matter whether we agree with hunting or not, nor whether we are for or against it. What matters is that this person could only express himself through hunting. If you saw him talking about hunting it was like seeing someone from the Amazon region, dressed and painted appropriately, like the people of the Amazon who become invisible in order not to be noticed by their prey. It was as if I was looking at a primitive ready to eat his prey. This man was transforming, he was passionate about it.

This is why I believe that people must uplift their spirit. Otherwise, we're just a straight line, like the EEG of a dead person. We must uplift our spirit through religion, through politics and through art. I, for example, never uplifted my spirit, neither through politics, which I don't even believe in, nor through religion. But I uplifted my spirit through art. And who am I to say that? No one, a zero.

Markos had something to uplift his spirit; thus, he became a poet. He became someone great. He went beyond his limits.

— *What was the thing that made Markos great?*

We didn't know Markos, there were no photos of him. We didn't even know how he looked like. When we were kids, we used to compare him to... Hitchcock[253]! Markos was a little bit rigid like Hitchcock. Then, when he grew a mustache, we used to compare him with Papadopoulos[254]. We didn't dare to say that, but some people thought so. Back then we had no stimuli, we only had images. We had the King[255], Papadopoulos and Frederica[256]. We had their portraits hanged and we used to compare everybody to them. But Markos really did look like Hitchcock. He was a huge man, like a closet. He would enter Lemonis's store and the place looked full! In addition, women adored him for his height. Greeks were not really tall back then and he was towering over pretty much everybody.

— *Maybe his height gave him this hoarseness in his voice.*

Most people used to speak like that back then. Lemonis had a muffled voice. I wasn't impressed by Markos's voice,

---

[253] Sir Alfred Joseph Hitchcock (1899-1980) was an English film director, producer and screenwriter. He is one of the most influential and extensively studied filmmakers in the history of cinema. Known as the "Master of Suspense", he directed over 50 feature films in a career spanning six decades. His films garnered a total of 46 Oscar nominations and 6 wins.

[254] Georgios Papadopoulos was the head of the military coup d'état that took place in Greece on April 21, 1967, and leader of the junta that ruled the country from 1967 to 1974. He held his dictatorial power until 1973, when he was himself overthrown by his co-conspirator Dimitrios Ioannidis.

[255] Pavlos (1901-1964) was King of Greece from 1947 until his death in 1964. He was succeeded by his son, Constantine II.

[256] Frederica of Hanover (1917-1981) was Queen consort of Greece from 1947 until 1964 as the wife of King Pavlos.

that is, by this hoarseness.

— *Markos had asked some record labels to release a record of his, but none of them wanted him. Then they heard a rebetiko record from America; they liked it and then they changed their mind and asked for Markos.*

Yes, because decorum was very important in Greece back then... It still is. The fact that he was talking the way he was talking didn't help him. It was how the common people used to talk.

— *Maybe it was cant, maybe it was the style at the time.*

I don't think it was cant. I was close to fishmongers all my life and I saw that most people spoke like that. Maybe their voice was affected from smoking, they were coughing, maybe from the cold too. I don't know. But they had that kind of voice. That's why I was never particularly impressed by Markos's voice and by the way he was talking.

— *Not even by his songs?*

His songs are another thing. But I remember something: Lemonis and Markos were in a room. Between them was Lemonis's safe, a huge safe with steel nails, and Markos was about the height of the safe. Their voices were the same, you couldn't tell them apart. I couldn't distinguish Vamvakaris because I could also hear Lemonis's voice.

— *I'd like to insist a little on Markos's poetry.*

Look, many people nowadays don't know Markos because

he hasn't been a part of their lives and because of that they could wrong him. But we, as elders who even met him, are now trying to think about what makes him so great. What ultimately makes a person great? The timelessness of his work for sure, but not only that. It's also his personality.

I believe that Markos was aware of what was going on around him. He was self-aware, he knew who he was. He knew his worth and he felt remorse. Society itself created remorse for him. Vamvakaris was someone who was feeling remorse. But he knew that what he was doing was important and that he was important too. And later, when the recognition came from others, after 1960, he felt accepted for the first time. It's a huge thing to be accepted while knowing during your whole life that you're worth a lot. And even when he said: "Thank you, my children" with gratitude to the younger generations, it was something that he expected, he knew that he deserved that.

— *We're talking about the students that Markos praised. I have the feeling that he did that to praise the youngsters themselves. I've talked to them; this is why I believe that. They'll never forget that.*

Of course, it's good fortune to write down Markos Vamvakaris's memoirs as dictated by Markos himself. It's what we said before: you must uplift your spirit otherwise it's like you're not alive. People like that may live a hard life, but they live intensely. Markos was a man of few words. He was close-mouthed and also he didn't waste any energy and didn't wander aimlessly. He didn't waste his time: off the stage, many thoughts ran through his mind. He spotted someone, he observed another person and he listened to everything. It's not necessary to say much; it's nonsense to expatiate.

220

— *So, he was a simple person?*

Yes, he was as simple as a Doric column. Tall and vertical. But he was also like that with lyrics too. His songs have nothing superfluous in them. I was once asked: "Why don't his songs have more verses?" Well, because he was like a Doric column, that's why they have few verses.

— *So, he was like a Doric column in his songs and in his life as well.*

Yes, you can see that mainly in "Frangosyriani". The tempo is fast. It's not like the Blues.

— *But what is it that made "Frangosyriani" impose itself?*

First of all, it's an authentic song. Secondly, it was original for that time. That's why it's ingenious, because there was no other song like that before. What came out of the turmoil in Markos's head was genius. In other words, he created something unique through all the influences he had. That's why I said that Markos was a rhapsode.

— *I will tell you something about Markos: he left Syros at the age of fifteen. Until then, he was influenced by the Jesuits and used to commune and confess. In 1971, he went to confess for the last time in his life, and in 1972 he died. Markos was in the Jesuits' choir. He knew all the hymns, so he was influenced by them.*

Yes, and do you know why? Because love at that time was a serious thing. A very serious thing. Up until World War II it was taken seriously. Maybe because it was imposed by society back then. There was no reckless love. So what is more serious than drawing a parallel of your religious knowledge in order to achieve your goal?

Achilleas Dimitropoulos

Achilleas Dimitropoulos
Still from a TV show by ERT dedicated to Syros, 2019.

38

AH! IF ONLY HE WERE STILL ALIVE TO HEAR HIS VOICE...

At the beginning of the 1960s, Mikis Theodorakis, who had released "Epitaphios", "Politeia", "Lipotaktes" [257] and other albums, was an idol for us high school kids. I'm the last of seven brothers, born in 1943. My three brothers became journalists. My fifth brother, Aloizios, with another young fellow, also an aspiring journalist, Dimitris Chalivelakis, sent a letter to Theodorakis when he left for Paris in 1961. It was after the "elections of violence and fraud" [258] and he had stated that he was "not coming back". This letter played a very important role and essentially turned Theodorakis's life upside down. He replied a few days later with a huge letter that I've saved and that's how they managed to bring him back. This was also the reason for the creation of the great

---

[257] "Epitaph", "Republic", "Deserters".

[258] Parliamentary elections were held in Greece on 29 October 1961 to elect members of the Hellenic Parliament. The result was a victory for the conservative right-wing party (ERE), which also had some prominent centrist members. However, the elections were quickly denounced by both main opposition parties, the leftist United Democratic Left and the Centre Union, who refused to recognize the result based on numerous cases of voter intimidation and irregularities, such as sudden massive increases in support for ERE against historical patterns, or the voting by deceased persons. Hence the elections of 1961 became known in the Greek political history as the "elections of violence and fraud".

Association of Friends of Greek Music. This association became the epicenter of young musicians and poets. We held many events up until 1967, when the junta seized power; after that the association was essentially disbanded.

— *Since when did you start loving rebetiko?*

I was a rebetiko addict from a young age, because I was influenced by my fourth brother, Giannis, the journalist, who systematically attended the rebetiko venues of the time and often took me with him. I was also influenced by Argyris, my uncle, who had joined Chatzidakis in the creation of the first core of intellectuals who were positive towards rebetiko music, which was then slandered by almost everyone. Subsequently, Manos Chatzidakis, with his lecture on rebetiko on January 31, 1949 at the Theatro Technis, paved the way for the final acceptance of rebetiko. Keep in mind that his lecture was also marked by the presence of Markos Vamvakaris and Sotiria Bellou.

— *How did you get acquainted with Nearchos Georgiadis?*

Back then, we used to play songs by Loizos[259], Leontis[260],

---

[259] Manos Loizos (1937-1982) was one of the most important Greek-Cypriot music composers. He was a self-taught musician. His first recordings were made in 1963, but he started gaining a larger audience after 1967. By 1975, Loizos had become one of the most popular artists in Greek music.

[260] Christos Leontis (born in 1940) is a composer. His interest in Greek folk song and especially the Cretan musical tradition, together with

Theodorakis, Chatzidakis during our concerts, and a couple of young fellows were also singing some rebetiko songs, like Markos's "Frangosyriani" or "Ta matoklada sou laboun" for example, or Kaldaras's[261] and Tsitsanis's songs and others. At one point, Nearchos Georgiadis, who was from Cyprus, came to the Association's offices and asked me who was in charge of playing these rebetiko songs in the concerts. That's how we got acquainted with Nearchos. On May Day 1963, we decided to do a big concert at AEK's [262] stadium in Nea Filadelfeia [263] with songs by Chatzidakis, Theodorakis, Loizos, Leontis and I suggested to also add songs written by Vamvakaris, Tsitsanis, Papaioannou, Mitsakis and Chiotis. But we couldn't find Vamvakaris in order to bring him to the stadium, because he wasn't playing that year. So Nearchos said to me: "I found him. Let's go." We went to Aspra Chomata, in 1964, at his house, which was opposite the small kafeneion. In fact, I had a tape recorder and cameras with me. It was the first interview I took from a folk musician. I was studying at the Polytechnic School and Nearchos was studying at Law School, so we didn't have much free time. We were going to visit him during Christmas or during some holidays. That's how 1964, 1965 and 1966 went by. We had visited Markos ten times and we were usually hanging out in the basement with the many birds. This shows how good a man he was. He loved birds and he was listening to them.

---

his early exposure to Byzantine music, determined his later musical personality.

[261] Apostolos Kaldaras (1922-1990) was a prominent Greek composer, lyricist and bouzouki player.

[262] AEK Athens Football Club, also known as AEK FC or simply AEK, is a Greek football club established in Athens in 1924 by Greek refugees from Constantinople in the wake of the Greco-Turkish War.

[263] A suburb of Athens.

That's how we started our story with Markos.

— *Describe to me your first impression.*

We were riveted to Markos's discourse. Of all the people in this field that I met – because I recorded them all – Markos was the most narrative. I mean, he would start talking and he wouldn't stop easily; he continued narrating and, with our help, given that we knew some things, he was ending his stories. Nobody among the old ones was doing that. Markos also had the fascination of sincerity; he talked about everything with great sincerity.

— *How and when did Markos start releasing records?*

What people need to know about Markos is that he is different from the others. Because Markos's story is a story that lasts through time. We know the facts day by day. The song "To minore tou teke"[264] came from America. An amazing piece of music. It was recorded in January 1932. A zeibekiko. Giannis Chalikias or Jack Grigoriou played the bouzouki. He was an underground bouzouki player in America. This record was a huge hit here in Greece. I mean, what's this guy playing in this track... People didn't know what a bouzouki was. So Peristeris re-released it in a Greek cover. In the meantime, Markos was going to the record labels and asking them to release his songs. Peristeris, who was a very intelligent and great man, took him to Matsas[265] in the winter of

---

[264] "The minor of the tekes".

[265] Minos Matsas (1903-1970), head of Odeon and Parlophone record labels. He is considered one of the pioneers of music recording and production in Greece (see page 255 for more information).

1932-1933 and said: "Play." Markos played and Matsas told him: "Let's record." So, the recordings of Markos's first two albums took place. But these were preceded by four songs of his in Columbia, which were however released after those two albums by Odeon and Parlophone. So, things got crazy and within a few months Markos became widely famous.[266]. In 1934, two of Markos's songs had been released. In the same year, he went to Drapetsona with Giorgos Batis, Anestis Delias and Stratos Pagioumtzis, and this band appeared with bouzoukia and baglamades for the first time: its name was the "Famous Quartet of Piraeus".

Markos is also a great singer. What I'm telling you is very important. Now that we've done some clean ups of Markos's records, it's clear how great a singer he was. We were saying to each other: "If only he were still alive to hear his voice..." What a great voice he has! Markos sings properly. This is the new conclusion that I haven't written yet and that you are the first to write it.

— *Was Tsitsanis influenced by Markos?*

In Trikala, Tsitsanis went to the conservatory and learned how to play the violin. In 1932 and 1933, he heard the records that Markos had released. At the beginning of 1936, he came to Athens in order to study. He met with Perdikopoulos, a singer and guitarist from the Peloponnese. Perdikopoulos saw that Tsitsanis was playing the bouzouki very well and took him to Peristeris and Matsas. The latter, who knew that Markos was commercially important because of his great voice, immediately made him collaborate with Tsitsanis; he

---

[266] "At that time, I had brought out a lot of my own songs on record because I was the first and so far none of these guys had yet appeared." (op. cit., p. 186).

sang some of his first songs. Markos sang 25 of Tsitsanis's songs. Proves how great influence Markos had on Tsitsanis. I can tell you that Tsitsanis used to play Markos's songs when we used to go to the music joints and were alone at the end. I mean, Tsitsanis evolved in the last years of his life to be the best performer of Markos's songs.

— *What was Tsitsanis's opinion about him?*

He had a lot of respect for him. Tsitsanis respected him, as did everyone else.

— *Can you tell me one of Markos's skill?*

Markos could see a nice girl passing in front of him, for example, and in five minutes he was able to write a song. Others had this skill too, but I don't know if anyone else had this ease that Markos had: he was transforming a feeling into a song. That's the huge difference between him and everyone else. That's why we get emotional when we listen to his songs. He was seeing an image and he was turning it into a song. He did this with every song of his. I mean, each of his songs is a short story. Markos was a mirror, a camera. He was photographing the image and turning it into a song, that's why he was so great. No one else had such an asset to such an extent. That's my opinion.

— *Were you able to find all of his songs?*

We preserved all of them, even those recorded at 78 rpm. There is no song written by Markos that we haven't found. We also have in our possession those written after 1960. We did a good job. We searched and collected all of them.

—   Who are the best performers of his songs?

Markos himself. He was playing, writing, singing, dancing and conducting. Markos, even when he was singing songs by other composers, was making his mark. Markos has sung 132 songs by other composers beyond him. No other famous singer has sung 132 songs by other composers. I mean, Markos was a commercially important singer, he was able to move us all. I list him in the top five voices of his time.

—   What was Markos's relation with the bouzouki?

He often said: "The bouzouki is a part of my body. If I didn't learn bouzouki, I'd chop my hand off." His hand and his bouzouki were one and the same. He loved the bouzouki very much.

—   Why?

Because of its sound. Unlike the violin, the bouzouki is a "harsh" instrument. Matsas, who had knowledge of politics and economics and was a connoisseur of the social milieu, was clever enough to say to Markos: "Come with me, don't run away."

—   What shook Matsas's world?

The cruelty of the lyrics, which was present in Markos's first songs, but also the sharp sound of the bouzouki.

— *What was Markos's relation with money?*[267]

Whatever money Markos was earning, he was spending it immediately. I think that, for Markos, every day was a lifetime. When he had money, he was spending it.

— *Did his colleagues love him?*

Markos was the most beloved among the composers. He was a recognized commander in chief[268]. An amazing rebetiko singer, Orfeas Kreouzis, told me: "Markos was like a father to us. If we had a problem, we were asking him his opinion. We loved him very much. He was our pillar." This is very touching. Markos was the informal commander in chief of the rebetiko band.

— *Did the rest of Greece love him?*

Markos was adored wherever he went, in all Greek cities. He was accepted from the working-class people and not only from them.

— *Was he aware of what was happening in the society he was living in?*

He was always informed. He used to read two or three

---

[267] "Maybe I had money and people were saying to me 'You're going to lose it.' I don't give a damn" (op. cit., p. 243).
[268] "Because Markos would be singing and they'd know that this guy singing is the leader of laiko music" (op. cit., p. 239).

newspapers with great devotion every day[269]. We would meet him usually in the kafeneion across from his house reading newspapers; then, we would go to his basement in order to record him.

— *What was Markos's relation with religion?*

Paradoxically, while coming from religious people, rebetiko makes no reference to religion. Markos was a religious man. He had good relations with the Catholic Church and was faithful to Catholicism. He believed in God all his life.

— *How did Chatzidakis discover Markos Vamvakaris?*

As I said, Markos was the informal commander in chief of the rebetiko band. He was a star. In 1949, Chatzidakis had just realized that rebetiko was something very interesting. During that period, he heard that people were talking a lot about Markos Vamvakaris and he started looking for him. The effort was also aided by director Nikos Koundouros[270],

---

[269] "I liked reading the newspapers. Even with all this work, you can be sure I always had a newspaper at hand. I used to buy one and read it" (op. cit., p. 91).

[270] Nikos Koundouros (1926-2017) was a film director. He studied painting and sculpture at the Athens School of Fine Arts. During World War II, he was a member of the left-wing resistance movement EAM-ELAS and, because of this, he was subsequently exiled to the Makronissos island (notorious as the site of a political prison from the 1940s to the 1970s). At the age of 28, he decided to follow a career in cinematography. After the release of his complex and innovative film

who had located Markos in downtown Athens, in a long hall, where he was playing with his crew. He has told me that himself. Koundouros informed Chatzidakis and they went together and listened to him. Chatzidakis gave a lecture about rebetiko at the Theatro Technis[271] on December 31, 1949, and he invited Markos to sing. But what's important is that Chatzidakis used Markos to give this lecture. He understood that Markos was the pillar of rebetiko and he also invited young Sotiria Bellou, who had just started out, to sing. He believed that Bellou was a rising star.

— *What was Markos's relation with Bithikotsis?*

Bithikotsis was greatly influenced by Markos. Markos was the reason why he started singing. He has categorically and publicly stated this; he has said and written it in the book he has published. Bithikotsis always admired him and he was also the one who brought him back to the recording studios, along with Tsitsanis.

— *And with Theodorakis?*

What I know is that Theodorakis searched and found him

"O drakos" ("The Ogre of Athens"), he found acceptance as a prominent artist in Greece and Europe, and acquired important awards in various international and Greek film festivals.

[271] Theatro Technis (meaning "Art Theater") is a theatrical production company founded in 1942 by Karolos Koun (a prominent Greek theater director, widely known for his lively staging of ancient Greek plays). Thanks to him, the Greek public got acquainted with great foreign and modern writers and, throughout his career, he introduced new Greek writers. Since the 1970s, mainly modern Greek theater plays have been staged.

at some point. Markos has told me that himself. But he was upset: "They told me a lot of things but they didn't help me. Manos Chatzidakis and Theodorakis." I remember this from what Markos used to say.

— *From all the interviews you've taken, which one was the best?*

Markos's. The simplicity, the discourse and the flow of Markos's speech cannot be described. We were twenty-year-old students and we stumbled upon a man who had such charisma. We had a great age difference, but we were drawn to him. No one else had Markos's narrative. This is why we remained close for so many years.

Panagiotis Kounadis

Panagiotis Kounadis on the right with the president of the "Companions of Markos Vamvakaris" fan club Apostolos Nanoulis.

39

MARKOS IS A REVERENTIAL FIGURE FOR THE NATION

"This is the Athens Radio Station"[272]; this is what Greeks heard for the first time on their radios on May 22, 1938. Until 1950, no rebetiko song whatsoever was broadcasted, with one exception: In January 1940 "Frangosyriani" was played on the radio. It wasn't only Markos's first transmitted song, but it was the first song with a bouzouki to be heard on the radio station. Either the person in charge of the records was from Syros, loved Markos and started a rebellion. He must've thought: "I'll just play it and whatever happens, happens", or he was unaware that the song was played with a bouzouki. Or maybe none of that happened. The fact is that Markos's voice was the first rebetiko voice to be heard on the radio and the first song was "Frangosyriani".

— *My dear Kostas, tell me about the words Markos used in his songs.*

He utilized in his songs what he was hearing in the grocery store and in the tavern when he was with his friends or with his acquaintances. When he would hear some word in a tekes or from some manghes, Markos would record it in his

---

[272] The Athens Radio Station was a radio station that began to emit in 1938 in Athens under the auspices of the Metaxas regime's Radio Broadcast Service. It was the forerunner of the eventual National Radio Foundation.

mind, and I can say that he would set it to music by incorporating it in a couplet or a quatrain so that he wouldn't forget it. He would fit it, somewhat roughly, as a kind of guide. Two days or a week later, he would add it in a new song.

— *Did Markos love knowledge?*

Markos, as a genuine man of the people, liked knowledge. This is why he was reading newspapers and the school books of his children; he was also reading Souris, Vizyinos, and was writing about Paris, Achilles, Socrates and the Lernaean Hydra. By acquiring knowledge, he was able to do things that for many, then and now, seem unthinkable.

— *Is there something inexplicable with Markos?*

Yes, Dimitris. Even he wasn't able to explain certain things in his autobiography. A mysterious force, which we'll never come to know or locate, led Markos and made him create his work – a work of worldwide scope.

I believe in fate, as did the ancient Greeks. Markos just happened to hear Aivaliotis, an amateur bouzouki player, whose way of playing changed Markos's life; as well as the lives of us all, of course.

— *Did Eleni, his first wife, play a role?*

The woman who made his life miserable was the reason behind some amazing songs of his. This happened to Markos too: she made his life a living hell. The suffering caused by Eleni's misconducts stimulated him and that's how he was inspired to write some of his masterpieces. The bottom line is the songs that Markos passed down to us because of her.

— What was his contribution to the working class?

Markos turned bouzouki playing into a profession. Those who went up on stage and played bouzouki prospered and earned money. They owe this to Markos's struggles.

— What do you think about Markos as a dancer?

He was dancing amazing zeibekiko. Tsitsanis told me that he saw him dancing once and he was astonished. He used to say that Markos was the best dancer he ever saw. An artist who dances his own songs lives and thrives.

— Did Tsitsanis love Markos?

The first rebetiko songs he heard on records and with which he grew up was Markos's. Even until the moment he died, when he was playing in the taverns, he was playing Markos's songs. Dimitris, not only did he love him, but he admired him very much.

— What about Chatzidakis and Markos?

Chatzidakis and Koundouros, when they heard Markos play for the first time, understood out of intuition that he was an intellectual, they understood what he had inside him and that what he was doing would last as long as Greece exists. When Chatzidakis had prepared his album "Exi laikes zografies"[273] with six songs by Tsitsanis, he went to the tavern where Markos was working with Bellou, his brother Argyris, Karipis[274] and Lili Nicolesco on the piano and asked

---

[273] "Six folk paintings".

[274] Kostas Karipis (1880-1952) was a guitarist and singer.

Markos to sing with Bellou during his lecture in 1949.

— *What role did being intoxicated play in Markos's life?*

Being high was a part of his life. It wasn't something he was doing to show off. We need to clarify this. It was an integral part of his creation process. Batis and Stratos were also in the hookah smoking game, but they were probably doing it because it was helping them. For Markos, it was a part of his life. He wasn't doing it to be better at interpreting his songs. He was doing it in order to be more authentic. But Markos's art was above that.

— *Did luck help Markos become what he became?*

Nothing in life is a coincidence. In my opinion, God told him: "You shall be born and you shall do this." Others say that it was fate. Others that it was an unfathomable force that told him: "You shall do this. Go on." That's why Markos, by instinct, never cursed his fate, despite the difficulties he went through at times – various wars, the Occupation, the Greek Civil War...

— *Tell me an unfulfilled desire of Markos.*

Both Papaioannou and Tsitsanis have told me: Markos's desire was to go to America and play for the Greeks. He didn't go though. He got sick.

— *Does Markos have a future?*

Even though our country is small, I believe that fifty years from now Markos and his work will be known worldwide.

It's still early, despite the fact that 112 years have passed since his birth. Dimitris, you too are contributing with your work in order to find out how this man appeared in our lives. I know it's not easy to find out. You believe in what you're doing; you have it in your DNA. Your work will make many young Greeks and foreigners of the next generation focus on Markos. Markos is a reverential figure for the nation.

Kostas Chatzidoulis

Tsitsanis and Kostas Chatzidoulis in the tavern Charama, 1978.
(Kostas Chatzidoulis's archive)

40

MARKOS'S SONGS ARE MADE
WITHOUT HAND

The photo I have with Markos is the only photo I have on my desk. It was taken in 1966, at the small kafeneion across the street from his house in Aspra Chomata, in Palia Kokkinia. I went there for the first time in 1966. He was still pretty healthy, as you can see in the photo. Then he fell ill and lost a lot of weight. This was my first or second visit. I remember this meeting well. He bought me an ouzo, it was around eleven in the morning or noon. We sat for several hours. A cheese pie seller passed by, you know, one of those street vendors carrying cheese pies, and Markos bought me one.

— *How was his professional situation then?*

He wasn't suffering when I met him. As far as I know, his poor years were from 1953 to 1960, when he was out of the recording industry and couldn't find a job in the music joints. He was begging his much younger brother Argyris, a great bouzouki player of the 1950s, to work with him. From 1960 onwards, Markos had some money either because his eldest son Vassilis went out to sea and had some income which he was sending back home, or because Tsitsanis and Bithikotsis took him to Columbia and re-released some records. Markos wasn't living in a basement per se, as some folklorists say. His basement was his studio. His house was on the ground floor and it was just fine. In fact, Domenikos had his piano downstairs. Next to the piano was a basket where Markos had some notebooks in which he used to write the lyrics of his songs. There were about two or three bouzoukia around. But he had apparently started having some health problems and was complaining that his old friends and colleagues weren't visiting him. He mainly referred to Tsitsanis and Bithikotsis.

— *Was he playing the bouzouki? Was he writing songs back then?*

At first, he was in the mood and he was playing the bouzouki. He even told me that he was still composing and that he had many, hundreds of songs ready. I asked him to play the dromoi[275] for me – some taximia actually based on the dromoi – and, because I had some music knowledge, I wrote them down on a music staff that I drew. In fact, we later checked these dromoi with Keromytis and both of them indeed called them by the same names. Because, you know, the bouzouki players changed some names in relation to how the church musicians and traditional folk musicians called them. This is a good historical record on Markos.

— *You also interviewed him. Since when have you been a journalist?*

I entered journalism in 1969. I worked for fifteen years in the newspaper "To Vima"[276]. I got a job in a magazine at around the same time. It was an entertainment guide called "Psychagogia"[277]. I've published an interview of Markos in

---

[275] Dromos (pl. dromoi) = the traditional musical scales played on the bouzouki originating from the makams (see page 209 for more information).

[276] "The Tribune".

[277] "Entertainment".

that magazine.

— *What did you talk about with Markos during the times you visited him?*

I was asking him several things about the old days. I was of course always talking to him formally and with great appreciation and respect. He was sharing his complaints with me. "I am Markos, my child", he used to tell me. I mean, in 1967-1968 he knew who he was because he had made his comeback, he had received some good reviews, he had met Theodorakis at Columbia's studio, who treated him with great respect. He leaned over, took Markos's hand, kissed it and said to him: "I am your humble apprentice." I've heard Theodorakis saying this publicly.

At some point, the family rented a house in Nikaia, at the bus stop "Farmakeio"[278]. I went to visit him in his new home with a good friend of mine. It was an elevated ground floor, a relatively spacious apartment in a building. The furniture we sat on was still wrapped in plastic, it was brand new. Markos was happy in that house. One day in 1968 he told me: "I want to read to you the novel I've written." I went one day at noon, it was August, and he read it all to me in about three hours. It was a text of about 150 pages; it was rather a novel, I guess. I think it was entitled "The Condemned Benefactor". I know he gave it to someone who typed it on a typewriter. Domenikos must surely have it in his archive. As he has told me, he also has 300 unreleased songs of his father's...

— *What made Markos a special artist?*

---

[278] "Pharmacy".

God gave Markos incredible talent. He was turning whatever he was feeling into a song with great sincerity, which sometimes was reaching the limits of rawness. His songs are as if they're made without hand, as if they're not man-made. You know how wildflowers grow? That's how Markos's songs are. Tsitsanis's songs seem to be man-made – and by a great craftsman, of course. Markos's songs seem to be made by something other than human hands. It's like they're gushing from somewhere, as if they've sprouted on their own. You come to a point where you say to yourself: "How can these songs be so nice and so simple?" That's Markos's big difference. Tsitsanis is a different kind of musician. He has put a tremendous amount of work in his songs. Markos could grab the bouzouki and play a new song.

— *How did you start playing rebetiko?*

When I came to Athens in order to study, I met several people and I began discovering the 45-rpm records and the extended plays that His Master's Voice[279] had released. This is when I heard a lot of rebetika songs, including some covers supervised by Tsitsanis, who, in the early 1960s, was the artistic director at Columbia. Around 1960, Markos released some old songs of his own, but also many new ones under the care of Tsitsanis. He later released a few dozens with other companies. But what I wanted was to hear the old rebetika songs of Markos and of the other composers that you couldn't find easily. So, I started looking for 78-rpm records

---

[279] His Master's Voice (HMV) was the unofficial name of a major British record label. The phrase was coined in the 1890s as the title of a painting of a terrier mix dog named Nipper, listening to a wind-up disc gramophone. It is a famous trademark in the recording industry.

in Monastiraki[280].

In 1969, I met with an amateur bouzouki player, Manolis Dimitrianakis, who was still a student. I became good friends with him and we started playing at amateur level, especially Markos's songs. We were playing together for three or four years in taverns, in our homes, wherever we were having fun...

Giorgos Kontogiannis

Markos and Giorgos Kontogiannis, journalist and publisher of "Laiko Tragoudi" magazine.
(Giorgos Kontogiannis's archive)

---

[280] Monastiraki (meaning "little monastery") is a flea market neighborhood in the old town of Athens and is one of the principal shopping districts of the city. The area is home to clothing boutiques, souvenir shops, and specialty stores, and is a major tourist attraction for bargain shopping.

41

ARE YOU MARKOS'S STUDENTS?

I was born in December 1945, in Ierapetra, Crete. I was playing the mandolin from a young age.

When I got into Law School, I went with some friends of mine to "Tetradio"[281], a boîte[282] in Plaka[283], where Alekos Stamatelis was singing, a very good singer when it came to Markos's songs. When I heard him, I went crazy and I said to myself: "That's it, I'm going to learn how to play the bouzouki." I bought a bouzouki from Monastiraki and started playing all alone.

In Law School, I asked if anyone knew Markos. Back then, there was a magazine, "Panspoudastiki", and a fellow student of mine, Nearchos Georgiadis, told me:

"Go get the magazine in which I've published an interview with Markos. I know him, I often go to his house."

"I want to meet him", I replied.

After getting some carnations, which he liked, as well as

---

[281] Tetradio means "notebook".

[282] From French boîte de nuit, meaning "nightclub". Boîtes were small nightclubs created shortly before the mid-1960s, and gave the opportunity to many young artists who didn't have access to big record labels to be heard and to stand out.

[283] Plaka is an old historical neighborhood of Athens, clustered around the northern and eastern slopes of the Acropolis and incorporating labyrin-thine streets and neoclassical architecture. It is built on top of the resi-dential areas of the ancient town of Athens. It is known as the "neigh-borhood of the Gods" due to its proximity to the Acropolis and its many archaeological sites.

some birdseed for his birds, we went to his home in Aspra Chomata. It was autumn. Markos was sitting inside the kafeneion across from his house.

"Hi, barba Markos", Nearchos told him.

"Let's go to my basement to talk", Markos replied.

When we got down to the basement, Nearchos told him: "My friend Manolis plays the bouzouki." So, Markos told me: "Let's hear you play."
I almost pissed my pants! I grabbed a bouzouki and played "Frangosyriani". "You don't really know how to play the bouzouki, but you have 'progressive' fingers." What he meant by "progressive" was that I was instinctively pressing down on the strings with my fingers.

I had no one to show me how to do it. I was learning all by myself and from some tapes that Nearchos had. I was listening to everything and playing whatever I could play and however I could. Markos told me: "My child, I cannot systematically teach you because I'm sick, but when Nearchos comes here you may also come and I'll show you some stuff. You may sometimes come by yourself too. I'm all alone here, I seek company..." And I would go every ten days and he would show me. Sometimes I would go once a week. In my house, I studied the bouzouki fifteen hours a day. In six months, I had become a proper bouzouki player.

After the summer holidays I went alone to visit him. Sideburns and long hair were the fashion back then. I saw him at the kafeneio. "Hi, barba Markos. I came back from Crete." He checked me out in a very strict manner and said to me: "Are you a hippie? Go get a haircut and then you can come back." I wished I could just disappear, so I left. I have the impression that I even apologized to him! I waited for Nearchos to come back from Cyprus to visit him again.

— *What was his office like?*

245

There were some stairs and you would go downstairs. Domenikos's piano was there, as well as many cages with birds on the wall and his bouzoukia. He had a very nice bouzouki made of unpainted dark walnut; it could have been mulberry though...

— *What did he teach you?*

Markos was showing me how he was playing. I learned the dromoi from Markos. He taught me five or six tunings, but because I never used them, I've forgotten them now. I no longer play with these tunings. Us new bouzouki players are now accompanied by guitars. These tunings are now obsolete... Playing with a specific tuning meant that each dromos could be played only from one specific tonality. One couldn't play every tuning from every tonality.

— *Tell me one characteristic of Markos's songs.*

He was very sensitive and very well-read. That's why his songs are reportages of his time. Here's an example:

I want to be as powerful	*Θέλω να γίνω ισχυρός*
as Mussolini,	*ωσάν το Μουσολίνι,*
tough as Hitler,	*ωσάν το Χίτλερ ζόρικος,*
who's a frightful meanie.	*π' ούτε ψιλή δε δίνει.*

— *Tell me a few words about Markos's voice.*

Tsitsanis used to say that Markos's voice was the voice of the bouzouki. His voice was so synchronized on the bouzouki. Dimitris, there was no other singer who was as synchronized with the notes of the bouzouki as Markos. Not even Stratos, Greece's greatest rebetiko singer, nor Kazantzidis.

— *Did you meet Stratos Pagioumtzis?*

People used to call us "Markos's students". In 1968-1969, Nearchos and I went to Stratos's house in Aigaleo in order to discuss about some concerts that we were planning to do about Markos in Plaka with Bagianteras[284] and he told us: "Are you Markos's students? Ah! Excellent. Come in!" So, Stratos welcomed us.

He told me one day:

"Where did you learn the dromoi?"

"Markos showed them to me."

"OK, so that means you know them. Improvise from SI[285] uşak[286]."

So, I improvised and he sang an amanes; I was dumbfounded and the pick fell off my hands...

What struck me most about Stratos was his vocal range. Stratos once went in a joint where Vangelis Perpiniadis[287] was singing. The latter asked Stratos to sing without a microphone; the people who were there used to say that if he had sung with a microphone, the windows would've been shattered...

---

[284] Dimitris Gogos (1903-1985) was one of the most influential singers, players and composers of rebetiko. Also called Bagianteras, a nickname that was given to him in 1925 for covering and playing in bouzouki Emmerich Kálmán's operetta "Die Bajadere", Bagianteras wrote songs that met great success and popularity in Greece.

[285] SI, also known as B, is the seventh note of the fixed-Do solfège.

[286] A musical scale.

[287] Vangelis Perpiniadis (1927-2003) was a singer, composer and bouzouki player, son of the famous rebetis Stelios Perpiniadis (1899-1977, see page ▌ for more information). Vangelis Perpiniadis started playing music from an early age, initially in his father's tavern. He also reinterpreted several Markos Vamvakaris's songs.

He released a lot of records. Zabetas, who had a soft spot for him and loved him very much, plucked him from obscurity. They were neighbors.

— *Can you tell me one of Markos's admirers?*

Bithikotsis loved Markos very much. He was his admirer. He would always say: "Markos is the 'Acropolis' of laiko music."

Manolis Dimitrianakis

Manolis Dimitrianakis on the left, Stratos Pagioumtzis and Dimitris Bagianteras in Plaka, 1970.
(Manolis Dimitrianakis's archive)

42

REBETIKO, MARKOS VAMVAKARIS AND THE ACTIVITIES OF SOME STUDENTS DURING THE YEARS 1964-1967

In 2017, at the premiere of Nasi Toumpakari's theatrical monologue "I, Markos Vamvakaris" presented at Thanassis Papageorgiou[288]'s STOA[289] theater, I met the unstinting educator Dimitris Varthalitis who, continuing his research on the life and works of Markos, was working on a new feature on him in the magazine "Syriana Grammata" with unpublished information and documents.

This year, in March 2020, during Dimitris's two visits to my office, I felt nostalgic for my youth activities and I provided all the information I had obtained about Vamvakaris when I used to hang out with Nearchos Georgiadis, Christina Lalioti, Giannis Kaounis, Thomas Gorpas[290], Sofia Chatzidouka, Marie Papadaki, Maro Limnou-Loizou, Elias Petropoulos[291], Angeliki Kalamara, Kostas Tzikas, Grigoris Niolis, Christos Kiskiras, Panagiotis Kounadis and with many

---

[288] Thanasis Papageorgiou (born in 1938) is a director and actor. In 2017, he portrayed Markos Vamvakaris in Nasi Toumpakari's theatrical monologue "I, Markos Vamvakaris".

[289] Stoa means "gallery".

[290] Thomas Gorpas (1935-2003) was a poet, publisher, journalist and writer.

[291] Elias Petropoulos (1928-2003) was an author, folklorist and urban historian.

other musicians, lyricists and singers during the years 1964-1967.

Our student life... 55 years ago

Two educators, one from Piraeus, Evangelos Papanoutsos (1900-1982) and one Cypriot from Morphou, Loukis Akritas (1909-1965), as part of the educational reform of 1964, established the "free academic diploma" for the admission exams in the universities. Several young people who were working and many others who were coming from the province managed to find their way to the university and contribute with their experiences to the strengthening of the student movement and the support of the cultural values of our homeland in the face of the cataclysmic and noisy influx of the Anglo-American culture that was to conquer Europe. Since 1949-1950, a handful of intellectuals had seduced the students of the time with their approaches to rebetiko and shadow-puppet theater.

Our abovementioned company explored these exact same topics and it all began because of Nearchos Georgiadis. I met Nearchos at the Students' Film Club of Athens (SFCA) when he was a sophomore in Law. We used to hang out with students from other schools and sing mainly rebetika songs in our gatherings.

From the SFCA to Monastiraki and Plaka

Until July 1965, the month of the Apostasia[292], we had

---

[292] The term Apostasia ("apostasy") is used to describe the political crisis in Greece centered on the resignation, on July 15, 1965 of Prime

gathered information and meager bibliographic material while wandering in Yusurum[293] and the taverns of Plaka. Nearchos, with his student pocket money, had already started in March of that year to collect 78-rpm records that we stored, protected in 35mm film boxes, in his room.

At the beginning of October 1965, in the tavern of Tsekouras, in Plaka, we first heard from a worn-out record a song that got us excited. An old man had taken out the record from a bag made from a kind of white cotton fabric and was asking the owner of the tavern to play it in a pushy way. It was Markos's song "O isovitis"[294].

"Are you selling it?" asked Nearchos.

"You don't have enough money to buy it, my dear lad", the old man told him.

"How much?"

"Ten grand!"

Everyone in the tavern heard the answer and we all laughed, except for Nearchos, who that night "abandoned" Tsitsanis and became obsessed with Vamvakaris.

Minister Georgios Papandreou and subsequent appointment, by King Constantine II, of successive prime ministers from Papandreou's own party, the Center Union, to replace him. Defectors from the Center Union were branded by Papandreou's sympathizers as apostates ("renegades"). The Apostasia heralded a prolonged period of political instability, which weakened the fragile post-civil war order and ultimately led to the establishment of the military regime in April 1967.

[293] Yusurum, the flea market in Monastiraki, was so named by Jewish merchants Noah and Elias Yusurum, who were prominent members of the local antique dealers' association in the late 19th century.

[294] "The lifer".

From Exarcheia to Aspra Chomata

We were walking and we were observing. In Nearchos's room, the 78-rpm records were growing in numbers and the rumor for the "students who are into rebetiko and Karagiozis"[295] in the summer of 1966 led three folk enthusiasts to our stomping grounds: Thomas Gorpas, Elias Petropoulos and Tasos Schorelis[296], who "pinched out" several documents that were useful for the organization of their events, and at the same time prepared the publication of their own books by approaching the old rebetes.

The visits to the old rebetes, which began in September 1965 at Markos's house in Aspra Chomata, continued in Peristeri[297], Aigaleo and Keratsini[298] in search of Bagianteras, Stratos Pagioumtzis, Batis and Keromytis until 1968. For the use of the tape recorder, Nearchos provided Kounadis (as a sort of "rent") with the ability to copy the records to magnetic tapes that have remained in the Kounadis Archive until today.[299]

After April 1967, when most members of the original

---

[295] Karagiozis is a shadow puppet and fictional character of Greek folklore, originating in the Turkish shadow play Karagöz and Hacivat. He is the main character of the tales narrated in the Turkish and Greek shadow-puppet theater.

[296] Tasos Schorelis (1923-1986) was an author and folklorist.

[297] Peristeri is a municipality in the western part of Athens.

[298] Keratsini is a suburb in the western part of Piraeus.

[299] The Kounadis Archive is one of the best organized urban folk music archives of the period between 1900 and 1960. It was founded in 2017 and comprises one of the richest collections of rebetika songs and documents, capturing the evolution of the times in music composition both in Greece and abroad. For more information, visit vmrebetiko.gr.

group found themselves isolated, persecuted or exiled[300], Nearchos, being a Cypriot with a British passport, continued his research with Kiki Kalamara and with new partners.

In 1969 and 1970 he organized three concerts, one with Markos and two with Bagianteras and Stratos Pagioumtzis. We saw each other for the last time in October 1971...

The first impression

— *When did you first meet Markos?*

In 1956. In Pasalimani, Piraeus. Late September. I was eleven years old. During the summer, we used to go to the semi-basement of grandfather Vangelis and grandmother Irini on 34 Moutsopoulou Coast. On the wide sidewalks of Moutsopoulou Coast, the Charidimos brothers[301] had a coffee-pastry shop where the walkers and the fans of the shadow-puppet theater used to come. In the afternoons, my grandmother would take out chairs with a small table on the sidewalk next to the Charidimos' chairs and tables, where

---

[300] Vavanatsos refers to the dictatorship of the colonels in Greece from 1967 to 1974. This dictatorship resulted from the coup d'état of April 21, 1967 by the military junta then dominated by Georgios Papadopoulos.

[301] The brothers Giorgos (1924-1996) and Sotiris (born in 1941) Charidimos became famous for their Karagiozis shows. Their father Christos Charidimos (1895-1970) began his involvement with shadow-puppet theater at the age of 17. In 1923 (according to others in 1925), Christos Charidimos acquired his permanent professional premises at the Hermes theater, creating a Karagiozis theater on 32 Moutsopoulou Coast. The Hermes theater, right next to the coffee-pastry shop maintained by Christos Charidimos himself, had 220 wooden seats for adults and 120 seats for children.

the older members of the family drank coffee and we, the younger ones, cooled off with vanilla in a teaspoon submerged in a glass of water.

One day, my father pointed to a huge man accompanied by a child younger than me and told me:

"Do you see this man getting ready to play the bouzouki? It's Markos Vamvakaris, the one who has written 'Frangosyriani', a friend of Batis."

"Why does he look sad?" I asked him.

"You don't want to know..." he replied.

He played for a very short period of time. I was just a kid and I didn't approach him. In 1956, Markos had "disappeared". He was 51 years old and he looked old... This was the first impression I got from Markos.

The Charidimos brothers' coffee-pastry shop in 1949.

— *Did your father know Markos?*

My father knew Batis. He was a movie buff and also a friend of my grandfather. Batis's trademark was that he was a rascal. He had a great sense of humor[302]. People were constantly after him, they wanted to meet him in Agia Sofia and his café-ouzo shop, which he had named "George Baté" in Lemonadika[303], in the port, where my father and my uncle Kostas used to go. My uncle used to say that Batis was Markos's teacher!

The second impression

In October 1965 I visited him for the first time in Ofryniou Street, accompanying Nearchos and Dimitris Riziotis, who had already met and been photographed with Markos in September together with Giannis Kaounis. He welcomed us with joy.

— *How did you feel when you saw him after ten years?*

As if I saw my father. He was wearing the same slippers as him. He was in better shape than in 1956, when I had seen him in Pasalimani. On my second visit, in January 1966,

---

[302] "Batis was a sort of comedian. He didn't even know how to play anything at all. And if he recorded a song on the radio, Stratos sang it for him. He was the life and soul of the party, he made us laugh right up to the last years of his life... He used to say that his father was from Syros too" (op. cit., p 149).

[303] Lemonadika was the seaside fruit market of Piraeus. At a time when road transport was non-existent due to lack of road network and land transport means, boats used to arrive from all parts of Greece loaded with fruits and vegetables. Out of all these, however, the smell of lemons dominated and this is how the entire fruit market was named "Lemonadika".

when Nearchos started recording the interviews with the tape recorder that he had borrowed from Kounadis, we were accompanied for the first time by Kiki Kalamara, a hard-working student from Elefsina[304], who was the same height as Markos; the latter was impressed by this fact and seemed a little shy around her since he kept saying: "Well... Maybe I shouldn't tell you all this stuff in front of the young lady..." But after a while he came out of his shell. He was just a man of the people who was visited by some students...

From left, Dimitris Riziotis, Markos and Nearchos Georgiadis.

— *What did you talk about?*

Give or take what is written in his autobiography, which

---

[304] Elefsina (or Eleusis) is a town and municipality in West Attica. Today, Elefsina is a major industrial center, with the largest oil refinery in Greece.

256

was, in my estimation, 60 % the work of Kiki, 30 % the work of Nearchos and 5 % the work of Kaounis. But, it was destined to be published as a book by Angeliki Vellou-Keil, who had the audacity in her preface to "thank" Kiki and Nearchos for the "help" they provided her with...

— *How long did you stay there?*

An hour and a half and then we left. Nearchos arranged with Markos to meet again in order to give him two records from Cyprus that "had Arab dromoi". Markos, self-taught, without any academic musical knowledge, understood all the dromoi and the makams by ear, without being able to read musical symbols.

— *What was the environment he lived in like?*

It was an environment that didn't favor him. He should've lived in another neighborhood. He should've been surrounded by people who would help him. Even the kafeneion he used to go to was unsuitable for him.

— *Where did he welcome you?*

In the basement of his house, a basement like all the others at that time, with humidity, pots and cages with songbirds, even parrots!

— *Describe it to me.*

I was looking at... his feet! I wasn't paying attention to the basement. I wasn't interested in the humidity of the basement.

— So, you're telling me that you were checking out his feet?

Markos was a man who maintained his relationship with the earth. He was like Antaeus[305]. He remained in contact with the earth. While arthritis was evident in his hands, his legs were in good condition.

When Markos composed on the bouzouki, he would adapt his zeibekika to the dancer's feet; when he would write a zeibekiko, he would try to dance it first.

— Did you talk with his children?

I didn't meet his children then; they weren't present at these first meetings. I met Stelios and Domenikos only once, in the autumn of 1966, when they accompanied Markos to the first concert we organized at the clubhouse of the Association of Cretan Students.

— How many times did you visit him?

Five times in total. Three times with Nearchos and Riziotis, one time with Nearchos and one time with Nearchos and Kiki until December 1966. Nearchos continued to visit him

---

[305] Antaeus was a figure in Berber and Greek mythology. In Greek sources, he was the giant son of Poseidon and Gaia, who lived in the interior desert of Libya. His wife was the goddess Tinge, for whom the city of Tangier in Morocco was named, and he had a daughter named Alceis or Barce. He was famed for his loss to Heracles as part of his twelve Labours. Antaeus would challenge all passers-by to wrestling matches and remained invincible as long as he remained in contact with his mother, the earth.

with different people until April 1967, when we were disbanded due to the junta. Kiki continued to meet Markos alone until 1971, completing his dictated memoirs.

— *Do you see any differences between Markos and the other rebetes?*

I would single out two: the first is the fact that he was a Catholic. Catholicism was his pillar of support all of his life. He spent the first 15 years of his life in Apano Syros and was constantly "under the supervision" of European Jesuits.

The second difference, the dominant one, is the fact that he didn't appropriate the work of his colleagues, as most did. Everything was his!

— *My dear Vangelis, it's impressive how he was nurtured by the Jesuits, how he was influenced by the music of the harmonium and by the hymns of the Catholic Church in the first 20 years of the twentieth century. You know, a lot of catholic chants are danced like chasapika!*

Yes, Dimitris, the years he spent close to the Jesuits and how much they influenced his life are highlighted both in your book and in his autobiography. Experts in both dromoi and solfège must comparatively study those hymns in order to conclude if and how much they influenced his music. Markos had in him what we call "vis vitalis", vital force. Markos stood on his own two feet because of his magnitude and Catholicism. He gave me the impression that throughout his life he was constantly apologizing, confessing!

— *Can someone easily read and understand Markos's memoirs?*

One needs to have studied all this stuff in order to understand them. Kiki had codified all of Nearchos's notes. Markos's autobiography is Kiki's and Nearchos's work, and one chapter referring to the bouzouki players was written by Giannis Kaounis, the most modest member of our fellowship, a working student who spent his free time meeting with Batis and Markos, as well as organizing the events of our informal Association.

We didn't have an office, there were no statutes, we were reffering to ourselves sometimes as "Association of Friends of Laiko Music" and sometimes as "Movement for Rebetiko Song", with Nearchos as the leader and Kiki, Kaounis, Dimitris Riziotis, me, Giannis Kazakos Christos Kiskiras, Grigoris Niolis and Phivos, Nearchos's brother, as members, after 1966...

In January 1966 I introduced Panagiotis Kounadis to Nearchos – they were living 60 meters apart from each other – and this is when the collaboration between the two of them began.

Giannis Kaounis
Still from a special report by ERT dedicated to Markos, 2000.

Markos's laryngeal-cephalic voice

Where is a person's character most reflected? Others say in the face, others in the way he or she moves, others in the "aura". The great masters say: a person's character is most reflected in the voice.

Markos had many talents that were reflected in his voice. By listening to his voice, we can remember the voices of our grandfathers, the "Byzantine" voices, the laryngeal-cephalic ones.

First of all, Markos didn't have just one voice. He had three: one as a singer, one as a father and one as a... lover! Markos produced his voice from the chest to the skull. His voice, just like Bithikotsis's voice, were voices that hoarded the "three Greek syndromes": poverty, valor and offence, in combination with the centuries-old musicality of the Greek language.

A poor man has a gritty voice and a fluctuation in its intensity. His voice comes from the skull, it's not a voice that is cultivated like the ones of the opera singers. The bouzouki matched perfectly with Markos's voice. You can't accompany his voice with a violin, for example, it doesn't click with a violin. His voice needs a bouzouki, a tzoura or a baglama.

Markos was a great singer[306] by nature, equal if not superior to Bithikotsis. He had a steady, cephalic and hoarse voice

---

[306] "In the end, they got me to sing the song 'Eprepe na 'rchosouna, manga, mes ston teke mas'. When I sang it they were speechless. I didn't think I had a good voice because in the singing lessons at school they had me doing second voice, not top voice. Anyway, I didn't understand that second voice is also important. I didn't know it. I'd see all these tenors here while my voice was taking the base line. But that was the voice they were looking for" (op. cit., p. 159).

that was also coming a bit from his chest (laryngeal-cephalic = voce rauca, according to opera terminology).

— *Whose voice is better: Markos's or Bithikotsis's?*

Markos's. Look, Dimitris, Markos was not interested in cultivating his voice and the record labels occasionally used him as a singer. The record labels defined this stuff. And if Bithikotsis became what he became, he owed it to the record labels and to Theodorakis. If the record labels had imposed Markos, his voice would have become the standard. But Markos wasn't interested in a career like Stellakis[307] or Stratos; these two made a career only as singers. Markos had it all.

Markos's first appearance at a student event

Until the beginning of 1966, Nearchos Georgiadis, Christina Lalioti, Sofia Chatzidouka and I got all around Athens in the evenings – mainly on weekends – and did "walking tour analyses". We were discussing two issues at once: shadow-puppet theater and rebetiko. We used to debate over why zeibekiko is related to life and death, how does the dancer find the courage, by taking the salt of the earth when he bends down and "caresses" or hits the earth, to continue living or to bury the vain hopes for the betterment of his life... We discussed how these two forms of expression – shadow-puppet theater and rebetiko – communicate with the afterlife...

---

[307] Stelios Perpiniadis (1899- 1977), better known as Stellakis, was a rebetiko musician who wrote, sang and played the guitar. He was the father of Greek folk musician Vangelis Perpiniadis (see page ??? for more information).

In 1966, Kiki Kalamara took the place of Christina and Marie Papadaki, a student of architecture, took the place of Sofia. By the fall of 1966, we were ready to organize an event presenting Markos as the "Patriarch" of rebetiko.

The Association of Cretan Students offered to host our first event; we called ourselves "Association of Friends of Laiko Music".

Giannis Kaounis and Giannis Kazakos helped Nearchos set up the hall and the program of the event. Two Cretan students, Niolakis and Noukakis – I think – made the posters for the event, Kaounis brought some chairs on a tricycle and read a text about Markos, while the then-rising actor Kostas Kazakos, brother of Giannis, acted as the host and presented the band. It was an event that caused a sensation.

Markos was accompanied by Stelios Keromytis, his 19-year-old son Stelios, his lastborn Domenikos and a guitarist – I don't remember if it was Lakis Chalkias[308] or some other young guy.

---

[308] Lakis Chalkias (born in 1943) is a famous songwriter, musician and singer.

Stelios Keromytis, Markos Vamvakaris and the then 19-
year-old Stelios Vamvakaris in 1966.

The impact of the event mobilized everyone: the record
companies, the environment of Mikis Theodorakis, Tasos
Schorelis, who used to organize Mikis's concerts, the Association of Friends of Greek Music with the rising stars Loizos
and Leontis, as well as a number of journalists including the
active Elias Petropoulos, who started visiting Markos before
Lefteris Papadopoulos and Mikis. By April 21, 1967, more
than 50 people must have visited Markos in his basement at
Ofryniou Street in order to meet him up close.

May 1968 - Event for Markos.

In December 1966, Markos appeared in a boîte in Plaka
and before April 1967 he gave a concert at the Kentrikon
theater, where Theodorakis addressed him as "Master"! After
that, during the first two years of the junta (1967-1969), he
made many appearances in Athens and other cities in
Greece, in the absence of "his" students. The record labels,
which had sidelined him, asked for new songs and Vamvakaris, believing that a new career would start, spent the last

264

few years of his life dealing with a number of people involved in rebetiko...

Due to the persecutions and the confirmed or potential arrests with the declaration of the dictatorship, most members of our company fell into a state of semi-illegality and/or illegality and were forced to distance ourselves. Those of us who remained "underemployed" watched in distress the developments with Markos, but also with the other less famous folk composers and singers whom the cunning "rebetiko embalmers" wandered around in boîtes and nightclubs for some glory before their end... In any case, Nearchos and Kiki, maintaining a less frequent contact with Markos, managed to finish the interviews.

Until 1965, everyone was talking about Tsitsanis and his successors. Nobody knew the ones that had come before him, or they just considered them... outdated. All this interest from the part of the students brought them back to the forefront, in a way. For example, Keromytis used to say: "I didn't even receive a day's pay and now I started getting one!" They were forgotten, marginalized...

Markos as Diogenes – Tsitsanis the "vlachos" – Theodorakis the ambitious one

There were many people who were excited to hang out with "primitive artists" like Markos. Chatzidakis, for example, got excited like a kid when he first met Markos at Koundouros's instigation.

— *Manos Chatzidakis, on January 31, 1949, gave his famous speech on rebetiko at the Theatro Technis; he was only 24 years old. Wasn't he very young?*

So what? These things are for young people who journey to discover who they are. Didn't we give our speeches too as young people? This stuff comes on its own.

Chatzidakis was an educated man. He was someone who didn't struggle to dominate, he wanted to contribute. That is why he left behind, as a legacy, a number of worthy artists who are proud to mention his name. Chatzidakis contributed to culture by creating. Theodorakis, then and now, wanted and wants to dominate culture. This has been their distinction all their lives...

— *How do you think Theodorakis viewed Markos?*

He was probably... afraid of him! Markos wasn't someone who could be manipulated. Theodorakis was capable of patronizing Tsitsanis. Tsitsanis was a "vlachos"[309]. Markos was like Diogenes. Markos was the one who said to Theodorakis: "You're the master musician, you shouldn't be calling me master!" It's like what Diogenes said to Alexander the Great: "Stand out of my light", "I do not ask you for anything", "leave me alone".

— *Is Markos like Diogenes?*

---

[309] Vlachs is a historical term from the Middle Ages that designates an exonym, mostly for the Romanians who lived north and south of the Danube. As a contemporary term, the Vlachs are the Balkan Romance-speaking peoples who live south of the Danube in what are now eastern Serbia, southern Albania, northern Greece and southwestern Bulgaria, as native ethnic groups. In Greek everyday language, "vlachos" is a general term used to designate those who come from a mountainous or rural area and refers to someone who speaks with a peasant accent. It is usually used as a pejorative term to designate someone uncivilized, uneducated and without manners.

But of course, Dimitris! There were always people like Diogenes in our homeland...

— *So, is Theodorakis sort of afraid of Markos?*

Certainly! That is why he doesn't mention him much, even though he knew him personally. He mentions Tsitsanis, Chiotis, Zabetas; the ones he "used"... Theodorakis had met Markos, had talked to him and is aware of his value, which cannot be compared. Theodorakis followed in Markos's footsteps.

— *What was Tsitsanis view on Markos's rebetika songs?*

He liked them a lot. But Tsitsanis's rebetika have nothing to do with Markos's.

— *Will Markos remain with us?*

Markos cannot fade away. Nor Tsitsanis. But, Tsitsanis is of another quality. One is a genius talented "vlachos" and the other is an entire civilization! Besides, Tsitsanis may have put the rebetes out of business, but he followed in Markos's footsteps too.[310]

— *Did he really follow in his footsteps?*

---

[310] It was from my songs, the ones I first brought out, that all of them learned bouzouki. From my tunes..." (op. cit., p. 186)

267

Definitely. Because he was no Tountas[311], no Peristeris. That is, he didn't possess the Asia Minor experience. Tsitsanis was a genius, he was extremely smart, sensuous and talented. He was educated, wrote great lyrics and was surrounded by important people who exalted him...

Three of Markos's songs

In 1955, the pre-war rebetika songs were almost forgotten. Only a few collectors of old gramophone records maintained the... reverberations of pre-war rebetiko and only the radio station of the Armed Forces broadcast laika songs, mainly by Tsitsanis and occasionally by others. The sound of rebetiko was being heard in a sort of marginal way, from gramophone records worn by frequent use...

When we started researching and studying Markos's lyrics, we admired their density. His songs contained indications of "inner light". It's difficult to measure the intensity of his lyrics. Knowledge from various fields is required: History, Mythology, Sociology, Physics, Law, Theology, even... Psychiatry! This was what amazed us the most. Markos, acting as a chronicler, implemented in verse and music what he

---

[311] Panagiotis Tountas (1886-1942) was a rebetiko composer. He made a notable contribution to the creation of rebetiko in Greece. He was born in Smyrna and from a young age he learned to play the mandolin. He joined many groups and traveled a lot, especially to the Greek diaspora. After the destruction of Smyrna, he went to Athens. In 1924, he became director of the local annex of Odeon Records. He worked with all the major record labels in Greece and was responsible for most of the recordings of the era. In 1931, he assumed the position of art director for Columbia Records and His Master's Voice (until 1940). He worked with many musicians and many of his rebetika songs were sung by renowned singers.

carried inside him.

As students, we were also looking in which other cultures there were lyrics like Markos's; we found some in the Arab culture. The Arabs were most famed for their work on mathematics and made representations of spacetime, but didn't go into depth, that is, to the topic of life and death. They didn't go to Aesop. They ignored Diogenes. They didn't have the background Markos had.

1. "Frangosyriani":

I've a swelling in my heart, *a flaming burst of heat,* *it's as if you've put a spell on me,* *Frangosyriani, my sweet.*	*Μία φούντωση, μια φλόγα* *έχω μέσα στην καρδιά,* *λες και μάγια μου 'χεις κάνει* *Φραγκοσυριανή γλυκιά.*
I'll come down to the shore *again to meet with you;* *with caresses and kisses* *how I'd like to shower you.*	*Θα 'ρθω να σε ανταμώσω* *πάλι στην ακρογιαλιά,* *θα ήθελα να σε χορτάσω* *όλο χάδια και φιλιά.*
I'll take you all around *Finikas, Parakopi,* *Galissas and Della Grazia,* *even if my heart fails me.*	*Θα σε πάρω να γυρίσω* *Φοίνικα, Παρακοπή,* *Γαλησσά και Ντελαγκράτσια* *και ας μου 'ρθει συγκοπή.*
To Pateli, to Nichori, *as far as Alithini,* *and at Piskopio romances,* *my sweet Frangosyriani.*	*Στο Πατέλι, στο Νιχώρι,* *φίνα στην Αληθινή,* *και στο Πισκοπιό ρομάντζα,* *γλυκιά μου Φραγκοσυριανή.*

If you take a map, enlarge it and put the place names mentioned in the song, you'll have the mapping of the entire island.

Who is this Frangosyriani? She's a Frankosyran girl. She has the West inside her, she's Catholic and, at the same time, she "breathes" in the East; we shouldn't overlook this. And

269

the lover declares that he'll "come down to the shore again to meet with" her, implying that he has met her in the past.

He also wants her so much, because he says: "with caresses and kisses how I'd like to shower you". But why doesn't he say: "I want"? Multiple answers are possible here... And the question is: can we demand this simplicity from modern lyricists?

2. "Plimmyra"[312]:

With this year's flood,	*Με τη φετινή πλημμύρα, βρε,*
I headed for the mountains;	*όρη και βουνά επήρα.*
I saw a mother crying	*Είδα μάνα να φωνάζει, βρε,*
and very deeply sighing.	*και βαριά ν' αναστενάζει.*
My baby, my little child,	*Το μωρό, το μικρό, το παιδί μου,*
save it	*σώσε μου το,*
and take me to the other side.	*και πάρ' τη ζωή μου.*
I fell down to save it,	*Έπεσα για να το σώσω, βρε,*
I almost didn't make it.	*κόντεψα να μη γλιτώσω.*
I was swept away by the flood,	*Με παρέσυρε το ρέμα, βρε,*
oh, dear mother, I swear to God.	*μάνα μου δεν είναι ψέμα.*
I was swimming in the stream	*Μες στο ρέμα κολυμπούσα, βρε,*
but I couldn't save the toddler;	*να το σώσω δεν μπορούσα.*
when I finally swam ashore,	*Μόλις βγήκα στη στεριά:*
I saw two kids and an oldster.	*δυο παιδιά και μια γριά.*
Climbed up on a tree,	*Σ' ένα δέντρο ανεβασμένοι, βρε,*
the poor people escaped free.	*εγλυτώσαν οι καημένοι.*
In Peristeri and Moschato[313]	*Περιστέρι και Μοσχάτο, βρε,*
everything was rowdy.	*τα 'καν' όλα άνω κάτω.*

---

[312] "Flood".

[313] Moschato is a suburb in the southwestern part of Athens. It is situated on the Faliro Bay coast, east of the mouth of the river Kifissos.

In Kaminia and Agia Sotira[314]	*Καμίνια και Αγιά Σωτήρα, βρε,*
all was swallowed by the flood.	*τα 'πνιξ' όλα η πλημμύρα.*

When Markos wrote this song as a... "chronicler" in 1935, without obviously having any special knowledge of plumbing and of the history of flood works in Attica[315], he was capturing the deterioration of the rainwater catchment area that took place 2400 years ago, that is, from 465 BC to 1935 AD!

The Athenians had the problem of "losing" the port, where the naval station was located due to the aggradation of the Kifissos river, since the Age of Pericles[316]. So what did the Ancient Greeks do? They diverted Kifissos. Instead of emptying into Kantharos, the old and actual port, they diverted it in order to empty into Faliro[317]. In this way, they changed the catchment area and created a flood problem in Moschato, Kaminia, etc.

---

[314] A neighborhood of Piraeus.

[315] Attica is the region that encompasses the city of Athens.

[316] Pericles (c. 495-429 BC) was a prominent and influential statesman, orator and general of Athens during its golden age, specifically the time between the Persian and the Peloponnesian Wars. Pericles had such a profound influence on Athenian society that he was acclaimed by Thucydides, a historian, as "the first citizen of Athens". Pericles turned the Delian League into an Athenian empire. The period during which he led Athens, roughly from 461 to 429 BC, is sometimes known as the "Age of Pericles".

[317] The Faliro Bay, a bay of the Saronic Gulf, is located 6 km southwest of Athens city center.

The map depicts the wider area of "rich" and "poor" Piraeus, where rebetika songs were glorified.

There is no other record up until Markos's lyrics describing this situation. Despite the flood works by Charilaos Trikoupis[318], the floods still occur. And they occur because of this diversion of the Kifissos river that hasn't been corrected until today...

3. "O Markos ypourgos"[319]:

Those who become prime ministers,	*Όσοι γίνουν πρωθυπουργοί*
all of them will die,	*όλοι τους θα πεθάνουν,*

---

[318] Charilaos Trikoupis (1832-1896) was a politician who served as a Prime Minister of Greece seven times from 1875 until 1895. He is best remembered for introducing the motion of no confidence to the Greek constitution, proposing and funding such ambitious and modern projects as the construction of the Corinth Canal, but also eventually leading the country to bankruptcy.

[319] "Markos the minister".

the people hunt them down	τους κυνηγάει ο λαός
for all the "good" they try.	απ' τα καλά που κάνουν.
I'm going to be a candidate	Βάζω υποψηφιότητα
to become prime minister;	πρωθυπουργός να γίνω,
I'll be all lazy, I'll just sit,	να κάθουμαι τεμπέλικα,
I'll drink and simply eat.	να τρώω και να πίνω.
I'll appear in the parliament	Και ν' ανεβαίνω στη Βουλή
to order them up,	εγώ να τους διατάζω,
I'll prepare the hookah	να τους πατώ τον άργιλε
and they'll be all stoned up.	και να τους μαστουριάζω.

"Those who become prime ministers, all of them will die"... The concept of vanity is challenged by Diogenes's irony. "All of them will die"! Life and death! And with the verses "I'm going to be a candidate to become prime minister" one can only laugh... Regarding the verse "I'll be all lazy, I'll just sit" (since the slaves who'll vote for me will also work for me): the key element is the power of the tyrant; Markos's "political analysis" contains the philosophy of cynicism[320] and the iconoclastic humor of Karagiozis. It reminds us of Diogenes who, through his jar, satirized the "normality" of the overlords. We go back to these roots with Markos...

Rebetiko is addressed to a wide audience and, at the same time, it's so dense that one can't really grasp it. It slips away from the genre itself and travels to the ancient rituals of life

---

[320] Cynicism is a school of thought of ancient Greek philosophy as practiced by the Cynics. For the Cynics, the purpose of life is to live in virtue, in agreement with nature. As reasoning creatures, people can gain happiness by rigorous training and by living in a way which is natural for themselves, rejecting all conventional desires for wealth, power, and fame. Instead, they were to lead a simple life free from all possessions.

and death, to the ancient individual arts of dancing, to folk-lore, but also to social sciences, since it's a product of the multi-phase folk inspiration.

— *What do you mean by "life and death"?*

Take as an example all the great theatrical drama creations, from the ancient theater to Shakespeare and even Samuel Beckett. All dialogues describe the difficulty of living until we die.

— *So where is "life and death" most reflected?*

It's reflected, from way back, in myths and rituals. What were the Eleusinian Mysteries[321], for example? In order to appease the souls of the people, they made the hierophant[322] reconcile the initiated with the idea of death through theat-

---

[321] The Eleusinian Mysteries were initiations held every year for the cult of Demeter and Persephone based at the Panhellenic Sanctuary of Elefsina in ancient Greece. Their basis was an old agrarian cult. The mysteries represented the myth of the abduction of Persephone from her mother Dimitra by the king of the underworld Hades, in a cycle with three phases: the descent (loss), the search, and the ascent, with the main theme being the ascent of Persephone and the reunion with her mother. The rites, ceremonies, and beliefs were kept secret and consistently preserved from antiquity. For the initiated, the rebirth of Persephone symbolized the eternity of life which flows from generation to generation, and they believed that they would have a reward in the afterlife.

[322] A hierophant is a person who brings religious congregants into the presence of that which is deemed holy. As such, a hierophant is an interpreter of sacred mysteries and arcane principles.

rical acts, passing to the darkness through the light by enjoying life without regard for death.

In his early years in Tabouria, Markos would slaughter animals and cry. Life and death. He lived with animals; it was hurting him that he was a skinner and that he was slaughtering animals...

— *How do you think rebetiko helped Markos?*

First of all, through rebetiko he was able to stand on his feet. He found his balance through art. He didn't perish. And secondly, through rebetiko he started a family. His eldest son Vassilis is now a ship-owner! I don't personally know Vassilis but, from what I hear, I think that he kept the natural kindness of his father's soul after "escaping" from the environment of deprivation he used to live in. The question is how Markos conveyed it to him. All of this sounds like a fairy-tale...

Vaggelis Vavanatsos

275

43

MARKOS AND I

The first meetings

Autumn of 1966. I had just arrived in Athens from my home country Cyprus in order to sign up in med school. My brother Nearchos, who was five years older than me, had already created the Association of Friends of Greek Music with his friends and they had rediscovered the long-forgotten giant and pioneer of laiko music Markos Vamvakaris. Among the other activities of the Association was to write down Markos's unreleased songs and record and disseminate them, if possible.

The problem was that even though Markos remembered, could sing and play many of these songs on the bouzouki, they had to be written down musically, that is, with notes, in order to be given to record labels for further action.

Nearchos found the solution: I, his little brother, who, in addition to being a medical student, was also an amateur musician and accordionist, could help. Thus, for the next few months of my student life, in parallel with my studies, I often traveled from the center of Athens – we lived in Exarcheia[323] back then – to Markos's house in Kokkinia in order to carry out the mission that was assigned to me.

I must note that from the age of twelve I had come in

---

[323] Exarcheia is a neighborhood in central Athens. The district took its name from a 19th century businessman named Exarchos who opened a large general store there. Exarcheia is renowned for being Athens's historical core of radical political and intellectual activism and is considered the anarchist quarter of Athens.

contact with Markos's songs that Nearchos had brought to our house in Cyprus in the form of 45-rpm records, all covers from 1960-1962 with the voices of Bithikotsis, Poly Panou, Katy Gray, etc., as well as Markos himself, so I was already a fan of laiko music, and especially of Markos.

My first impressions, when I visited Markos at his house with my brother, were entirely vague. Markos was warm and friendly. We drank coffee and ate confections from his wife, there were flowers in his basement and we could hear the birds chirping in their cages.

So, we got to work just like that! During our repeated meetings, five or six in total, Markos would take his bouzouki and play whatever songs he remembered all the while singing with his rigid but now broken – due to his age and illnesses – voice. I would bring a stave notebook with me in order to write down the songs with notes. In our meetings, except perhaps in the first one, I would bring my accordion with me, an Italian Marinucci 120 bass, which was quite heavy. I would bring it because I found it easier to write down the songs after first playing them on the accordion by ear. You see, I wasn't a professional musician and I wasn't able to directly write down the notes. It was easier to first play them on my own instrument and then transfer them to paper.

Our collaboration continued like that for two months. Visits were made nearly every week. It was also the first months of my studies, you see... We must've written down six to eight songs in this way. In the following period and for the next few years of Markos's life, a few of these songs, as well as others, were released on 45-rpm records, some with Markos's voice.

Some additional memories from those meetings:
• I met his son Domenikos, who's the same age as me; he

277

was an amazing bouzouki player! I remember him playing the four-stringed bouzouki Chiotis-style and we committed the "sacrilege" of playing together – he played the bouzouki and I played the accordion – virtuosic songs.

• In some of Markos's recordings there are some taximia, that is, an improvisation off the beat. When it's part of a song, it's placed at the beginning of the track, usually lasting 20-40 seconds, always off the beat; then, the intro and the rest of the song follow. However, it's possible for the taximi to be autonomous, i.e. without a song, or to be combined with another instrumental rhythmic part, for example in a zeibekiko rhythm.

I'd like to comment on two of Markos's characteristic and masterful taximia: the first one has been recorded at the beginning of his emblematic song "Ta matoklada sou laboun", in the 1960 cover by Grigoris Bithikotsis. It lasts about 35 seconds – the voice of Grigoris Bithikotsis saluting Markos is heard in between – and literally serves as an irreplaceable intro (overture) to the song; I can't avoid the association with corresponding intros from classical music. This taximi is one of the reasons that none of the innumerable subsequent covers can be compared to it.

The other example is his famous song "Taxim zeibekiko", an older recording on a 78-rpm record.[324] What we have here is an extended taximi of an extremely high level of improvisation, followed by the second part, an instrumental in zeibekiko rhythm, probably originating from a traditional tune, which later served as the basis for the well-known song "Enas mangas ston Votaniko"[325].

---

[324] Recorded in 1937.

[325] "A mangas in Votanikos". First recorded in 1934, this song was allegedly composed by Spyros Peristeris, but, as Phivos Georgiadis argues, it probably originates from a traditional tune.

In both examples I mentioned, Markos's protean technique is distinctive, his way of playing is "clean", his melodic lines are unexpected and we get the feeling that what we hear comes from somewhere deep. At the same time, however, one feels that, no matter how much freedom the artist experiences, he cannot escape from an invisible thread that connects each note with the previous and the next one.

Concerts

I had the good fortune to participate, as an accordionist, in two concerts with Markos. The first was the one given on November 2, 1966, at 8 pm, in the clubhouse of the Association of Cretan Students. It was organized by the Association of Friends of Greek Music. It was the first laiko music concert ever.

The success was unexpected. The hall, with a capacity of 250 people, was packed. My parents, who had come to Athens for a visit, were in the front row. Markos also sat in the front row with his wife Evangelia, who both arrived a little late from Kokkinia.

As soon as Markos entered, my mother, not being accustomed to such situations, suddenly heard him say: "I want to wee-wee", like a child. For many years this was a joke between my brother, our mother and me.

So, the night started in a somewhat humorous way and turned into a moving, as well as unprecedented – I believe historically significant too – tribute to the unique artist. What I remember was the emotional stress both on stage as well as from the audience. Markos's thrill was evident.

The poster for the reappearance of Markos was designed
by the architect/musician Antonis Doukakis.

The second concert took place on December 5, 1966, at
the Kentrikon theater. It was organized by Tasos Schorelis
and was successful. This concert was more organized, there
were microphones. I was playing the accordion once again.
Stelios Keromytis was also present. Even though the large
hall wasn't completely full, I believe that this concert contributed, together with the previous one, to the revival of
Markos's fame and presence in the foreground for the few
years that he was still to live.

Contributing to this was the fact that, this time, several well-known scholars and artists were in the audience. Nevertheless, for me personally, the authenticity and emotion of the first "small" concert in the Cretans' clubhouse remains unbeatable.

A poster and a flyer for Markos's concert at the Kentrikon theater.

The birds

When I first visited Markos, I noticed that in the basement he used as his workshop there were cages with birds – canaries, goldfinches, I can't really remember – which of course chirped from time to time. Apart from the pleasant feeling that their presence created for me, I hadn't understood from the beginning their importance for Markos.

As our acquaintance and collaboration progressed and as we were writing down songs, I began to realize the essential role that birds played in the way Markos composed his songs. This was more evident when Markos would pick up the bouzouki and play an improvisation. At times he seemed to listen to the birds' chirps and then try to imitate them! Just as the birds chirped, stopped, started again, sometimes in a different pitch or rhythm, so did Markos pluck the strings of the instrument, composing these famous taximia...

This is the greatness of Markos, the "Patriarch" of rebetiko, with his deeply spontaneous and improvisational character.

Phivos Georgiadis

Phivos Georgiadis   Nearchos Georgiadis

44

LIKE A ROCK LASHED
BY THE WAVES OF THE WILD SEA

In the mid-1950s, early 1960s, what dominated were the songs of Stelios Kazantzidis and a number of singers and composers of that style. The only traces of a robust production from the past that seemed to have been violently interrupted – what many call rebetiko – were some four or five 45-rpm records with medleys by Tsitsanis, Papaioannou, Bagianteras, Lafkas[326], Mitsakis.

Markos Vamvakaris, the first master of them all, did not have the honor to be part of those records; he was completely forgotten. However, Grigoris Bithikotsis had the good fortune to sing two or three of his songs, given that, in that time, he was constantly rising in popularity. This is how his cover of "Frangosyriani", together with Tsitsanis's song "Synnefiasmeni Kyriaki", hold the reins until today in Greece.

I first heard Markos's voice from the tape recorder of my friend and fellow architecture student Antonis Noukakis and I was surprised. He was of course no Pavarotti[327], not even Kazantzidis. He had an ancient, strange and frog-like voice. It took me a while to get used to it, but my acquaintance with Nearchos Georgiadis, a Cypriot law student, with whom we

---

[326] Giorgos Lafkas (1919–1972) was a composer, singer and bouzouki player. Lafkas was born in the village of Metamorfosi, Laconia, and came to Athens in 1943 to study agronomy, but music won him over.

[327] Luciano Pavarotti (1935-2007) was an Italian operatic tenor who during the late part of his career crossed over into popular music, eventually becoming one of the most acclaimed tenors of all times.

shared another common passion, cinema, gave me the pleasure to deliver myself to the "magical world of rebetiko", as Nearchos characteristically used to say.

So it happened and we found ourselves one morning at Markos's home in Kokkinia, in a small yard on the ground floor of his house, after having previously sat in the living room, where Mrs. Vangelio, his wife, treated us to some confections and coffee. I think we also met the youngest of his children, the then teenager Domenikos. I remember that he had a sofa there or maybe a sort of carpeted ledge where he used to sit and play his bouzouki. He dominated in this small yard, and I, with my artistic spirit, rightly thought of the title "the 'Patriarch' of rebetiko". He also had cages with birds, canaries, to which he used to speak. He had also given them names. He told us that when he played the bouzouki the birds would start singing and that's how he would give birth to his nice songs.

I was impressed by this big man who, despite having a ramrod posture, looked much older than his real age, with his carved face, as if all his difficult life had been painted there. I was also impressed by the fact that, while on some occasions he was quite talkative, he often seemed sad. I was accustomed to talk to older people, but Nearchos had mastered a simple and at the same time journalistic way to do that, which usually worked. Markos was a simple man, someone among the common people. With his ordinary virtues and vices, let's say. But, above all, he was an artist, a great artist. And, without being an expert, I think that Markos, with his subject matter transcending the narrow confines of the underworld, as a family man and also as a worker, inaugurated and justified the designation "laiko" music, as it's a music style that embraces all the popular masses.

During other visits, we also met his other two children, Vassilis, the eldest son, who was studying at the merchant marine college, and Stelios, who left us last year... He loved his children and was proud of them.

It's known that most rebetes smoked pot, as did Markos, but at the time I met him he didn't even smoke a simple cigarette, and he considered hashish to be responsible for all the illnesses he had. He used to list them one by one: "I have asthma, arthritis, bronchitis, diabetes..."

One day, I made a couple of pencil sketches of him. But the most interesting portrait of Markos was the one with the "Famous Quartet of Piraeus". Nearchos lent me a photo that he treasured, the now well-known photo with Markos and Anestos standing behind Stratos and Batis. I made a painting on an approximately 2.50 m x 1.50 m canvas, with acrylic colors in the red color hue range and with a garland representing mermaids with bouzoukia all around. I'm guessing that today it must adorn some Turkish tavern – at best – somewhere in the occupied areas of Cyprus, since Morphou was Nearchos's homeland...

The "Famous Quartet of Piraeus", 1934.

285

The event I am referring to took place in the clubhouse of the Association of Cretan Students, "in a big house", as Markos says in his autobiography.[328] It was done with the collaboration of the Association of Cretan Students, of which I was a member of the Board, and the Association of Friends of Greek Music, led by Nearchos.

About 1,000 tickets were sold (for 2 drachmas each) and the attendance was unexpected; people were hanging by the windows like grapes. They were students and people who loved this kind of culture. Markos was excited. He, his children Stelios and Domenikos and Manolis Dimitrianakis were playing the bouzouki. Panagiotis Chrysinis[329] was playing the baglama, Phivos Georgiadis[330] the accordion, Kostas Tzikas was the drummer, and Giorgos Chatziantoniou[331], Eleni Roda[332] and Soula Stavrou were singing.

---

[328] "The students helped towards this. They organized big events about me. Not just here, but also when I went to Thessaloniki the whole student population came to see me. [...] It seemed like they knew my story, they learned my story, they knew who I was and they loved me very much. I mean, wherever I go now I have my students with me. They turn up. This story began when we did a concert with Nearchos Georgiadis and Kiki Kalamara in a big house" (op. cit., p. 237).

[329] Panagiotis Chrysinis was Stelios Chrysinis's (1916-1970, composer and musician) older brother. The brothers began working in movie theaters where they played music for silent films. They both followed a career in music, despite both being blind from a young age.

[330] See page ▌ for more information.

[331] Giorgos Chatziantoniou (1941-1997) was a singer.

[332] Eleni Roda is a singer. She has appeared in many Greek films as an actress, but ultimately devoted herself to singing.

Domenikos M. Vamvakaris, Markos Vamvakaris, Phivos
Georgiadis and Eleni Roda.
(Eleni Roda's archive)

The introduction was made by Nearchos. The preface to
the event was made by the actor Kostas Kazakos[333], and I read
excerpts from Markos's memoirs. The event had a great impact, received positive comments in the newspapers and was
the starting point for other concerts organized shortly after
by Tasos Schorelis at the Kentrikon[334] theater, but also for
the concerts organized by Elias Petropoulos at the Hilton, a
year after the establishment of the dictatorship. Many scholars, as well as people in arts and media occupations, focused
on these issues in one way or another. However, I think that
the backbone of this entire story was Nearchos, who worked
tirelessly, with consistency, imagination and selflessness up
until the very end of his life. Let me also honor the memory
of my good friend and fellow student Kiki Kalamara, with

---

[333] See page █.
[334] Kentrikon means "central".

whom we collaborated as regards Markos Vamvakaris.

Kiki Kalamara-Molocthou
(1946-2009)
Still from a special report by
ERT dedicated to
Markos, 2000.

Nearchos Georgiadis
(1944-2013)
Still from a special report by
RIK[335] dedicated to
Markos, 2004.

I think it's worth noting that, in addition to the colossal chapter of his work, he was also a significant hoarder of "stray" lyrics and of some melodies that would otherwise have been lost forever. He himself used to tell us that he was sometimes inspired by verses written in the back of calendars that he was collecting and using them creatively in fresh compositions. Years after his death, I heard him talking about the wonderful song "Giati mikroula mou"[336] in an interview he had given when he was still alive: "This melody isn't mine, it's a very old melody, a Byzantine one!" Well, if he hadn't "adopted" it, this tune would have been forgotten!

In the introduction of my book "Δυο τραγούδια με ουρά"[337], published by Kalenti publications, 2005, I mention somewhere: "I believe that singing in general is perhaps the

---

[335] Cyprus Broadcasting Corporation (CyBC or RIK) is Cyprus's public broadcasting service.

[336] "Why my little one?".

[337] "Two songs with a tail".

most important form of art, at least in terms of social functionality. As it is usually completed in a few verses and is at the same time so simple, but also so complex, there's nothing more to be done: music, singing and dance, many times intertwined together, constitute an invaluable little bindweed. These are the most concentrated creations that our soul and senses can savor." When I was writing these lines, I mostly had Markos's songs in mind; singing, music, dance.

I would finally like to mention that I cannot recall the color of his eyes. I only remember that his gaze was usually sad, even though sometimes sparkling. At other times, his eyes roved away, beyond space and time. Was he thinking about the past? Or was he anxiously looking to the future?

Grigoris Niolis

Engraving by Grigoris Niolis, 1968.

45

MARKOS IS THE MOST ROBUST EXPRESSION OF OUR MODERN POPULAR CULTURE

— *My dear Kostas, where were you born?*

In Pyrgos.[338]

— *When did you first hear Markos's voice on a record?*

From what I remember, the first Greek bouzouki record I heard in my house was Markos Vamvakaris's "Frangosyriani", which was recorded in 1935, the year I was born. have been listening to rebetiko music since I was in my mother's womb, from some records that my grandfather had brought, along with a Columbia gramophone, when he came back from America in 1915. They were recorded in America in the early 20th century, but the style was still mixed, a blend of dimotiko[339] and music with influences from Asia Minor. They used to sing rebetika songs back then, even with just a guitar. The bouzouki prevailed and locked in to rebetiko after the 1920s. By the 1930s, the way was clear for the protagonists of rebetiko. Thus, the "Famous Quartet of Piraeus" was created, consisting of the master Giorgos Batis with his baglama, Markos Vamvakaris, who was to become rebetiko's most genuine and profound exponent, Stratos Pagioumtzis,

---

[338] Pyrgos is a city in the northwestern Peloponnese.

[339] Greece's traditional rural music.

whose voice was to indelibly seal his career, and Anestos Delias, this sensitive young man with his unique songs, who left this world too soon.

People in Pyrgos were crazy about rebetiko. The songs of Markos, Tsitsanis, Papaioannou, were the songs I loved during the first years of the war and the Occupation. There were prominent manghes in Pyrgos. I had relatives who wore their jackets over one shoulder only and their cummerbunds were hanging and touching the ground. They were high and mighty manghes, full of confidence and prestige, who were highly esteemed in Pyrgos. They weren't bums.

I used to sing all of Markos's songs, as well as "Vangelitsa"[340] by Papaioannou, and when I came to Athens I was surprised that the Athenians knew them too. I was completely taken by surprise. I thought they were ours, from Pyrgos!

— *When did you come to Athens?*

I came to Athens in 1948 and settled in Vyronas. My father was in exile and I had three younger brothers, so I had to work to make a living. The jobs I did were hard. But I loved rebetiko. Through rebetiko, I understood music. It's the most genuine manifestation of Greece, a basic pillar, the buttress of our culture. I used to go wherever I could hear the sound of the bouzouki. This is how I met all the rebetes of the time and chatted with them, especially with Markos, whom I was especially fond of. I established friendly relations, which lasted many years, with many of them, such as

---

[340] Affectionate name for Vangelio or Evangelia. The song was first recorded in 1937.

with Sotiria Bellou, Stratos Pagioumtzis, Prodromos Tsaou-sakis[341], Giannis Papaioannou...

— *Describe Markos to me.*

I'll describe to you what I remember from the meetings we had in the joints where he used to play. I remember that he was an ill-fated, tortured and very serious man. I thought he was inaccessible, distant. But, in fact, he was a soft and very tender person. He had an unusual sophistication. He had all the folk tradition inside him and that gave him a sort of nobility which I couldn't understand where it came from. I couldn't suspect that this man had the subtlest, noblest feelings. He was generous in his dealings with the other rebetes. He was made of the noblest material. It was like... You know how there are noble and heavy metals? Iron and lead belong to one category, and silver and gold belong to another. Markos was made from the materials that belong to the second one.

— *Did you ever ask Markos any questions?*

I once asked him for his opinion on a young singer. He made a not so nice face and told me: "He's so tense! He stretches his neck to release the sound. He forces it. A good singer shouldn't make any effort. The voice should go up, go down, but the face must remain inexpressive. The listener must think that it can go up some more. Nobody must be able to recognize that it hit its limits. When the singer is tense,

---

[341] Prodromos Moutafoglou (1919-1979), better known by his stage name Prodromos Tsaousakis, was a popular rebetiko singer, songwriter and composer.

the 'e' on the high notes sounds like an 'i'. If you pay attention, you'll hear it too."

— *How was Markos's voice?*

His voice was his great advantage. It gave rebetiko its character. Rebetiko is a fine art. Markos hadn't taken care of his voice. He used to sing using his natural tone. And that was in his favor. Like wild flowers... You see wild flowers among the weeds and you say to yourself: "What's this?" You find yourself in a green meadow and you suddenly see a threshing floor full of red poppies and you wonder how did that happen... This is what nature does. These are the nature's revolutionary touches. Markos's voice is such a touch.

— *What do you think of the way Markos was playing?*

He was sensational. He had a sort of power which almost rendered the singing part of the songs unnecessary. Rebetiko doesn't absolutely need the lyrics. When they're good, it helps. But rebetiko, for the most part, is the sound of the bouzouki.

— *What was Markos trying to express with his bouzouki?*

As I said, the way he was playing was sensational. It gets inside your mind and agitates you because it expresses the great pain of the people on the margins of society. The trampled lives of these people could only be expressed through the bouzouki. Markos externalized his pain with his bouzouki without being a philosopher or an intellectual. But he was a true artist-creator.

— *Is zeibekiko a proud dance?*

No. It's a modest, simple, unpretentious dance. Zeibekiko has no steps, it's all about improvisation. It has very few moves. Someone who dances zeibekiko converses with the underworld. It's a matter of life and death. No jumping or gyrating is allowed. Below the ground is the melting pot of the dead and the zeibekiko dancer is heading there. It's like saying: "Manghes, save a spot for me too, I'm coming!" A rebetis lives a reality that he cannot bear. His life has become a mess. And death is the great doctor. Death arrives and misery is automatically gone, hunger goes away, the policeman with his whip disappears and the bitterness of unfulfilled love is cured. A ritual is taking place! It looks more like a funeral than anything else... The zeibekiko dancer at some point bends down and touches the ground with his fingers and says to the dead: "Manghes, hear me out: I'm coming!"

— *Does rebetiko have a class-ridden nature?*

For me, rebetiko is absolutely class-ridden. It expresses the people who are lying on the floor and are looking up. The social pyramid is an exploitative one, it's based on the exploitation of man by man. Whatever level of the pyramid you're in, you'll have those who exploit you above you and below you are those who are exploited by you. Those who do not exploit anyone, because they're at the last level, are the rebetes. They're free from this "social illness". They're healthy. This is the honorableness they possess. They just look up and see the entire class stratification. They're the dregs of society, broke, crushed, drowned, and they're noble by nature, precisely because they don't exploit anyone. They're free from the "cancer of society", which is private property and capital. Rebetes were no intellectuals. Most of them were illiterate, but they were deeply aware that they were expressing the pain of an entire people.

I think that this is the heart of rebetiko. Rebetiko takes these people under its wings and they rejoice. It oxygenates our brain and tells us about the dreams that were stolen from us, but we, riding on rebetiko's wings, won't stop dreaming, because that is how we keep our humaneness alive.

— *Where was Markos's character shaped and how did he become the exponent of these people?*

His character was shaped and he became an exponent of these people when he was a child in the port of Syros and a young man in the honky-tonks of Piraeus.

— *What do rebetika songs express?*

Love songs, blue-eyed enchantresses, gypsy women represent the unfulfilled dreams of people. And the more unfulfilled they are, the more the rebetes sing them as if they were real. For this reason, just like fine art, rebetiko will never be lost.

— *How would you characterize Markos's lyrics?*

They consist of people's daily conversations. They don't have anything intellectual. The way he plays and his voice offer us a tragic element. Markos was extremely observant. Whatever moved him, he turned it into a song.

— *Did birds play a role in rebetiko?*

The birds that chirp, the sound that the rain makes when it falls on the reeds, the water that falls into the river and hits the stones are the first sounds recorded by the human ear; this is how we began to make music. Markos, with his songs, was in contact with the natural environment, and especially with the chirping of birds.

Photo of Markos taken by Giannis Kazakos, Kostas's brother.

— *Will Markos be remembered?*

Oh! Rebetiko is a pillar of our culture. We're still standing because we rely on our great poets, our great novelists, our great painters and of course our great musicians. Rebetiko music is a great chapter of our music and Markos Vamvakaris is the first among the first!

— *What did Markos bring from Syra?*

My dear Dimitris, you have dedicated yourself to Markos's life and you've done a lot of good work. Congratulations! In the book that you wrote about Markos, you also recorded all the dimotika songs that his father played with his

297

gaida while little Markos accompanied him with his drum to the festivals of the island. When Markos was a young kid, in Ermoupoli, there was also a dance school where they taught zeibekiko and Markos attended it. When he came to Piraeus at the age of fifteen, in 1920, he brought this tradition with him. It was a great deal of wealth.

— *To close the interview, can you tell me what does Markos mean to you?*

Probably the most robust expression of our modern popular culture.

Kostas Kazakos

Kostas Kazakos dancing zeibekiko in the late 1960s.

46

IT TAKES 62 MILES TO GO TO SYRA

When Markos died in 1972, I was young, I was just entering middle school. But then I met his two children, Domenikos and Stelios, as well as his wife, Mrs. Vangelio. I have the autobiography compiled by Angeliki Vellou-Keil and the conversations I had with his children, mainly with Stelios, as a main reference about Markos.

In 1987, we held an exhibition in Syros entitled "The Music of the Aegean". And this is where, for the first time, his children and Vangelio gave us various items of his to exhibit, his amulet and two manuscripts. A red amulet, which Markos used to wear close to the heart. It's shaped like a little red heart that has various things stitched in it, as they used to do with amulets in the old days, and with a cross embroidered on it. There's also a photo taken by Giorgis Christofilakis that shows him wearing it close to the heart. I donated the amulet and the two manuscripts to the Benaki Museum and they are now on display at the Museum of the Generation of the 1930s on Zalokosta Street, in the old house of Chatzikyriakos-Gikas[342], in a showcase dedicated to Markos Vamvakaris. Markos has written on the front of one of the manuscripts: "It takes 62 miles to go to Syra". From the back Zabetas has written his phone number and, further down, Markos has noted the name "Susie" and another phone number. The other manuscript is actually a box of candy on which Markos has written lyrics about a lot of sufferings. These items were

---

[342] Nikos Chatzikyriakos-Gikas (1906-1994) was a leading painter, sculptor, engraver, writer and academic.

given to me by Stelios, who was deeply moved when we held the exhibition in Ermoupoli. I had the amulet for a long time, as if I really had a kind of energy with me. Markos was a superstitious man.[343]

— *When did Markos first adore the bouzouki?*

Basically, from what he himself has said, he adored the bouzouki in Piraeus in 1925 when he heard Nikos Aivaliotis play.[344] But he must've heard it before in Apano Syros and in Ermoupoli.[345]

---

[343] "You can't imagine the spells she shoved under our door. [...] Every kind of bad voodoo" (op. cit., p. 277).

"What doctors didn't they take him [Linardos] to? [...] Even to some bogus witches who said they could make him better" (op. cit., p. 143).

"I had another dream. I saw a Turkish gypsy girl dressed in red" (op. cit., p. 125).

[344] "Just before going to the army, late in 1924 or early in 1925, I happened to hear barba Nikos Aivaliotis playing his bouzouki. I loved it so much I made a vow: if I didn't learn bouzouki I'd chop my hands off with the bone chopper they use in the butcher shop. [...] From then on this instrument held me in chains. There was nothing else for me in the world" (op. cit., p. 105).

"So Nikos came one evening at home [...] and when I happened to hear his first strums [...] I was struck dumb. [...] Six months after my father brought him to the house, I had already learned to play so well that when he heard me he was speechless. In just six months I was playing really well. I had excelled, I had become a proper beast on the instrument" (op. cit., p. 108).

[345] "But it wasn't the first time I'd heard this instrument. Apart from the gaida, my father used to play a bit of bouzouki, just a little. Even in Syros as a boy, I had heard many old bouzouki players. Manolakis,

— Tell us a few words about the history of the bou-zouki.

This type of bouzouki that currently exists in Greece is the evolution of the tambouras. The tambouras is a string instrument that was played in ancient Greece. The byzantine pandoura[346] is the instrument of Digenis Akritas[347]. Around the middle of the 19th century, the tambouras evolved into a bouzouki. The bouzouki is essentially a combination of the tambouras with some elements from the mandolin and was manufactured in Athens's and Smyrna's instrument-making stores. I haven't found any data and haven't done any research as regards the presence of the bouzouki in Syros.

Trisimisis from Apano Chora, Stravogiorgis the blind man, Maoutsos, Andrikakis, the barbers Vafeas and Karagiannis and Pankalakis who played excellent tzoura. These guys are all from Syros" (op. cit., p. 106).

[346] The pandoura, an ancient string instrument, belonged in the broad class of the lute and guitar instruments. The ancient Greek pandoura was a medium or long-necked lute with a small resonating chamber, used by the ancient Greeks. Ancient Greek artwork depicts such lutes from the 3rd or 4th century BC onward. Its descendants still survive as the Greek tambouras and bouzouki.

[347] Digenis Akritas is the most famous of the Acritic Songs (epic poems that emerged in the Byzantine Empire). The epic details the life of the hero Vasileios, whose epithet Digenis Akritas ("Twain-born Bor-derer") refers to his mixed Byzantine-Cappadocian Greek and Arab blood. The first part of the epic details the lives of his parents, how they met, and how his father, an Emir, converted to Christianity after abducting and marrying Digenis's mother. The remainder of the epic refers to (often from a first-person point of view) Vasileios's acts of heroism on the Byzantine border.

—   Did Syros have an urban culture at the time when Markos lived there?

Ermoupoli had many barrel organs, a theater, Karagiozis shadow-puppet theater, meaning that it had an urban folk culture at the beginning of the 20th century. I believe that Apano Syros, where Markos lived, did not have an urban culture. It's an island area like the rest of the Cyclades. The bagpipes and the drum dominated.[348] Markos's father, Domenikos, played the bagpipes and Markos accompanied him with his drum.

—   Tell us something more about the bagpipes.

The bagpipes, as far as we know, came to Greece from Asia in the 1st century AD. I don't really know when it arrived in Syros. The bagpipes Markos is referring to in his autobiography are accompanied with a drum. The musicians didn't play zeibekika with the bagpipes. Zeibekika were played by the barrel organ.

This means that Markos had two sources that made an impact on him: the traditional Aegean one, that is, the one with the bagpipes, which he learned with his father by accompanying him with the drum. He was playing traditional Cycladic songs. The other source that influenced him was the barrel organ. It was the jukebox of the time. You could rent a barrel organ and have fun. The organ grinders would kick him because he wanted to hear the sound directly from the case of the instrument.[349]

---

[348] "I used to play the drum from the age of six" (op. cit., p. 61).

[349] "I used to press my ear against the barrel organ" (op. cit., p. 59).

The barrel organs had a repertoire from all over Greece.[350] While with the bagpipes you could play the two or three local songs.[351] The barrel organs were playing the melodies. Markos had melodies in him. With the bagpipes you can play mostly the rhythm, some patterns; but what really matters is the drum. The dancer listens to the drum, he doesn't listen to the bagpipes so much. This is why Markos learned from rhythm. I mean, rhythm was inculcated in him while playing the drum and while accompanying his father as a child.

— *What influenced him most in his musical education?*

I very much believe that the barrel organ played a big role in Markos's musical education. That is, if I were to emphasize something that influenced him the most, this would be the western barrel organ. It came from Constantinople and went all over Greece.

— *What was the biggest influence on Markos's soul in his childhood?*

The people of Apano Syros, as poor farmers and stockbreeders, were living on the fringes of Ermoupoli's society. Officially, Ermoupoli and part of the local community kept a very long distance from Vamvakaris. On the one hand, they wanted him, because Markos was a name that constituted advertising for the island, but the city of Ermoupoli does not accept him even now. They consider him a matter

---

[350] "Waltzes, quadrilles, syrta, kalamatiana, chasapika, zeibekika, servika" (op. cit., p. 61).

[351] "I was beating out the rhythm of syrto, ballos and Cretan" (op. cit., p. 61).

303

of Apano Syros and of Piraeus.

I don't think that Markos, after all, and this might annoy some people, is just a "product" from Syros. Markos though owes to Syros his initiation to the centuries-long Aegean tradition through the sound of the bagpipes. Moreover, this tradition coupled with the urban tradition of the barrel organ, the one that connects us with Constantinople. In Ermoupoli, though, for the first time, he felt what it means to be marginalized because of being a Catholic and poor. He felt for the first time what it means for others to profit from his work because of being small and weak. What it means to work all week and earn very little money...[352] And this is where he felt for the first time what it means to be chased for unlawful conduct. So, he left for Piraeus, where the second great cycle of his life began.[353]

— *He however had many religious experiences from Apano Syros.*

Markos must've been religious. His first marriage took place in the Catholic Church of Piraeus, but he got divorced. And because the Catholic Church didn't allow him to marry for a second time, he remarried in an Orthodox ceremony. But at some point, the Catholic Church arranged for him to start receiving communion again and Markos was going to

---

[352] "1912 came along and they took my father off into the army. Then my mother took me with her and off we went to get work in Deligiannis's cotton factory. My mother was pregnant with her belly way out. [...] She was getting three and a half drachmas a day and I was getting three and a half drachmas a week" (op. cit., p. 64).

[353] "I stowed away on a boat and ran away to Piraeus. [...] Here ends the drama of Syros. But my life is an entire series of dramas" (op. cit., p. 80).

the church of Saint Paul on Sundays. However, he was saying: "I'm persecuted by both God and people." So, what he cared about was not being persecuted by God, he was taking it hard and considering it a double marginalization. He was sidelined both by people and God.

— *What is it that makes a song so popular? What's Greeks' relation with "Frangosyriani"?*

Most people sing it without knowing what it's about. I mean, how many people associate the song with Catholicism and Apano Syros?

— *Why doesn't any of his songs mention Ermoupoli? Did he reject it, as the city rejected him?*

Indeed, he wasn't even referring to the city as "Ermoupoli" or "Kato Chora". While, on the contrary, he was mentioning Apano Syros. I believe that he had no connection whatsoever with Ermoupoli. The city didn't love him and he didn't love it. For Markos, it was a place of torment; factories where he was forced to work, a place haunted for him. He must've been through some difficult situations there. He was an underage kid in with all kinds of folks. Markos was an Oliver Twist of the time, mutatis mutandis. He must've experienced marginal situations similar to London's.

When Markos came to Piraeus at the age of 15, he had gone through some experiences, he had struggled and knew what it was like to be marginalized. And all this not in Apano Syros, but in Ermoupoli. So, why would he feel good in this environment and why should he sing about it?

— *Why are people saying that Markos is the "Patriarch" of rebctiko?*

Markos is the "Patriarch" of rebetiko because he's the one who dynamically transitions from smyrneiko[354] music and the santouria[355] and the violins to the Piraeus style and the bouzoukia and baglamades, who are considered to be the classic sound of rebetiko. Markos is the one who introduced us in the classical era of rebetiko music. Markos knew smyrneiko very well because musicians came to Kokkinia after 1922 and he had heard all them refugees playing.

— *Who was the first to record while playing the bouzouki in Greece?*

Markos was the first to record while playing the bouzouki[356], which was marginalized by the record companies

---

[354] Musical style originating in Smyrna. It appeared in the 19th century and reached Greece after 1922. The influences of smyrneika (the songs of smyrneiko) are manifold. This musical style is a reflection of the communities that populated the city (Greeks, Turks, Jews, Armenians but also French and English). Typical instruments of this genre were the violin, the oud, the santouri, the tsimbalo (an instrument similar to the santouri), the qanun (a type of large zither with a thin trapezoidal soundboard), the lyre from Constantinople and the clarinet.

[355] Santouri (pl. santouria) = a stringed instrument in the hammer dulcimer family. There are Greek, Persian and Indian types which are distinct from each other in style, construction, tuning and technique. The Persian and Indian instruments are more generally respectively known as the santur and santoor.

[356] Actually, the first ever bouzouki recording in Greece took place in 1931 by bouzouki player Giorgos Manetas. He recorded two songs: "Ta disticha tou manga" (meaning "The couplets of the mangas") and "Kale mana den boro" (meaning "Mother, I cannot" – see page 177, Columbia DG-139 1931).

306

in Greece. Of course, bouzouki recordings had been made earlier, mainly in America. Many musicians left and went straight to America, where there were many Greek record companies. In Greece, the first records factory essentially operated in 1930.

— *Is Markos a role model?*

In all of life's challenges, I would venture to say that I have Markos as a role model, as a whole person, as a man who struggled in his life with his values, his identity and his principles, which he maintained to the end and who was at the same time a very tender family man. He cared a lot about his children. He was a man who needed the female presence as a partner, as a companion and as beauty.

— *Are you moved by Markos?*

I'm deeply moved by Markos. I admire Markos as a human being, as an attitude towards life, as a complete personality. Markos is life. Markos is the society; he's written history and he was a man who fought the establishment. Markos is Syros. Markos is Piraeus. Markos is Greece.

Lambros Liavas

47

I BECAME MARKOS'S PASSIONATE FAN AT THE AGE OF FIVE

— *Are you a fan of Markos?*

Markos is my beloved one.

— *When did you start playing the bouzouki?*

In 1974. My first teacher was Stavros Daralas[357] and then I met Giorgos Zabetas and many others. I have met many rebetes, who had given me information about Markos, such as Kalfopoulos[358], Keromytis, Papaioannou, Georgakopoulou[359] and Giorgos Mouflouzelis[360].

---

[357] Brother of Loukas Daralas, the father of the famous singer Giorgos Dalaras.

[358] Spyros Kalfopoulos (1923-2006) was a bouzouki player, singer, composer and lyricist. He was born in Piraeus from parents coming from Asia Minor. He made his first appearance during the German Occupation.

[359] Ioanna Georgakopoulou (1920-2007) was a singer. She began her career before World War II. She began recording 78-rpm records around 1938. Just after the war, Ioanna Georgakopoulou sang some of Tsitsanis's finest songs that had been written during and after the German Occupation.

[360] Giorgos Mouflouzelis (1912-1991) was a tzoura player, composer and singer. He was born in the island of Mytilini. He stopped going to school and from the age of ten he started working in construction.

My grandfather, Vassilis Konstantakos, from the village of Potamia in the region of Laconia, came and settled in Athens in 1948. In 1955, he opened a tavern which operated until 1995. He brought the must from the Mesogaia[361] and ferment it in the tavern. His strength was his wine. He made twenty thousand barrels of wine and, by Easter, there was not a single drop left. He himself used to fill jars with herrings and serve them with his famous wine. But his specialty was chitterlings.

All of Pagrati[362] used to come and drink the wine of Vassilis the "Regga"[363]. Big names were coming too, and, for many years, from 1958 to 1968, Papaioannou and Tsitsanis used to come to the tavern; Markos Vamvakaris joined them later. Sometimes, only Papaioannou and Markos would come. When the three of them met, Papaioannou would take his baglama and he or Markos would play. Tsitsanis never touched it. They used to come to my grandfather's tavern to drink good wine, but also because the area of Kareas, where the tavern was located, was a marginalized part of Attica, with residents counted on the fingers of one hand. Thus, they knew that they wouldn't have the... paparazzi chasing them.

I will never ever forget the three of them drinking wine together, eating chitterlings and joking. I remember the sound of the baglama that Markos used to play and the tone

---

From 1930 to 1940 he worked as a builder in his homeland, but during that time he traveled several times to Piraeus and Athens, since he had a great desire to meet professional bouzouki players. He permanently settled in Athens in 1958.

[361] The Mesogaia (or Mesogeia, the "Midlands") is a geographical region of Attica.

[362] A neighborhood of Athens.

[363] Regga means "herring".

of his voice. It was a divine gift for a kid. That was the reason why I became Markos's passionate fan and why I played the three-stringed bouzouki.

— *Did Syros play a role in the formation of Markos?*

The place where someone is born and spends his or her childhood is the be-all and end-all of life. Syros is a harsh island. It's whipped by north and south winds, but at the same time it's a blessed place. There is no water but there is fragrant thyme and thus beekeeping exists. There is sage, magical caper... I have been there at least twenty times. Syrans are lucky to live on such an island.

Markos was born in Danakos and, since he was poor, he was forced to walk all around because he and his father used to uproot thyme and take it to the bakeries in order to receive a loaf of bread. His father played the gaida and Markos accompanied him to festivals, weddings, baptisms, carnival celebrations by playing the drum. He understood rhythm from a young age, something very important for a musician. He also liked to be close to barrel organs.

At the age of five he settled in Apano Syra, in Skali. The way Apano Syra is built, with its narrow streets, is not coincidental. People communicated with each other from one door to another. They had created a society that was not intrusive, but participatory. Markos grew up in this environment from the age of five to fifteen, and I consider this to be very important.

He gazed at the sea from the balcony of his house. The sea offers us broadmindedness... You can't get bored in Syros! From wherever you look, you can see the sea, and, within a few minutes, you can be close to a beach; thus, your emotional makeup changes.

When Markos came to Piraeus in 1920, he wasn't lucky

enough to get a decent job. His life was not strewn with rose petals neither in Syra nor in Piraeus. I believe that this fueled his doctrinal, stoic behavior. Eventually, the bouzouki was the instrument that set him free. He gave everything up for it. The talented and oppressed Markos externalized all the knowledge he had acquired and couldn't somehow express it through the bouzouki. How many singers can you recall singing four octaves like Stelios Kazantzidis? How many artists can you recall playing the bouzouki like the amazing virtuoso Chiotis? But, Dimitris, does any of their songs express suffering? No. Only Markos's.

The music of each artist has a truth depending on his or her experiences. Tsitsanis wanted to go to law school. He had a more revolutionary style. Markos had the performative power of authenticity. "I play what I see".

— *Do you believe that Markos's songs are of value?*

A song that has been recorded fifty, even eighty years ago, and is now sung by musicians in their twenties, thirties and forties, is something very important. I believe that Markos's songs are of an incredible value.

— *What is Markos's most important feature?*

He never deviated from his own path, he never strayed from his principles. This is formidable. All Markos's songs are "simple" and, as a result, the philosophy that he espoused characterized him.

It is very important to stick to your style and Markos did it consistently. Also, Markos was incredibly observant; he recorded everything he saw.

— *What did Markos offer to the bouzouki?*

311

Markos did unique things with his three-stringed bouzouki. He changed the tunings. While all the three-stringed bouzoukia were and still are tuned in RE LA RE, Markos played in LA SOL LA or SI LA SI.[364] He changed the tuning of the instrument so that his voice could be heard in the same pitch he was playing. Markos's authentic karadouzenia were unique in their conception. Markos is equal to Beethoven, Bach, Mozart. Always keep in mind that Markos hadn't studied music. He was self-taught. This means that he was an incredible and inexhaustible source of pure talent.

— *Tell me one of his most important songs.*

I consider the original version "Antilaloun oi fylakes" from 1935, as well as the cover from Grigoris Bithikotsis from 1960, retaining most of the elements of the original version, to be one of his best songs. Markos was able to set to music the pain of the prisoners and especially of those who were being imprisoned because they were caught holding a bouzouki in their hands. Also, when I hear the original version of "Charamata i ora treis", I immediately rejoice.

— *Did Tsitsanis love Markos?*

He respected and loved him a lot. Once, he told me, in the

---

[364] The origin of the syllabic musical notation is due to the Italian monk Guido of Arezzo (born 992 AD) who used the first syllables of a Latin hymn to name the music notes and is regarded as the inventor of the modern musical notation: DO – RE – MI – FA – SOL – LA – SI. The alphabetical musical notation is mainly used in Anglo-Saxon countries and uses the letters of the alphabet: A (LA) – B (SI) – C (DO) – D (RE) – E (MI) – F (FA) – G (SOL).

presence of my friend Dimitra Galani[365], that he would've liked to be the one to compose the song "Oloi oi rebetes tou dounia"[366]. It was one of his favorite songs and one of the few songs that he sang except his own. It's a grand thing to acknowledge that what another artist has written is huge.

— *Has your friend Victoria Tsitsani told you anything more?*

Tsitsanis's daughter has told me that her father did not help Markos unintentionally. He knew his great value and all his work and helped him in order to also bring all the other rebetes to the fore.

— *My dear Vassilis, close this interview for me.*

Markos was a wonderful person. Unique, great, aristocratic, but also very creative. And as Manolis Chiotis once said: "Vamvakaris gave us the true rebetiko music."

Vassilis Zikas

---

[365] Dimitra Galani is a famous Greek singer and composer.
[366] "All the rebetes of the world".

48

ROBUST FIRE IS COMING OUT OF MARKOS

Manos Eleftheriou [367], in his 419-page book entitled "Black Eyes, Markos Vamvakaris and the Syran society in the years 1905-1920", Metaichmio publications, Athens, 2013, presents the local society of Syros as it emerges through class and economical conflicts.

It also features a text written by Thomas Korovinis[368] (pp. 15-17) entitled "Markos burns you", in which he describes, in a poetic and almost riveting tone, the redemptive feeling of Markos Vamvakaris's songs: "It's as if he delves into the soul, as if he's soaking it. [...] Robust fire is coming out of Markos that burns your guts. [...] The others [...], no matter how much they burn you, cool you down as a relieving break at some point. Markos always burns you."

Nikos Ordoulidis[369], in his 311-page book entitled "The discographic career of Vassilis Tsitsanis (1936-1983), Analysis of his music and the research problems in Greek music", IANOS publications, Thessaloniki, 2014, refers to Markos Vamvakaris in the context of the separation of laiko and rebetiko music. The characterization attributed to Markos Vamvakaris by Ordoulidis is that of "Patriarch of rebetiko".

---

[367] Manos Eleftheriou (1938-2018) was a prominent poet, lyricist and prose writer. He wrote poetry collections, short stories, novels and the lyrics of more than 400 songs. He also worked as a columnist, publishing editor, illustrator and radio producer.

[368] Thomas Korovinis (born in 1953) is a Greek writer.

[369] Nikos Ordoulidis is a musician, professor and researcher.

He regards him as the most prominent representative of rebetiko music, unlike Tsitsanis, who is classified as a laiko musician. He differentiates them based on the beginning of their recording career.

Markos Vamvakaris began recording his first records in 1933. His beginnings were marked by: his heavy rebetika songs, his characteristic voice and the arrival of refugees from Asia Minor. The catalyst for the transition from rebetiko to laiko was the Metaxas dictatorship from 1936 to 1941, as it imposed censorship. Indeed, 1936, the starting year of Tsitsanis's recording career, explains why the singer is characterized as a laiko musician; it looked like he had no other choice. He was a laiko musician because he couldn't be anything else. After all, he was born in Trikala (1915), ten years after Markos (1905), and he was de facto abstinent from the migratory flow (1922). Therefore, he was mildly affected by this music, since he was only seven years old at the time when Markos had already established a family in Piraeus. No one but Markos could've served the rebetiko repertoire. It was as if the whole universe had conspired for it.

In his autobiography, Markos Vamvakaris makes some references to Vassilis Tsitsanis. He recognizes and acknowledges him as a good musician, noting that he and the rest of the musicians of his generation learned playing the bouzouki from him and that they all carved out their career paths by following in his footsteps. "I gave these guys the first shove, that made them come and start playing the bouzouki. Tsitsanis, Chiotis, Papaioannou, all these guys, from my songs. And even now I can assure you they still follow in my footsteps." (p. 186)

Makis Matsas[370], in his 419-page documented book "Behind the marquee, 40 years of Greek music as I lived it", Dioptra publications, Athens, 2014, recounts two incidents (p. 52) with Markos Vamvakaris, "the history of Greek music, the cornerstone of Greek laiko music", as he calls him. He remembers through the narration of his father Minos Matsas the acquaintance and collaboration with the then unknown and later legend of rebetiko music Markos: "The first person my father talked to me about was Markos Vamvakaris. Before the war, Markos Vamvakaris had recorded the first four songs of his life in Columbia, but the company was reluctant to release his records. Disappointed by their attitude, he decided to visit me", Minos told me. "My father heard something new, [...] an unprecedented sound for the time. He immediately booked an appointment with Markos in order to record his songs. [...] Indeed, the crew from Germany came a few months later and the recordings started." It was a big risk for Minos Matsas to accept to record Markos Vamvakaris's songs, given that he was unknown to the public and that the record company already had a successful collaboration with Nikos Chatziapostolou[371]: "At that time, he was the most worthy but also the most commercially important person in the Greek music scene." Chatziapostolou left the company because of Minos Matsas's collaboration with Markos

---

[370] Makis Matsas (born in 1937) is Minos Matsas's son. In 1960, at the age of 23, Makis Matas signed an important deal founding the "Minos Matsas and Son" record label and started an ambitious effort to restructure and reorganize the company of his father. Over the course of his career, he discovered and supported numerous promising artists in their early steps who later became famous performers in Greece.

[371] Nikos Chatziapostolou (1884-1941) was a composer, conductor and bassist. He is considered to be the main representative of the Greek operetta.

Vamvakaris. The opportunity given by Minos to Markos proved to be decisive, as it contributed to the evolution of the history of Greek music.

The second incident (p. 141) concerns the return of Markos Vamvakaris, this time thanks to Makis Matsas: "Everyone talks about how Chatzidakis's historic lecture at the Theatro Technis in 1949, where he talked about Vamvakaris, our own Bach, as he named him, played an important role in the revival of rebetiko. But that would not have been possible had Minos Matsas not discovered and imposed Vamvakaris." In the 1960s, Makis Matsas, decided to re-release the songs of Markos Vamvakaris, as well as to record a new album with the great rebetis entitled "Markos Vamvakaris – forty years" (1967). "I wanted to find the 'Patriarch' of rebetiko Markos Vamvakaris and record with him a brand new 33-rpm record with his own compositions. The album was a great success. However, the greatest significance and contribution of this success was that Markos constituted the stepping stone for the revival and the vindication of rebetiko music."

Dimitris. V. Varthalitis

49

MARKOS IS MY GREAT LOVE

— *My dear Markos, what does Markos Vamvakaris mean to you?*

Markos is my great love... I was born to a bourgeois family. I grew up in Kolonaki[372]; I mean, I was the child of Filippos Dragoumis, MP and minister, and Elena Valaoritis. I developed a passion for rebetiko in such an environment. It was in my soul. Deep down inside, I'm a rebetis. This was the result of my desire for anything authentic, every type of music, every corner of the earth that genuinely expressed the souls of people. If Markos had met me, I know he would have loved me because I love him too. Dimitris, you brought back memories that took me to the happiest moments of my life...

— *Did your parents listen to rebetika songs?*

Even though my father wanted me to get into dimotiko and folk music, he didn't know that rebetiko also existed.

— *Was Markos a phenomenon?*

Markos was no phenomenon; he was something... expected. I'm telling you this because out of twenty thousand people, one musician will be born. And when the environment is the right one, he or she will bloom and bear fruit.

---

[372] Kolonaki (literally "Little column") is an upscale neighborhood in central Athens.

I'll tell you my own story so that you can understand Markos's as well: we didn't have musicians in our family. We had poets from my mother's side and we had scholars from my father's side. Of course, there were also painters from both sides. I myself couldn't even draw a straight line. But from the age of three or four, I was attracted to everything related to music. Keep in mind that no one had taught me anything about it.

I was born in 1934, and all the memories I have from the period 1934-1939 are related to music. I remember my mother taking me to a store to buy a radio; this is a memory of mine. Another one is when my mother fell ill and suffered otitis. Why do I recall this? Because, while she was in the hospital, she sent me to an aunt of mine who had a gramophone and her daughters were playing records.

I started playing the piano in 1939 but I stopped in 1940, because the war started. I was lucky though in 1942: a cousin of my mother's, chased by the Germans, came and hid in our house. She had just graduated from the Vienna Conservatory as a pianist, and was about to give a recital, so she was studying the piano every day. This was the first time I heard Mozart, Beethoven, etc. And I remember that even though I was like a wild goat – you know, just like Orpheus's animals that used to sit upright when he played the lyre – I used to sit upright too and listen to her as she practiced. While my teacher was teaching me the notes, my mother's cousin was playing the piano in the other room and I knew that a particular note was LA or FA, for example. Other children really struggle to be able to reach that level.

— *And what about Markos?*

He was born with music and poetry.

— *How come?*

Well, Dimitris, you'll turn over a bunch of stones and one of them will be sculpted, carved...

— *What role did Syros play in his life?*

Life sometimes offers you the raw material. One does not start from scratch. Syros was the melting pot. It's a central island with a great natural harbor. Before the Greek Revolution, the Syrans were already going to work in Constantinople and Smyrna, and this is from where they were influenced. During the Revolution, many refugees from all over Greece, the mainland, the islands, but also from Asia Minor, including many musicians, came to Syros.

— *What was the most important event of his life during his years in Syros?*

The fact that he went to a dance school. It was there that Markos found his interest, that's where he was shaped. Also, the fact that his grandfather and father played the gaida and he himself played the drum. Markos had rhythm inside him, it was something innate. A musician is born, not made. Markos had music inside his head... As I said, he was born with music and poetry.

— *What does "Frangosyriani" say about Markos?*

His love for his birthplace. We all have a place within us that we love most of all. It's usually where we were born and spent the first years of our lives. He needed to praise Syros. It was a strong inner impulse.

— Why did this song become so popular?

Because it's easy for someone to memorize it. It's not complicated rhythm-wise and the music is a bit like a march. People like it because it's attractive. It's like seeing a beautiful woman: you might like one and don't like another one.

— Was Markos a creator?

Markos had great creative talent. He made music; that was the hardest part of it all. And he did what any worthy musician would do. He gathered all the elements that were around him and were interesting to him. He assimilated them, made them his property, had them inside him and, when the time was right, he produced them as songs. Markos is the foundation. There were others before him, but they hadn't developed more rounded-out personalities like Markos. Markos "absorbed" more stuff and managed to create an original work.

— Describe Markos's voice to me.

It's a unique voice. It has a heavy timbre. It's a voice with a character, with power that is immediately imposed. If you're in a café full of people and a big personality or a very nice girl comes in suddenly, everyone usually stops and looks at him or her. This is how Markos's voice is imposed on us. But it's not a cultivated voice from a conservatory; it's like the most beautiful wild flower.

— Did Markos have elements from the antiquity?

Many great folk artists have them without knowing it.

— And from Byzantium?

Yes, of course. He had listened to Byzantine music.

— *From folk poetry?*

He had elements from folk poetry and island poetry, but he merged them with his own.

— *Did rebetiko mark Greek culture?*

My dear Dimitris, after rebetiko, whose founder is Markos Vamvakaris, there is no other folk culture. It ends there, after rebetiko. There will be composers, but there's no more folk culture. It's over. Rebetiko is the last flower of Greek culture, and academics despise it.

— *Does the official folklore acknowledge Markos?*

Folklore will hardly acknowledge him. The point is to keep him "alive", as we do. Markos is a big deal.

— *Do you believe that Markos will continue "living"?*

It's always dangerous to make predictions. In any case, Markos is still "alive" and inspires us. Over time, he'll become better known and he'll be more loved. I will add, however, that as humanity is becoming more robotic, everything that we've loved, all this stuff that created our emotions, may not exist in the future... On the other hand, it might still exist. The future will be so different from what it is today that we don't even know what will be left and what will not. People are slowly losing their sensibilities and even great personalities are fading.

— Speaking of great personalities, how did Chatzidakis get involved with rebetiko and give that great speech about rebetiko at such a young age?

I knew Chatzidakis very well. We used to hang out a lot from 1954 to 1958. We used to listen to music together at his house and mine. He had a strong, original personality as well as a lot of courage; true grit. He was very considerate and classy. It was because of him, in part, that I became a musician. He used to tell me: "If you don't dare, you won't do anything in your life." Thus, despite the fact that I was studying law, I dropped out of school and got into music.

He gave that speech because he was a genius. When rebetiko became a trend in the '80s and the '90s, he used to say: "The songs that are worth listening to are only eighty; not one more." But that's not really true...

Markos F. Dragoumis

50

MANOS CHATZIDAKIS,
LET ME SHOW YOU A GOD

Manos Chatzidakis had introduced me to the mysteries of rebetiko. How would I ever have known such things? I was a bourgeois, I had an utterly bourgeois culture, I had no clue. Manos, who was at the center of my life, had initiated me into all of this. But, one day in April 1949, I told him: "Manos, I've ferreted out a magician in a 'burrow' in Omonoia. I want us to go there and show him to you." The magician was in a very long space, disproportionate to the entrance. We went in, I showed him the magician and Manos was enchanted. He said to me: "You gave me a great gift, Koundouros."

— *Did you talk with Markos?*

Yes, I did, in the tavern. I had been there several times before, under the care of a friend of mine, who worshiped Markos.

— *How did that happen?*

He said to me: "Let me show me a bouzouki 'god'; you'll get to know him too." He wanted to show me a god. That's how he called him. And I said to him: "Let's go see him." So, we went once, we went for a second and then for a third time. And then I said to myself: "We must not leave this god far from the other god, our god, Chatzidakis. I must get them together." So, I took Chatzidakis there and I told him:

"Manos, this god's name is Vamvakaris." And I withdrew myself. From then on, there was a secret and wonderful relationship between Chatzidakis and Vamvakaris. This is where I stopped. I was, however, always and following them. In any case, I was the first one to introduce Chatzidakis to Vamvakaris. After all, Chatzidakis had familiarized me with rebetiko. Manos had already written about rebetiko; I know that because he was fascinated about it. He also gave that famous lecture in 1949, in the presence of the magician Markos Vamvakaris. And I'll tell you something else: I also ferreted out Tsitsanis in that renowned joint on Syngrou Avenue, "Triana". I found him and took him to Chatzidakis. I was curious about things.

— *What else fascinated you about these places?*

It wasn't only about the music. It was also about what came with the music. The people, the spaces, the images. I was really charmed by those things. His orchestra, the entire stage. Markos wasn't alone, there were other people in the orchestra. His team was flexible. Sometimes there were five, sometimes there were three of them.

— *Was his voice, his stature, his playing charming?*

All of these things charmed me. All of these things make up Vamvakaris.

— *When was rebetiko first heard in cinema?*

Cinema was a snob to rebetiko. Rebetiko had never been heard into any Greek film. I was the first to add rebetiko music and rebetiko dances for the first time in Greek and world cinema in 1956. Chatzidakis had introduced and prepared me for the sound of rebetiko, he had gotten me in before I took him to Vamvakaris.

The hall where Markos Vamvakaris was singing was an oblong room. Opposite was the famous Kotopouli[373] cinema; just opposite, at a distance of fifty meters.

— *Were you fascinated by Markos's voice or by his playing?*

Now what you're asking me is to describe you Markos Vamvakaris. I cannot do that. But I remember his figure. But above all, what mattered to me was the sound of his voice and of his bouzouki. All of these things combined. These things make up Vamvakaris.

— *Did Manos Chatzidakis love Markos Vamvakaris?*

Of course. How could he not love him? He was visiting him very often. Besides, Manos embraced all rebetiko musicians, particularly Markos Vamvakaris and Tsitsanis. All of them together constitute the pantheon, they are the exponents of the awakening of Greek culture. I'm saying this because Greek folk culture was suffocated either by the pseudo-European renaissance – the very least it offered to Greece – or by dimotiko[374] from our tradition. Our folk culture was brought to the fore by two or three glorious Greeks. Giants were standing next to them though. There were also "semi-giants" and the lesser giants who consolidated what is now called "folk culture". Fortunately, the people followed.

---

[373] Marika Kotopouli (1887-1954) was a famous stage actress during the first half of the 20th century.
[374] Greece's traditional rural music.

— *Is it true that Engonopoulos[375] worshiped Markos Vamvakaris?*

Engonopoulos was a righteous man and knew how to share his devotions. He knew very well to choose. So did Markos Vamvakaris. So, it was only natural to love each other.

— *Costas Ferris[376] talks about a travel documentary in which Markos Vamvakaris appeared. You shot this on behalf of the British BBC and is now considered lost... How was it lost?*

Here's what happened: Papagos[377] had launched a campaign to attract tourists in Greece and any film that portrayed slums or humiliating images of Greece was being banned. So, this is a confiscated film from the state of which I don't even have a copy...

---

[375] Nikos Engonopoulos (1907-1985) was a painter, writer and poet. He was a major representative of the surrealist movement in Greece.

[376] Costas Ferris (born in 1935) is a Greek film director, writer, actor and producer. His 1983 film "Rembetiko" won the Silver Bear at the 34th Berlin International Film Festival.

[377] Alexandros Papagos (1883-1955) was a Greek Army officer who led the Hellenic Army in World War II and the later stages of the Greek Civil War. The only Greek career officer to be raised to the rank of Field Marshal, he became the first Chief of the Hellenic National Defence General Staff from 1950 until his resignation in 1951. He then entered politics, becoming the country's Prime Minister after his victory in the 1952 elections. His tenure saw the start of the "Greek economic miracle" (period of sustained economic growth in Greece from 1950 to 1973) and rising tensions with Britain and Turkey over the Cyprus issue.

But, Dimitris, I would like to stop, because all these memories got my heart racing. Let me catch my breath...

Nikos Koundouros

Nikos Koundouros

Manos Chatzidakis

Markos Vamvakaris

51

SUFFERING CREATED MARKOS

I

I was born in Piraeus in 1929 from an affluent family. From a young age I was going to the opera and I can't say I liked the bouzouki. But I had heard a lot about Markos Vamvakaris, the bouzouki player, and I considered it an honor for me to live next to his house. I was mentioning that to all my visitors.

When I got married, I settled in Nikaia, next to Markos Vamvakaris's new house. It was a two-storey building and he was living on the first floor. His house also had a balcony. As I was going up or down the stairs, if Markos was sitting on the balcony, I could grab his hand.

Evangelia, his wife, looked very young with her black hair. She was a slim, beautiful woman. She was dressing elegantly. She seemed to have a big age difference with her husband Markos Vamvakaris. She was polite and took great care of Markos, Stelios and Domenikos. I don't remember seeing Vassilis. I knew he had sailed out.

Markos was normally dressed, like a man of his age. He was very social. Every time I would go out, he would tell me: "How are you, Marika? Everything all right?" He was talking and chatting with me. I was feeling proud when I was speaking to him because I knew he was a great man. Sometimes he would ask me for a cigarette. But I didn't give him any.[378]

---

[378] "Two or three years ago I quit smoking. I was in such a bad state that I couldn't walk. [...] Now that I stopped I realize what a mistake it was to smoke cigarettes" (op. cit., p. 251).

But Markos was always melancholic because he had learned to live life to the fullest, he had learned to live with the bouzouki and it seemed like such a bad thing to him to be on the sidelines now. From what he was saying, I could understand that he was missing the life he used to lead and that it cost him dearly. When I think of him, that image of a melancholic man comes to my mind. I knew that the cause was neither his wife nor his children. His family was excellent. Something else was going on. He was suffering, not only from illness, but from life itself. He was expecting visitors that did not come. All those people he had helped were not coming to visit him. They had followed in his footsteps and now they were not paying him a visit in order to give him some joy. He was sitting on the balcony feeling all sad and waiting for them...[379]

I did not attend Markos's funeral because I had a young child. It was crowded. What can I say! There were many people, we were so moved and what struck me was that they had put a tiny bouzouki – it looked like it was golden – on the coffin and that they took him to the Third Cemetery on foot. It was a like huge demonstration in Dedalou Street. My son, Kostas, who is a teacher, likes to say that his mother knew Markos Vamvakaris. He admires him a lot. He often talks about him because he had met him as a child; he was born in 1966.

On the day of the funeral we went out of the house and he was afraid not to lose me, as the crowd was pressing in on us and he was weeping. He claims he was crying for Markos...

Maria Papouli

---

[379] "I got ill and nobody came to ask how I was. Nobody. It's unbelievable. Your teacher, dammit!" (op. cit., p. 243).

II

My mother was from an aristocratic family and my father was a man of the commons. He was open-handed and I think he was also a bit of a lady-killer. He was both good-looking and folksy.

We were living in Kokkinia. Our family home was there, but my entire education took place in Piraeus. I went to Ralleios School[380], to the French Institute, to the Piraeus Conservatory and then to the Athens Conservatory. Aspra Chomata was in Kokkinia, deep in the neighborhood, but it was a depraved district. People couldn't afford to eat. They were begging for money. There were poor folks, starving migrants from internal migration. They were devastated, they needed to survive somehow. Men were working very hard if we think about the situation at the time, without any machinery. They had the bouzouki though, which was completely forbidden, and they were gathering and smoking the hookah... When you were stumbling upon these people you were walking the other way. It's like today, when you see someone who's unfortunate-looking and you say to yourself: "Ah! I shouldn't cross his path..." That's how these people were like. Those were the days of poverty. That's how they made their songs, the banned ones. We're talking about songs that were very sad; but I wasn't listening to them because I was supposedly receiving another kind of education. I was the girl learning the piano and French. I despised rebetiko music, I couldn't even listen to it.

When we went to the store to buy a piano, I saw on the shelf a musical instrument that looked like a mandolin – which my mother was playing very well – and I told her to play a little bit. But it was a bouzouki! If my mother could've

---

[380] Ralleios School is an all-girls school in Piraeus established in 1885.

vanished into thin air, she would've been very happy! She was so embarrassed. I wasn't aware that the bouzouki was something different than mandolin and that it was forbidden. When we went out of the store, she gave me a good beating.

"How dare you utter that word?"

"But, mother, don't you play the bouzouki at home?"

That's a mandolin!"

And because the bouzouki was the entertainment of this circle of people, the means of blowing off steam, it was forbidden for us.

I got to know Markos Vamvakaris because a cram school, where I taught one summer, had opened near his house. I saw him frequently. He had trouble breathing, his eyes were bloodshot and he had a big belly. I never spoke to him. We were just greeting each other. He was moved by the bouzouki because of its sound. It suited him, he bonded with it. And when you're bonded with something you don't leave it easily; especially when you're charismatic, like Markos was.

People didn't tell me not to listen to this music, but they were creating such an atmosphere that I couldn't listen to it. I was listening to the Third Programme all day long. Nowadays, although I like this music, when I listen to it, this particular image comes to my mind and it spoils it for me a little bit.

Chatzidakis, with whom I had worked on the piano, was a very sensitive person. He liked to do research. If it weren't for Chatzidakis and Theodorakis, rebetiko might not have remained marginalized, but it could have survived as a special kind of culture.

My father Vassilis knew Markos very well. He used to go to the kafeneion where Markos was also going. My father used to tell us that he was helping Markos financially. He was going to the kafeneion and Markos was playing the bouzouki for him. He was also giving him money, meat and milk.

When my father died, all these people came to his funeral and cried like crazy. I once asked him:

"What was it that created Markos Vamvakaris?"

"Suffering, my child."

Anonym[381]

---

[381] The interviewee requested to remain anonymous.

52

MARKOS'S REQUEST

The phone woke me up. I heard a voice from the other end of the line: "Today is Markos's funeral. Get ready, so you don't miss the burial." Markos had managed to buy a small apartment in Korydallos. I went there and found him lying dead on a bed. He was huge, a man of 1.90m tall; he was like a rock. I couldn't believe that this "Universe Man" was dead. I cried.

"What are we waiting for?" I asked after a while Mrs. Vangelio.

"Argyris, from America. If the 'Ungrateful One' doesn't come, there will be no funeral. This is what Markos requested from me as his last wish."

Markos had been holding a big grudge against Argyris. "I raised him, fed him, I bought him pairs of shoes, I taught him how to play the bouzouki, I took him to a teacher to learn the piano", he once confessed to me. "I refer to him as the 'Ungrateful One', I no longer call him Argyris."

"Why, master?" I asked him.

"Because when Argyris became a great and famous bouzouki player, he didn't take me with him in the joints where he was working", he replied.

I sat alone for a while. Soon, a stranger wearing an American hat entered the room. I understood. The "Ungreatful One" had come. I didn't talk to him. The Catholic priests were waiting by the phone. Everything was now ready. There were lots of people in the cemetery. Common people, workers and laborers, women holding children in their arms! I also saw Giorgos Mitsakis, Sotiria Bellou, Elias Petropoulos,

Grigoris Bithikotsis.

Domenikos and Stelios, Markos's sons, took out the instruments. They started playing the last farewell at the send-off of their father. Bithikotsis started singing "Frangosyriani".

Thus, so simply, accompanied by the most beautiful Greek love song ever recorded, the "Patriarch" of rebetiko was buried on February 9, 1972, in the Third Cemetery of Athens.

Vassilis Daifotis

Markos Vamvakaris's funeral.
(from Elias Petropoulos's book "Rebetika Tragoudia",
Kedros publications)

53

MARKOS VAMVAKARIS'S DEATH

Rigas Anastasios, one of the doctors who was looking after Markos, told me: "Markos Vamvakaris was very sick. Us doctors did everything we could to cure him. It was impossible." He died on February 8, 1972.

On Tuesday, February 8, 1972, Christos Chachlakis, 47, a private-sector employee, declared to the Registry Office of the Municipality of Nikaia that Markos Vamvakaris, resident of Korydallos, born in Syros, 67, Greek, Catholic, music composer, son of Domenikos and of Elpida, husband of Evangelia Vergiou, daughter of Eleftherios, died at the hospital of the Hellenic Red Cross on Tuesday, February 8, 1972 at 1:30 pm. Dr. Spyros Pontikopoulos confirmed his death, which occurred from chronic nephritis, diabetes mellitus and heart failure. He was taken to 24 Dedalou Street in Korydallos [to be mourned].

The Department of Administration, Organization and Operation of the Third Cemetery informed us, upon our request, that Markos Vamvakaris was buried on 9/2/1972 in the 12th section of the cemetery, tomb no. 70. Nephritis is listed as the cause of death. On June 1, 1977 his body was exhumed and his bones are kept in the charnel house of the Third Cemetery, ossuary no. 15355.

Dimitris. V. Varthalitis

TIMELINE

Date	Event
1630	Birth of Giannoulis, Markos Vamvakaris's child with the daughter of Giannoulis Salachas.
1631	In a list of churches of Syros, the chapel of Saint Sebastian is located outside the settlement of Chora. On March 7, 1829, it is turned into a parish that comprises some villages of the island.
1633	The Capuchins settle in Apano Syros, where they build their monastery.
1744	In March, the Jesuit monastery in Ano Syros is founded. The Jesuits shape much of Markos's psyche.
13/11/1807	Markos Antoniou Vamvakaris or Rokos, the great-grandfather of Domenikos, Markos Vamvakaris's father, is born. The ruins of the house where Markos Vamvakaris was born and spend his early childhood are preserved on Tsygros hill, in Plati, Pouletos, between Danakos and Galissas.
28/10/1842	Leonardos, son of Frangiskos Provelengios or Balas and Anna Stefanou, Markos Vamvakaris's maternal grandfather, is born in Skali, Apano Syros.
20/4/1848	Maria or Marigitsa, daughter of Nikolaos Vidalis or Koukoulas and Irini Daveroni, Markos Vamvakaris's maternal grandmother, is born in Apano Syros.
9/10/1859	Rosa, the daughter of Antonios Vardas or Liontas and Nikoleta Gad, Markos Vamvakaris's future grandmother, is born.
20/5/1882	Domenikos, firstborn son of Antonios Vamvakaris (brother of Petros or Pieros) and Rosa Varda, Markos Vamvakaris's father, is born in Danakos.

9/7/1884	Markos Antoniou Vamvakaris buys a plot with trees, a bucketed water well, a tank and a stable in Pouletos.
15/4/1887	Markos Antoniou Vamvakaris, Markos Vamvakaris's grandfather, dies at the age of 30 (date of birth unknown) in Pouletos, bequeathing the plot he had bought on July 9, 1884 to Rosa, his wife, and to his three sons, Antonis, Morfinis and Domenikos, Markos Vamvakaris's father.
16/10/1887	Markos Antoniou Vamvakaris or "Rokos" (born November 13, 1807), Markos Vamvakaris's great-great-grandfather, dies, bequeathing his house to his second son, Petros or Pieros. This is the house where Markos Vamvakaris was born (1905) and where he spent his early childhood.
4/12/1889	Elpida Provelengiou, the ninth child of Leonardos Provelengios, Markos Vamvakaris's future mother, is born in Apano Syros.
19/1/1892	Leonardos Provelengios, Markos Vamvakaris's maternal grandfather, dies at the age of 50.
11/11/1896	Leonardos Provelengios's two-storey residence is seized due to owed debts. Markos Vamvakaris's family never owned a house in Syros. In fact, Markos Vamvakaris never in his life acquired a privately owned house.
1901	Iosif Chalavazis or Arakas, son of Nikos and Florentia, who became Markos Vamvakaris's best friend and "betrayed" him in 1937, is born.
25/7/1904	Domenikos Vamvakaris marries Elpida Provelengiou (Markos Vamvakaris's parents). The wedding ceremony takes place in the church of Saint Sebastian in Apano Syros. The young couple lives in Tsygros, in the house inherited by Petros or Pieros Markou Vamvakaris. Markos Vamvakaris was born in that house and this is where he spent his early childhood.
6/5/1905	Eleni Dimitriou Mavroudi, Markos Vamvakaris's first wife, is born in Piraeus.

10/5/1905	Markos Domenikou Vamvakaris is born in Tsygros, Danakos, Syros.
10/1/1908	Leonardos Vamvakaris, Markos Vamvakaris's brother, is born in Tsygros.
14/1/1908	Domenikos Vamvakaris no longer owns any land in Pouletos due to sales and seizures.
1909	The Vamvakaris family settles in Skali, Apano Syros.
1910	Markos Vamvakaris goes to school.
12/7/1910	Frangiskos Domenikou Vamvakaris, Markos Vamvakaris's brother, is born in Apano Syros.
17/9/1912	Domenikos Markou Vamvakaris is called up to serve in the armed forces during the universal military conscription.
7/3/1913	Antonis Domenikou Vamvakaris, Markos Vamvakaris's brother, is born.
7/4/1913	Antonis Domenikou Vamvakaris, Markos Vamvakaris's brother, dies in Apano Syros
10/9/1913	Domenikos Vamvakaris is discharged from the army and never served again.
18/9/1914	Margitsa Domenikou Vamvakari, Markos Vamvakaris's sister, is born.
1/2/1916	Petros or Pieros Vamvakaris dies.
17/3/1917	Margitsa Domenikou Vamvakari, Markos Vamvakaris's sister, dies from bronchitis.
14/2/1918	Grazia Domenikou Vamvakari, Markos Vamvakaris's sister, is born.
10/4/1918	Evangelia Vergiou, Markos Vamvakaris's second wife, is born in Piraeus.
1920	Markos Vamvakaris, along with Iosif Chalavazis, Nikolaos G. Maragos, and Petros N. Provelengios leave for Piraeus. Markos Vamvakaris is hosted in Tabouria by his aunt Irini Altouva.
1920	Markos Vamvakaris's family leaves for Piraeus.
7/12/1923	Markos Vamvakaris, 18, marries Eleni Mavroudi, also 18, at the Catholic Church of Saint Paul in Piraeus, without having an Orthodox ritual.

25/4/1925	Rosa Domenikou Vamvakari, Markos Vamvakaris's sister, is born in Piraeus and is baptized at the Catholic Church of Saint Paul on May 3, 1925.
10/2/1926	Markos Vamvakaris was assigned to the 34th regiment in Goudi.
27/2/1927	Marigitsa Provelengiou, Markos Vamvakaris's beloved grandmother, dies in Apano Syros at the age of 79. It is unknown if her daughter Elpida attended the funeral.
17/11/1927	Anargyros-Kosmas-Damianos Domenikou Vamvakaris, Markos Vamvakaris's brother, is born.
2/12/1927	Markos Vamvakaris is discharged from the army after serving 1 year, 9 months and 22 days.
9/2/1930	Anargyros-Kosmas-Damianos Domenikou Vamvakaris, Markos Vamvakaris's brother, dies.
18/10/1930	Anargyros-Kosmas-Maria or Argyris Domenikou Vamvakaris, Markos Vamvakaris's brother, is born.
19/4/1931	Domenikos, Markos Vamvakaris's father, basket maker, dies at the age of 49 in Piraeus.
1931	Markos returns to Syros for the first time since leaving the island.
1933	Markos Vamvakaris moves with Eleni Mavroudi to her mother's house in Aspra Chomata, 42 Nikis Street. So does Domenikos Vamvakaris's family: they move from the sheds of Drapetsona to Aspra Chomata, 40 Nikis Street.
1933	First appearance of Markos Vamvakaris in the music industry with the song "Eprepe na'rchosouna, manga, mes ston teke mas" (or "Karadouzeni").
1937	One summer evening, Markos and his wife Eleni are hosted at the house of Iosif Chalavazis, his childhood friend, 59 Vitolion Street, in Piraeus.

	That day marked the beginning of Markos's separation with Eleni.
1938	Markos Vamvakaris asked for a divorce from the catholic Archbishop of Athens Ioannis Baptist Filippousis. "You shall stay married. It is God's will", he replies to Markos.
28/3/1939	Markos Vamvakaris is seeking the annulment of his marriage with Eleni Mavroudi held on 7/12/1923 for infringement of the law regarding the sanctity of marriage at the Court of First Instance of Piraeus.
1/3/1940	The marriage of Markos Vamvakaris with Eleni Mavroudi is declared invalid by the Multi-Membered Court of First Instance of Piraeus.
1941	Leonardos Vamvakaris, Markos Vamvakaris's brother, dies in Piraeus.
3/3/1941	Markos Vamvakaris, during World War II, is ordered to report to the 41st General Battalion, where he serves for one month and 28 days. He is discharged on May 1, 1941.
1942	Elpida Provelengiou, Markos Vamvakaris's mother, dies.
1942	Markos Vamvakaris asks Lefteris Vergiou, Evangelia's father, to marry his daughter.
11/7/1943	Markos Vamvakaris's (aged 38) second and Evangelia Vergiou's (aged 25) first marriage is held by Michalis Manolakakis, pastor of the church of Saint Nikolaos in Piraeus. The wedding merriment is held in Aspra Chomata.
9/4/1944	Domenikos Vamvakaris, Markos Vamvakaris's first child, is born.
10/4/1944	Vassilis Vamvakaris, Markos Vamvakaris's son, is born.
27/8/1944	Markos Vamvakaris baptizes Domenikos at the Cathedral Basilica of Saint Dionysius in Athens.
23/3/1945	Domenikos Vamvakaris, Markos Vamvakaris's first child, dies in Athens from bronchial pneumonia.

30/5/1945	Varvara Markou Vamvakari, Markos Vamvakaris's second child, is born.
12/3/1946	Varvara Markou Vamvakari, Markos Vamvakaris's second child, dies and is buried in the Third Cemetery.
2/3/1947	Stelios Markou Vamvakaris, Markos Vamvakaris's son, is born.
2/2/1948	Elpida Markou Vamvakari, Markos Vamvakaris's third (illegitimate) child is born.
8/1/1949	Domenikos Markou Vamvakaris, Markos Vamvakaris's son, is born.
19/5/1949	Elpida Markou Vamvakari, Markos Vamvakaris's third (illegitimate) child, dies.
3/4/1963	Frangiskos Vamvakaris, Markos's brother, dies at the age of 53.
1964	Panagiotis Kounadis photographs Markos Vamvakaris and gets his first interview with a folk musician.
1965	Panagiotis Kounadis and Nearchos Georgiadis record Markos Vamvakaris recounting his life in Aspra Chomata.
1966	Markos is very much involved in his children's studies. He attends all conferences held at their school. I met him at such a conference on December 18, 1966.
1967	With the actions of the Catholic Archbishop of Athens Venediktos Printezis, Markos Vamvakaris is allowed to receive communion.
1967	Angeliki (Kiki) Kalamara, a law student, meets Markos Vamvakaris in the summer of 1967 and writes down his accounts.
1969	Angeliki Vellou-Keil comes from America in order to take Markos there and present him at the School of Fine Arts at Buffalo in New York State University. She also asks him some questions and records them with a tape recorder.
22/12/1971	Markos Vamvakaris confesses and receives communion for the last time.

8/2/1972	"Markos Vamvakaris, resident of Korydallos, born in Syros, 67, Catholic, music composer, son of Domenikos and of Elpida, husband of Evangelia Vergiou, died on Tuesday, at 1:30 pm".
9/2/1972	Markos Vamvakaris's funeral takes place. He is buried in the 12th section of the Third Cemetery of Athens.
1973	Markos Vamvakaris's autobiography, compiled by Angeliki Vellou-Keil, is published by Papazisis publications.
1/6/1977	Markos Vamvakaris's body is exhumed and his bones are kept in the charnel house of the Third Cemetery, ossuary no. 15355.
1983	Argyris Domenikou Vamvakaris dies.
27/5/1988	Markos Vamvakaris's bust is erected in Apano Syros.
1995	Opening of the Markos Vamvakaris Museum in Apano Syros.
22/9/1995	A marble slab is immured in the facade of Markos Vamvakaris's old house in order to honor him. Mayor: Vassilis Trapalis.
1997	Giorgis Christofilakis's book "Rebetiko myth – Markos Vamvakaris" is published by Tegopoulos-Maniateas publications.
17/3/1998	Eleni Mavroudi dies of heart failure in Aspra Chomata and is buried in the 28th section, tomb no. 120 of the Third Cemetery.
1998	The book "Markos Vamvakaris, my songs", compiled by Domenikos Vamvakaris, is published by Papagrigoriou-Nakas publications.
2001	The documentary "I like hearts like mine, Markos Vamvakaris", directed by George Zervas, is released.
2005	Manos Tsilimidis's book "Markos Vamvakaris, the saint mangas: Stelios Vamvakaris about his father" is published by Kaktos publications.

2005	Panagiotis Kounadis's book "Markos Vamvakaris 1905-1972: I was born mangas and I will die mangas" is published by Katarti publications.
11/2/2010	The ""Vamvakareio foundation – Arogi", funded by Vassilis Vamvakaris, is completed.
2013	Manos Eleftheriou's book "Black Eyes, Markos Vamvakaris and the Syran society in the years 1905-1920" is published by Metaichmio publications.
29/9/2014	Evangelia Vamvakari, 96, dies of senile cachexia.
30/6/2015	Markos Vamvakaris's autobiography "Markos Vamvakaris: The Man and the Bouzouki", translated in English by Noonie Minogue, is published by Greeklines.com.
27/6/2017	Dimitris V. Varthalitis's book "MARKOS VAMVAKARIS: FROM MYTH TO HISTORY 1600-2017" is published by Saint Paul Educational Establishment publications.
17/6/2019	Stelios Markou Vamvakaris, Markos Vamvakaris's son, dies.
2/9/2019	Markos Vamvakaris's autobiography "Markos Vamvakaris : le patriarche du rébétiko – Autobiographie", translated in French by Christos Poulakis, is published.
5/2020	The feature documentary "MARKOS", directed by Nikos Skarentzos, is released.
/2020	Dimitris V. Varthalitis's book "MARKOS VAMVAKARIS: FROM MYTH TO HISTORY 1600-2017", translated in English by Christos Poulakis, is published by Saint Paul Educational Establishment publications.

Printed in Great Britain
by Amazon

53692416R00206